STRADDLING THE BORDERS
The Year I Grew Up In Italy

by

Martha T. Cummings

Branden Publishing Co.
17 Station Street
Box 843 Brookline Village
Boston MA 02447

Library of Congress Cataloging-in-Publication Data

Straddling the borders ; the year I grew up in Italy
/ Martha T. Cummings.
    p.   cm.
    ISBN 0-8283-2036-5 (alk. paper)
1. Italy--Description and travel.
2. Cummings, Martha T.--Journeys--Italy.
DG430.2.C85 1999
914.504'929--dc   99-18280
                                   CIP

BRANDEN PUBLISHING COMPANY
17 Station Street
Box 843 Brookline Village
Boston, MA 02447

For My Aunt

MARTHA HOFFMANN RAGONESE

We miss you.
We love you.

Little 'M

NOTE

A percentage of the author's profits from this novel will go to The American Cancer Society.

Cover design--Martha T. Cummings and Gail Mardfin Starkey. Front cover photograph--Martha T. Cummings. Back cover photograph--Joseph F. Cummings, Jr. Author photograph--David F. Saul.

TABLE OF CONTENTS

1	Pre-Italy	It Is Mine To Do Now 6
2	Perugia	Veronica Wipes The Face Of Jesus 7
3	Perugia	Max Feeds The Face Of Jo 20
4	Perugia	Petra Spots The Ass Of Orca 33
5	Firenze	The Day Michelangelo Was Outed 42
6	Firenze	Uncle Sam--We Aren't In Kansas Anymore 54
7	Perugia	Mourning The Death Of Naivete´ 61
8	Perugia	The Recipe Card Club--Membership Is Now Closed 68
9	Roma	High Anxiety--Cyclopes, Lions And Plaster-Of-Paris 82
10	Roma	Drove My Chevy To The Trevi But The Trevi Was Dry 96
11	Roma	At Whom Is He Pointing, Anyway? . 110
12	Perugia	Nonno And Signora Gala-- The Human Cheat-Sheets 118
13	Perugia	Getting Pretty Hot--Feeling Pretty Cool 126
14	Tutti	Walls 134
15	Tutti	Holy Week At The Hofbräuhaus 140
16	Firenze	Michelangelo--Artist, Architect, Matchmaker 149
17	Perugia	Italian Red Tape Versus The American Middle Finger 158
18	Roma	Shrinkage--Personal, Clothes, Anxiety And Time 164
19	Roma	Isabella Is A Bella 170
20	Roma	Truth, Dare, Consequences--Promises But No Repeats 179
21	Perugia	You Can Run But You Cannot Hide . . 185
22	Tutti	Crusty Gusts And Lusty Busts 191
23	Sicilia	There's No Place Like Home 200
24	Perugia	Good-cries, Good-sighs, Good-ties, Good-byes 209
25	Perugia	What's It All About, Nonno? 219

Chapter One
It Is Mine To Do Now

He died before I was born.
I was born after he died.
Facts that make me unique in my family. Different.

I am the only one who never touched his skin. I am the only one who was never held in his hands. I am the only one who was not the object of his brown-eyed affection. I am the only one who is not in the last photograph that was ever taken of him.

I'm not completely sure why it matters so much. But it does. So to his homeland. To parts I can see, touch and taste, smell and hear. To streets where he once strolled. To air that he once breathed. To places his sweet eyes once rested upon. As a young boy. As the keeper of their hope.

He died before I was born.
But I was born after he died.
So, it is mine to do now.

Chapter Two
Veronica Wipes The Face Of Jesus

I was definitely getting signs in New York. Hurricane Gloria had swept into town just hours before I was scheduled to take off on a charter flight. Duncan, the friend I was staying with, had her apartment windows x'd with enough masking tape to protect us from death, as well as disease and pillage. She was cautious, for good reason. Her tiny dancer's body would have been sucked from the East Village to the outskirts of Long Island if Gloria had taunted her through the unprotected panes.

The timing of Gloria's late September arrival could not have been worse. I was already nervous about going across the Atlantic, alone, for a year, with the only command of Italian being some very distasteful expressions, passed down in the oral tradition of our family, surviving the trips from Abruzzi and Sicily, only to be embellished in these great United States.

I was fluent in profanity.

A profanity that was practiced in a household that leaned in the direction of Italy over Ireland. Lasagna over shamrocks. Words that ended in "o" over words that began with "o." Red wine over green beer. And lots of kissing and hugging and loving interspersed with worrying and yelling and guilt.

I was the youngest in the family. But was lucky enough to have a precious name reserved for me. Jo. After my Aunt Jo. Who was lucky enough to have a precious personality and character and spirit reserved for her. I was born Catholic and to parents in or near their 40s. Born spoiled. Born on a Thursday. My mother sent me into the world 10 minutes before *Zorro* came on the TV. Like the masked hero, I was blessed with a full head of pitch black hair which my mother promptly tied up with a large yellow ribbon. I ripped it off my head with a vengeance--eager to send a painfully clear message about the role of little "pretties" in my life. It was a sign of a feistiness to come. And to linger. And to grow--since, in time, frilly underpants, patent leathers and kindergarten dress code rules that prevented me from climbing up the jungle gym came to symbolize a national plot. I think it stemmed from the whole Original Sin problem. Adam. Eve. Serpent. Apple. Spending our lives trying to let people know that not all of us would have taken a bite.

And so I hated dresses, Barbie Dolls and the fact that I couldn't be an altar boy. I loved playing basketball with one brother, going on Indian hikes with another brother, riding the purple bike with the banana seat that my father gave me and dragging it to a halt with my PF Flyers. My sister and I sold lemonade and hunted for and hawked golf balls on the nearby course to buy U.S. Savings Bonds at school. I rode our sheep and collected fresh eggs from the chicken coop and played tether ball at my cousins' house while my *nonna* (grandmother), with her big toes sticking through her open-ended shoes, looked on with love from her long, plastic lounge chair. I clung to the white, short-sleeved, Ozella Dodge t-shirt my Uncle Americo gave me, and I savored my Aunt Elvira weekends when we watched game shows, ate homemade ice cream cake and straightened out her ridged bedspreads with a broomstick. I loved it when Aunt Lu placed her silky hands on my silky cheeks to play the Italian game, *Moscia Male*, which, to a little kid, sounded like *Moosha Ma*. And I spent countless hours with my mother, who sent me off to school each day, from kindergarten through high school, with a "God bless you," and an "I love you," and an "I'll be here if you need me." And she always was. Except for the morning of the day I would fly to Italy, to live for a year, in relative ignorance and absolute panic. The day I looked for the things that had comforted me. No PF Flyers. No grandmother's gaze. No tether.

I was on the phone to Kennedy Airport about 10 times that fateful morning. My small frame wrapped around the receiver--hunched in anticipation of doom. My fingernails losing the battle to my teeth. My olive skin replaced with the paleness of panic. My normally straight, black hair tossed in messy patterns and my anxiety planting the eggs for the crow's feet that were waiting to be born. Each time I called, the dispassionate employee informed me, via recording, that all flights would go on with minor delays--an announcement that exponentially escalated the tension of those of us who would prefer not to fly straight into or even near a storm with projected wind speeds of over 75 mph. Still, three hours before takeoff, I gathered my baggage, seven pieces in all--two suitcases, a tennis racquet, an enormous box of cosmetics, (as if I couldn't have found all of them in Italy), a fanny pack, a knapsack and a luggage carrier. Duncan and I hoisted it all, stumbled outside in the rain and hailed a cab.

The ride to the airport was very quiet.

I was convinced that I was headed for death, one way or another, but I was too stubborn to turn back and rethink the logic of quitting my teaching job and heading to a country where I would be voiceless and friendless and clueless for most of the year. Plus, there had been two going-away parties--one in Boston, one in New York. If I decided *not* to go, they'd all think I was pathetic. If I decided *to* go, only I would think I was pathetic. They won.

Duncan could feel the tension along the way and, mercifully, opted not to name it. If either one of us had started to host a Neurosis Party, which we, when together, were known to have done, we would have found ourselves with party hats and streamers, and I would have found myself ringing up a $4,000 taxi bill to New England. Instead, she questioned me about what I had packed. Passport? Visa? Traveler's Cheques? Tickets? Walkman? It was a little late for all that. Still, it gave me something to focus on that I could handle.

After the seventh time I had zipped and unzipped my fanny pack, checking to see if my passport and Traveler's Cheques had leapt from the vaulted enclosure in the intervening 90 seconds, we were pulling up in front of the terminal, and my possessions were being emptied onto the cold sidewalk by a team of support personnel who struck me as conspiratorial. There they were. In one big heap. The only things that would be familiar to me thousands of miles away from home. The only things that were being transplanted with me and that were kind enough and sensitive enough and bold enough to make the journey, too. I had an instant and supreme fondness for the socks and toothbrushes and Q-tips that rested inside. I wanted to rip open the bags and box and check to make sure they were OK. I wanted to carry them all onboard with me. To make sure that if I went down, if the plane went down, that at least I'd have something I knew as I plummeted into the Atlantic. That at least I'd have warm feet, fresh breath and clean ears as my body heaved itself onto the ocean's surface.

I was losing it. Totally losing it.

And then Duncan said good-bye. Gripping my body with her strong arms as we let loose mutual sighs of loss. As she waved to me from the back seat of our cab, her cab, I could barely focus on her face and her expression through the dizziness--a dizziness that worsened as I realized that my brand new tennis racquet was resting in the taxi's trunk. A $150 tip for a man who didn't speak two words to me and who would later dream of shorts and sneakers to match his cat-gut toy.

Pared down to six familiar pieces, I made my way, alone, to the British Airways terminal. After standing in line for 45 minutes and feeling for my passport and Cheques with absolute precision, I got to the desk and to an employee who looked as if she'd rather be anywhere else, doing anything else, than waiting on any living specimen who deign think it appropriate to ask something of her. "Oh, you're at the wrong terminal," she said, with a tone that visited a different version of the Four Corner States--with Arizona, Colorado, New Mexico and Utah making way for Arrogance, Condescension, Neglect and Unparalleled Spite. "You need to go to the United Airlines terminal." "Is it far?" "No, it's just down the road there--100 yards or so. It shouldn't be a problem unless you have a lot of luggage."

And with that she expelled her relief--the relief of passing one more poor slob onto some other airline employee clone down the block. She'd loom behind her big desk and wait to see whether her cohort on the other side of the net would return her serve or succumb to the power and surprise of the ace. I needed my racquet. And before I could manage to peel my elbows off of her too-high counter or open my mouth to express my mounting frustration, she managed a breathy, "Next?," neither caring to notice nor noticing to care that it would, of course, be a problem because I did, of course, have a lot of luggage. So, there we headed--out the door, over the curb and down the sloping, winding and bumpy tar to another exchange from hell.

Within seconds, two things were obvious. First, my luggage carrier was a piece of *merda*. Second, "luggage carrier" was a major misnomer. How about "dragger," "tumbler" or even "piss-me-off" gadget? That item, falsely marketed as a timesaving, stress-reducing device, fell over five times on the way down the hill. As people brushed by me, headed for their own adventures, unconcerned about my possessions that rattled within, I placed myself at the center of their universe and was confused by their unwillingness to stop and help me carry my comforts to the gate. The cosmetic box took the biggest hit. I was very worried about my Q-tips.

We finally got to the United Airlines Terminal and its much shorter lines with New York asphalt wedged into the luggage handles, spilled orange soda on the bottom of my knapsack and water from Hurricane Gloria's wrath soaking my heels. It was only when I arrived at the check-in counter and faced a woman whose hair was sprayed to paralysis and whose buttoned collar reeked of frigidity that I was told, again, "Wrong terminal." I was supposed to be at the British Airways Terminal, where I had started.

In record-time, inspired by the clear images of me having to restack my goods on the carrier-from-hell, kick my luggage to the top of the rain-soaked road and curse, with emphasis, those pedestrians who blatantly ignored my needs for their travels, I spewed, spit and screamed my way to hysteria. An hysteria that pushed the s-shaped vein that resides behind my left ear to the surface of my flesh, widening its banks to resemble the Amazon. An act that was aped by all other blood-carrying vessels as arteries mimicked the Nile and capillaries the Mississippi. And while that approach would prepare me brilliantly well for Italy, in The United States the fit was met with a stare of utter intolerance and disconnect. Within a few minutes, I found myself dragging my luggage carrier, 30 underpants and enough Tampax for 12 serious periods back up to British Airways. Do women menstruate in Italy? Could I have purchased those exact same tampons across the Atlantic? Was I that ethnocentric that I was afraid I'd be forced to use moss pads, Huggies or toilet paper rolled in the shapes of cigars?

Back at the beginning I arrived. Sweaty. Angry. Irritable. More intolerant than ever. Just soaking up the aura of the sexy European adventure. I got checked in right back at the desk where I had started, where no one was willing to admit the error that had sent me downstream. To the contrary, I was reprimanded for my cosmetics box, innocent victim of the piss-me-off carrier. So much was jammed inside that the bulging corners created a "packing hazard." All for the sake of some familiar toothpaste, shampoo and toilet paper.

"Fine. Thanks for letting me know. Take it anyway."

"OK," she said, with perfectly patronizing pauses. "But we can't be responsible." Like that represented a major shift in personal policy and attitude.

I dumped three of my six items into their custody, leaving me with my fanny pack, knapsack and luggage carrier, and headed for the lounge, buoyed only by the image of my cosmetics box exploding in the hands of Little Miss Sunshine as I made my way through security. Game, set, match.

I wanted to go home.

Instead, I headed for a thickly-padded seat with a built-in cup-holder in the airport lounge. I filled the cup-holder with a Bloody Mary and respectfully played my part (despite lingering sweaty intolerance and frustration) in a conversation with an elderly man who shared my Scorpion birthday. Another chat with a mother-daughter pair who ended up sitting next to me on the plane and the aspirin that were starting to put a dent in my anxiety headache brought refreshing reprieves as did *Bye, Bye, Miss American Pie* on my Walkman and finally, finally, Hurricane Gloria's steady demise. I could see her waving good-bye from the enormous windows on my left, windows that were then far less tortured by her pelting rain and raucous winds.

By the time they called our flight number and began boarding the rows in groups of five or 10 or 20, the Bloody Mary, my stomach and my head were happily coexisting. And I was surprised to be void of much of the fear--of loneliness, of rash decisions, of doubt. And filled, instead, with a sense of calm, of peace, of pride in the boldness of my move.

We were down the runway and airborne in record-time, soon over the cold, turbulent Atlantic waters and on a surprisingly smooth flight toward my destiny. Since, with any luck, we would not touch ground again until the Roman asphalt stepped up to greet us. Miles away from my American turf.

Soon I was lulled to relaxation by the steadiness of the metal beast and the constant buzz that surrounded me. The peanuts and sodas to get us started. The distribution of cheesy slippers and headsets and dinner menus and American and British newspapers. The pilot interruptions. The beeping and blinking of the seat belt signs. The red wine that accompanied our *pasta* dinners, the sleep that immediately followed, the search for the in-flight movies and the scanning of music stations--an activity that made me chuckle as I found Mozart sharing an airplane seat with Johnny Cash, Kool and The Gang and Herb Alpert and The Tijuana Brass.

All of the logistics were gratefully enhanced by the polite chatter with my mother-daughter neighbors--a pair that expressed their respect for my risk-taking, my interest in tracing my roots and my desire to learn the language and experience another culture. I felt proud of myself for making it onto that plane as I sipped my last drop of red wine and swigged my water. Life was good. *I* was good. My PF Flyers would slow me down no more, I thought, and Eve's spinelessness was nearly forgotten.

And then we landed.

The touchdown at Ciampino Airport, the destination for charter flights on the outskirts of Rome, was flawless. Finally, safe, in Italy, having stared into the faces of Hurricane Gloria and the women at the check-in counters and not blinked first. Italy, the land of love and life and culture, and I was allowing myself to breathe freely for a minute and to dream freely for a minute about my future. My fate.

And a minute it was for within a finger-snap of touchdown, the nightmare began to unfold. We found ourselves being ushered into a lobby that sported two archaic, Neanderthal carousels, barren walls, stained windows and gray, soiled, cement floors. It wasn't the exact look of love and life and culture I had been expecting. My utopia had been exchanged for a roundup of the locals for a banjo-fest on the front porch of *Deliverance II*. Locals who created a luggage handling display that embraced their deepest faults--irrationality and unpredictability. A display that emerged as a metaphor for life.

One carousel would turn on, and all 300 passengers, with me in the lead, would press the flesh to the front to vie for a space to spot our luggage. For several minutes, the carousel would just spin, spin, spin. No luggage. Just spinning. And then, for no apparent reason, the other carousel would turn on, and the first one would abruptly stop. And, on cue, all 300 passengers would scurry across the passageway, elbowing and pushing and jockeying to be closest--to what, we weren't sure. The dance repeated itself 10 times. Ten pressings of the flesh, 10 scurryings, 10 times 300 angry cries. The only solace I could find was in the consistency of the inconsistency. Finally, I sat down on my luggage carrier and paused to examine the scene.

And then, it happened. They came. One by one. My first suitcase was the third piece of luggage out of the chute. When it got closer, and I saw it was in good condition, the relief was palpable. I tried to remember what was inside. Which shorts. Which shirts. Which pajamas. The sudden appearance of my brutalized large green duffel bag, ripped so badly that the hole on the top was big enough to expose my Jockey Hipsters and three bras, my stained socks and faded t-shirts, jerked me back to dismal reality. And then, right behind it, the most dismal reality of all. The cosmetics box. Or, the cosmetics. As the remains of the moistened carton glided along the tracks, my eyes were drawn to things that were unrecognizable at first. But as they approached and got into clearer view, the silhouettes were obvious. Tampons. Dozens of tampons. Some intact. Some severed from their cords. Some crushed and wedged into the outer edges of the carousel. The international crowd parted, allowing the owner to step forward to gather her parcels, totaling at least 61. Piece by piece I reached for my collapsed Crest, some baby powder and spilled Listerine. Leaking Seabreeze, tattered cotton balls and a broken comb. Shampoo-soaked toilet paper, flattened cortisone and 48 brutalized sanitary items. And fractured Q-tips. I was right to have worried about them.

I collected all of my belongings as quickly as I could, amidst the sneers and cheers of my people, and grimaced as I thought about my welcome to the land of art and architecture, of food and wine, of landscapes and opera, of carousels and unscented Super Plusses. Thank God I couldn't understand a word they said--though the body movements told a story of their own. They were the same vibrant gesticulations that greeted me at the money exchange booth when I discovered that they accepted only *currency* for exchange at Ciampino Airport during those hours. I had to exchange dollars for *lire*. And the 11 lonely singles at the base of my pocket were clearly not enough to pay for a cab to Rome, which was critical, since I certainly could not have gotten on an Italian bus with all of my belongings and moss pad replacements emanating from every pocket and orifice.

I managed to get outside, throw my things on the ground and fixate on mass hysteria. Right behind a rust-colored bus with toxic fumes that was set to emerge from Ciampino with 123 passengers aboard despite the legal limits of 65. Forcing strangers to break through the American lines of demarcation. The American demands for personal space. Within seconds, a handsome, dark-haired, English-speaking Italian, with worn jeans and a crisp white t-shirt, approached me to say that a British couple and an American man were going to hire him out to take them to the heart of Rome. He asked if I were headed in that direction and if I would be interested in going along for the ride. I looked up to find comfort in his exceptional eyes. Deep-set. Dark brown. Smoothly welcoming. Enough to obliterate the following cautions. A woman traveling alone. Close to incapacitated. Maniacal and vulnerable. Exhausted and dirty. Climbing into an unmarked taxi with four strangers (one of whom was an olive-skinned god) and little cash.

Three minutes into the ride, one of the two British folks, choking on her muffled vowels, grew furious when she learned that I was unable to pay the full one-quarter of the fare to Rome, especially since I had the most luggage. She was indignant. Borderline belligerent. And her moaning ensued as we wended our way through the outskirts of the Eternal City. Adding some icing to the already overbaked cake. Adding more doubt as to why I thought this would be a good idea. Not just the taxi ride. The whole trip. Just before I launched a slew of particularly immature, but highly effective, attacks of all shapes and sizes, the Texas gentleman in the front seat leaned back and pressed more than enough *lire* into my sweaty palm. Silencing her. Calming me. Bringing all of us back to the setting of the moment. And bringing me back to The Stations Of The Cross.

An Easter ritual with my mother and brothers and sister. In an empty, dark church and carved scenes of a tortured man being forced to carry a heavy cross while we prayed and walked around the perimeter of the pews. The only station we liked was the one called *Veronica Wipes The Face Of Jesus*, the one with the woman who reached out to refresh the poor, tired man, a gesture which left her towel with an exact replica of His face. She was our peace in a scary setting.

It didn't take long, however, as we moved out of our prepubescence and into our cynical teens, to redirect Veronica's message. To move her age-old repertoire out of the church and into our home. We stuck to the overarching theme of relief but extended it to include all of the daily mini-miracles and none of the religious maxi-miracles. It wouldn't be out-of-character, for example, to hear my sister say "Veronica Wipes The Face Of Jesus" when I agreed to dust the downstairs living room so she could leave early for a football game. Or to hear my brother utter the same when someone would offer him a magazine as he raced, unprepared, to the upstairs bathroom. Or to hear that same brother say "Jesus thanks you, Ronnie," when one of us would be willing to scratch the itch that was just out of his reach.

This more versatile version of Veronica was everywhere. So I knew I'd run into her sooner or later. I just didn't think it'd be in the front seat of an illegal Roman cab. And I didn't think she'd be a 50 year-old Texas businessman with a big hat, a deep voice and a lot of money.

When we got to Rome's Termini Station, the train hub of Europe, I paid my respects only to those taxi cohorts who had paid their respects to me, visited the cash exchange, loaded up with *lire* and sprinted to the ticket window. The next train to Perugia left in seven minutes. So after purchasing my first class ticket, securing my 400 pieces of luggage on the piss-me-off carrier, and half-walking, half-running to the tracks to Umbria, I climbed aboard with time to spare.

As the train slowly squealed out of the Italian capital, I began to take stock of my possessions, salvage the Super Plusses and rub the conveyor belt grease stains out of my Jockeys. In the middle of my singularly focused obsession, a beautiful, Italian woman with perfect skin, thick, flowing, blonde hair and vibrant blue eyes that matched the silk suit that fell over her tall, thin frame, reached across the aisle to bring calm to the arms that were moving with a rabid feverishness. We struck up a conversation in broken English. Her name was Beatrice. That was my grandmother's name. Pronounced with a classic Italian rhythm and melody--far away from its American counterparts.

As the train said good-bye to the rows and rows of poles and electric wires that flood the outskirts of Rome and bid hello to the cypress trees and distant views of the Italian countryside, we talked. About my roots and my dreams and her bird's-eye view of an Italy that differed from the ones foreigners lust after from afar. We talked about her job in Rome and her birthplace in Umbria and her father who would meet her at the station. We talked about my course in Perugia and my birthplace in New England and my father who would not be at the station.

It was then that Beatrice dropped a bomb. She hoped I had already booked my lodging in Perugia because, she said, there was a major *festa* (celebration) going on in the city that weekend, and it would be virtually impossible to find a room that night. I was relieved to tell her that she need not worry since my travel agent had made arrangements for me weeks ago. "See? Here's the voucher." She gently took it from my hand, read it and started to shake her head from side-to-side as her pointer finger followed its lead. "This," she said, "is for a room in a city 50 km outside of Perugia. This train isn't going in that direction."

Beatrice must have been able to read the immediate defeat. The immediate surrender. The white flag that was circling above my head in jerks and starts. Not that it would have taken much. My head was slouched down on my chest, and teardrops were pooling up on my light gray t-shirt. I was exhausted. And angry. And beaten. Zorro had been stabbed and was bleeding and wanted to get on another plane that might search for and head into the half-opened eye of Hurricane Gloria. Sucking me in and flailing me around until I wasn't merely next to death. But in it.

It was all too much. Already. First, just saying good-bye to all that I knew and loved. But then Hurricane Gloria, the tennis racquet, the terminal mess-ups, the luggage carrier, the check-in women from hell, the carousel sideshow, the exchange of dollars to *lire*, the Parliamentary *Prima Donna* and then, a train to nowhere.

Beatrice put her arm on me again and told me to let her take care of it. The human-to-human contact allowed me to give in. And let go. So I did. Blindly. Aimlessly. I simply didn't care anymore.

At Foligno we were greeted by her *padre*, a thin, elegant man with graying hair, a bright, beautiful smile, sharply pressed clothes and a car that was big enough for three people and all of my luggage. When they kissed and hugged each other, it highlighted too well what it felt like to be hugged by someone who offers unconditional love. It was something I wouldn't feel, hold, smell, dance in for months, at best. I wished I had turned away before I saw it because I couldn't get it out of my head. And I wanted it out of my head.

It was in a whirlwind of Italian that the family of two drove me to a nearby *pensione* (a low-key hotel)--an aging, stucco building with three small terraces, dozens of thriving plants, red copper-tiled floors, a stone fireplace and wooden-beamed ceilings with empty straw-covered wine bottles that hung every 12 inches from side to side. Father and daughter communicating in song. Punctuating their points with a delicate gesture or two to direct their music. To reinforce their notes. To add to the flow. I watched. And listened. And longed for the day when someone would admire my Italian as much as I admired theirs. Graceful, passionate, loving.

With that as a backdrop, I realized that despite every single obstacle, every single challenge, every single doubt, every single disappointment, I had made my way there. To an Italy and a *pensione* I had dreamed about in my wild Italian fantasies. I felt proud again. And happy. And aware of my emotional schizophrenia. My eyes welled up with tears. From disbelief. From exhaustion. From gratitude.

Beatrice led me to my room, a simple rectangle with white, plastered walls that were invaded by only a dusty, mass-produced picture of Jesus Christ and a shower head. No curtain. Just a head. There were also a twin bed with a thin, white blanket, a sink and an old-fashioned, rotary dial phone.

We dropped my luggage on the bed, with the exception of my fanny pack, which carried my opportunities, and Beatrice brought me out to the main dining area for dinner. She ordered me a wonderful spaghetti dish, some red wine and lots of breadsticks, told me to set back my watch for daylight savings and, before she left, booked me a train to and hotel reservation in Perugia for the next day.

And there I was. Alone. In Italy. Where, on my first night, I ate nearly one bread stick for every strand of spaghetti, slept nearly one hour for every bread stick and showered in a stall that expelled less water onto my tired and dirty flesh than I would have expelled if I had spent half the evening spitting on myself.

Early the next morning I awoke to Beatrice's voice on the other end of the rotary phone. She had called a taxi to meet me at the *pensione* within the hour and get me to the train on time. After her call, another attempt at showering, some fresh clothes and a continental breakfast with *cappuccino*, I dragged my luggage to the Registration Desk to pay my bill. As I pulled out what I thought would be enough *lire* to cover one night's lodging, one night's dinner and breakfast, the young man behind the desk put his warm hand on top of mine and gestured for me to put the cash back in my pocket. All expenses had been paid, he said. By Beatrice. Leaving no phone. No address.

So within hours of stepping down in Italy, two different Veronicas at two different stations had brought towels to my face. A western cowboy with ruddy cheeks, a turquoise belt and large hands and an Italian model with a huge heart, velvet skin and voluminous hair. And both, of course, carried a lot of cash. If I had known that as a child, as we marched in step to The Stations Of The Cross, I might have paid a lot more attention.

Amen.

Chapter Three
Max Feeds The Face Of Jo

I believe that the first 36 hours of torture were meant to test me, a test that I would handle differently today. Today, I would never board Air Gloria. I would leave the cosmetics at home with 23 of my 30 sets of underpants, drink away my remaining $11 in the airport lounge to offset the fear of terrorist attack, ignore the 48 dismembered tampons on the luggage carousel and tell that woman in the taxi where to get off. But back then I was only five years out of college, still untainted, still unseasoned, still unprepared to unleash my bottomless arsenal of sarcasm and still headed for an adventure in *bella Italia* where, I was certain, I would find my soul mate, *la mia anima gemella*. A twin spirit who surfaced on the first day of school.

I arrived in Perugia on a Sunday. The university was closed so I had to wait until the next day to learn about my housing and schooling. With newness I like structure. With comfort I like spare time. At that point, I was hardly comfortable so I was looking for anything to fill up some 24 hours of freedom. A freedom I appreciated more as my life got more busy. More complicated. More crowded. Less free.

Early on Monday, I left my hotel and headed to school to be first in line for registration. When I arrived there, the holding pen for students was teeming with foreigners and reeked of disorder and chaos. Just a squared-off space with a ballooning collection of anxious young people. A replay of the airport carousel antics but with post adolescents playing the role of luggage.

I waited from 8:00 A.M. to 1:00 P.M., in a pack of pulsating, pushing, frustrated human beings, and was only partially registered when the university employees decided to break for lunch despite the lingering masses. Fortunately, I had accomplished enough in the five-hour, international hostage crisis to get into class the next day--which would meet down the street in a branch of *L'Università Per Stranieri,*

The University For Foreigners, or as a young Greek girl next to me translated, The University For Strange People. After the day I had spent, I believed she was more right than wrong.

The rest of the afternoon I bided my time by registering for a Visa extension with the police, buying two European notebooks with the small-blocked graph paper and visiting a few of the homes that the university had recommended for student housing. I wandered through Perugia trying to make some sense of the local maps and the system for numbering homes--numbers painted on blue and white ceramic tiles or embedded into the aged walls which sometimes traveled from 40 to 38A to 46 to 10 in one row. I walked down dark alleys and suspended stone pathways and little streets that were decorated with thriving green plants in copper-colored ceramic pots. And hiked the city's sloping lanes and tried to imitate the older citizens' method of zigzagging upward--an approach which is easier on the heart but harder on the watch. Four names down on my list, I found my sanctuary. Signora Estelle Palmisano. I pressed the intercom button and assumed that the syllables she sang out were summoning me to the top. So up I went.

Signora Palmisano had beautiful silver hair, a very huggable shape, no understanding of English and intense pride in her reliable cold and hot water, new closets and clean floors. Three times she informed me she had *acqua fredda e calda, fredda e calda, fredda e calda*. Her indisputable pride at offering both made me wonder if that combination of temperatures were a rarity in Perugia. And as we were shaking hands to confirm the arrangements before I found myself sleeping next to another anemic shower head, I realized she had more business savvy and shrewd marketing techniques than one would expect from an innocent, elderly, perfectly-coifed grandmother. She knew her audience, sensed the needs and threw out the line that hooked the water-obsessed American woman. It didn't matter to me. I got what I wanted, all for $2.91 per day *including* cold and hot water, and she got what she wanted and a little bonus. A half-Italian tenant. I would give her some company in her microcosm of The United Nations, a group which would include one German woman, one Greek woman, one Italian-American woman and one full Italian *padrona* (boss). My blood gave me an in and her immediate insistence that I call her Mamma was as sure a sign of that as anything could have been.

Mamma's home was located near the base of a sloping street that led to another street that led to the heart of Perugia. She lived on the top floor of a four-floor building that what it lacked in elevator service was made up for in character. It was a dark tan, almost but not quite brown, stucco building, a sort of ancient row house, that was adorned with large green shutters, vibrant planters and wrought iron lamplights. It was just a five-minute walk from both the main branch of the university and the side branch where my grammar and culture classes would be held. I'd go out the front door, take a right, pass (or not pass) a pastry shop, and head right down the wide, two-lane road with the stone wall that framed the view of the Umbrian countryside. Rich with farm plots, tall, thin trees, rolling hills and huge blue skies. The large black, metal university gate was on the left. Class would start at 8:00 A.M.

I moved in that afternoon.

I celebrated that night. First by taking a steaming hot shower and then by getting dressed up and going to dinner at *La Trattoria di Mamma e Papà*, a little restaurant I had found on a dark and narrow side street in Perugia. It was the size of my parents' living room and held four small tables draped in stiff white tablecloths. Red and white napkins were standing on their own in the center of the chipped and seasoned dishes.

The menu was handwritten on half of an 8.5 x 11 inch sheet of paper and was inserted into a plastic sheath. Between the different handwriting and the new vocabulary, I couldn't decipher anything except *antipasto* and Coca Cola; so that's what I chose. As I reveled in my ordering independence. Offered as some proof of my increasingly confident status and my decreasingly needy existence.

As I prepared the napkin on my lap and took notice of the restaurant's emptiness, I conjured up images of the kind of *antipasto* I knew--lots of lettuce, *provolone, mozzarella,* artichokes, roasted peppers, *mortadella* and some Genoa *salame.* And I salivated as I could taste the *salame* wrapped around an artichoke and the *provolone* sharing a space on my taste buds with the roasted peppers. With that, a plate the size of a saucer landed under my nose just after I had rearranged my silverware. No lettuce. No *mozzarella.* No artichokes.

Almost nothing familiar. Instead, I got liver pate´, four black olives and four green olives, and a piece of bread whose role, unbeknownst to them, was to ward off the gagging impulse that pate´ and olives incited.

As the elderly couple proudly hovered, he with a large fork in his hand, balding, painfully thin, somber and half of *American Gothic*, she with an apron in her hand, built like potato *gnocchi*, gawking, smiling, nodding to see if I'd nod back in approval, I began by choking down each morsel of food with a swig of Coca Cola. One for one over the course of 60 long, torturous minutes. One bite, one swig. One bite, one swig. It was an adult force-feed that brought back memories of being eight years-old and being required to eat one out of every two canned peas that stood coagulating on my plate. Partially hidden under the remnants of rice.

I had one bottle of Coke for every two olives I ate that night. And in-between each olive and each gulp I nodded joyous approval to the parents who were flanking me. Two more Cokes for the pate´ alone brought the food bill to 60 cents and the drink bill to $16. Worth almost six nights' lodging. So much for frugality. And so much, too, for a good night's sleep on my first night in my new home. With dreams invaded by roaming pate´, a caffeine high and visions of farmers nudging peas around my plate with pitchforks that had an olive on each tine.

The next day I was the first one up and out of the house and the fourth one into the third classroom on the left on the first floor. I waited quietly in my bolted-to-the-floor chair and spoke to no one as I stared at my blank block notebook and brand new Italian-English dictionary. The classroom crowded up quickly, and I remained focused on my four important tasks. Staring at my notebook. Staring at my dictionary. Not making eye contact with the international crowd that was sauntering in but listening to every word that was uttered. I could be very shy. Painfully shy, at times. But I could be nosy. Painfully nosy, at times. It was an effective combination.

Just before 8:00 A.M., a short, skinny and very young instructor with small, round glasses, a Modigliani face, long, somewhat stringy, brown hair and dark brown eyes flew into the room. She said something in a high-pitched voice. Welcome to Italy or my name is whatever or how are you or bite me. I didn't know. But what I did know is that within five minutes of Italian class beginning, I was completely out of my league. Total Italian. Total immersion. Total submersion. Ms. Modigliani had obviously misjudged, misunderstood, misread the bottomless depth of our ignorance. We didn't speak Italian. That's why we were there. Such as the couple in the front row from Great Britain who were trying to learn the language to take over a parish in Rome. The Mexican trio of friends (two girls and one boy) from the Yucatan who had the richest, blackest hair on earth and eyes that could bring anyone straight to their souls. The mid-20s Australian nurses, the late-teens Palestinians and the hormone-raging Greek twins who were already charting a course on their social maps. And the two Americans, one from Boston and one from Florida, who found a comfort in each other that would have never existed within their normal boundaries.

But Ms. Modigliani didn't care. Sentence after sentence. Gesture after gesture. Question after question met with wrinkled foreheads and stupid looks. I searched for any recognizable words. *Mangiare. Ciao. Nonno. Nonna. Arrivederci. Pasta.* Absolutely nothing. So then I searched for the clock and for the face of a classmate that was also insinuating "I am a total moron."

Time dragged by, one whining woman and 25 people stunned into extreme anxiety. After about two hours, she shooed us out of the room to go get an *espresso*. We shuffled out of the class, eyes half-closed, and moved cattle-like down the narrow hallway to the cafè at the end of the cold, tiled floor. Bumping into each other. Yawning. Smiling. Catatonic.

I hadn't had one sip of coffee throughout my entire life until that very moment. I had survived college and its 12-hour study days, fruitfly checks at 3:00 A.M. to prevent mating and to preserve virgins, and a 100-page thesis on primitive tribes near Papua, New Guinea without it, but that educational dictator, on day one, scared me into it. And I bless her--for in time I spoke a little more fluently with a shot of *espresso* and a glass of red wine, felt downright bilingual with a pot of *espresso* and a bottle of red wine and was a dead ringer for Sophia Loren with a jug of each. Or so I thought.

The caffeine kick made the classroom minutes pass much more quickly and squelched my inclination to wallow in ignorant shame.

I was more focused on the buzz than my submersion. On the bean than my dismay. Soon it was time for lunch. *"Allora, potete mangiare adesso. Ci vediamo dopo."* Hearing *mangiare* was all I needed. Any Italian who can't translate that should be cast out to sea.

As I began fantasizing about eating some good Italian food, absent olives, absent pate´, absent two sweet but needy, restaurant owners, I was interrupted by a tap on the shoulder and a greeting in English-with-a-sharp-German-accent. And a massively, toothy grin. "Hello. My name is Max. Massimo, in Italian. Would you like to have lunch together?" "Sure. My name is Jo. Gio in Italian. G-I-O. But it's pronounced the same way." When we stood to leave, I was grateful for his gesture. It beat eating alone.

I followed in Massimo's tall shadow to the *mensa*--the student cafeteria right down the hill from school. Since he seemed to know the routine, I took whatever he took. Bread (warm and fresh baked, so good it was regarded as sinful to smear it with butter), *pasta* with red sauce, veal (thinly cut and just the right portion--they didn't supersize their meals for an additional 39 cents), green beans and carrots (dressed simply with salt, pepper and olive oil), roasted potatoes, *Bel Paese* cheese (wrapped in a silver and green foil to protect the soft, creamy, spreadable cheese inside) and a miniature bottle of wine, Chianti. Then fruit for dessert. Pears. You might have thought we had just come from basic training. The cost--1,000 *lire* or 50 cents.

We grabbed a table for two and did a getting-to-know-you routine as we tore through the meal--with the *Bel Paese* on bread and the Chianti adding as much to the adventure as the words of my new acquaintance. I studied his looks and mannerisms as he spoke, and they invaded my thoughts as I learned his life history. A privileged youth within the Berlin Wall. Relative success in school. The eldest of three children. A second home in Bavaria. Profound pride in his family's accomplishments. And an imminent partnership in the family business--men's clothing. "Being able to talk with the top Milano fashion designers in their native language would be a major plus," he said, as he peered through his horn-rimmed glasses and awkwardly rearranged his brown, curly locks with his large, smooth hands. "A lot of our clothing is made exclusively for our company by the best of the Italian best," he delivered in modest fits and starts--with the most key words earning the most emphatic German influences.

I hesitated before sharing my personal history--suddenly aware that my upbringing in a farming town felt pale in comparison to life inside the Berlin Wall. And that my relatively uneventful teaching career in anthropology, mathematics and athletics didn't have me mingling with Giorgio Armani and Gianni Versace on a Saturday night. Still, there was a part of me that felt more privileged by what brought me to Italy. Mine was personal. Not financial. Mine was Nonno. My grandfather. My mother's father. A family hero. Who boarded a ship in Palermo, Sicily in the late 1800s, with three siblings at his heels, and waved good-bye to the hopeful parents who remained on the Italian shores. Shores he would never visit again. And shores his parents would never leave.

He bravely turned to a new land, my *nonno*. With no grasp of English. No job. And no mission other than fulfilling the promise to his parents. To care for the youngest and to ensure that they had a better life. It had to become worth the pain of their separation. A balance that my *nonno* insisted could never even out.

Nonno helped parent three children that turned into nine grandchildren--five of whom were born in time to be held in his arms. An honor that was reserved for my three siblings but not for me. Four years dragged by between the time his toes last touched the earth and mine first came to light. I was the only one in my family. And my difference is documented in that legendary last photo. That holds a place of dignity in each household. Taken two weeks before he said good-bye.

I watched Max listen to me as I spoke. His handling of my story would tell a story of its own. A story of our future as friends. He listened earnestly. And interrupted only to ask a question. And then quieted down again. To hear more of what I knew of the small, balding grandfather with the round glasses, classic sense of humor and warmth of rare proportions. And to learn of my need to know more. Within his country's borders. In Italy. As I was schooled in his language, ate his foods, breathed his air, walked his streets and made my way from Perugia to Tusa to catch glimpses of a lineage he left behind. Children of siblings who were born after he left--to parents who were consumed by the loss of their family.

Max was riveted. And that was the first of hundreds of signs. Soul mate signs.

After a *passeggiata* (walk) and another shot of *espresso*, we made our way back to class for the culture portion. On the way, Max asked if I'd like to come over for dinner that night. He had rented a nice apartment on the lower part of the hilltown. We'd shop together and head there after school. Still, a woman traveling alone. No longer incapacitated, hysterical, vulnerable, exhausted and dirty. No longer climbing into an unmarked taxi with four strangers and little cash. Just having a little dinner with someone who received my words with compassion and tenderness. I was relieved that I already had a friend.

The tampon debacle was a distant memory.

Culture class went a little more smoothly. We had a different teacher--also short but with a porcelain-tone face which was nearly perfectly round. She was absolutely hyper. Wired. And didn't speak a word of English but was astute enough to recognize when we weren't understanding a single syllable she had uttered. She wouldn't rework the sentences, she'd just say them a little more loudly, with a few more gestures and facial contortions, until we could get the gist. Then an irresistible smile would spread across her face--almost epiphanal. Annie Sullivan to a bunch of Helen Kellers.

I butchered my first Italian sentence that day. *"Gio, vieni dagli Stati Uniti?"* (Jo, do you come from the United States?) *"Si, sono gli Stati Uniti."* (Yes, I am the United States.) I had already made a name for myself. A pompous name. But a name.

After school, Max and I walked to my house together. Leisurely. Peacefully. Smoothly. I was aware of a ritual that was not yet routine. And aware that I hoped it would never become that. That the *espresso* smells from the nearby bar would never be taken for granted. That the roses on the wrought iron gate would never go unnoticed. That the ancient buildings that lived to tell a story would never lose my respect. And that my process would never surrender to my product.

When we arrived, and Signora Palmisano caught a glimpse of him on the landing, her eyes widened like saucers. Evidence of the shock of post pubescent male genitalia in her all-female household. So I asked him to wait outside as I grabbed some money and a jacket, said good-bye to Mamma and ran to the street for the beginning of our magical tour--starting with the bread.

Our pure white, tasteless American bread bears not even a distant resemblance to its foreign relatives. My first entrance into the land of the real stuff was through a set of glass beads from the 1960s into a hollowed out, shallow, hole-in-the-wall from the 1460s. Without Max, I would have walked right by, mistaking it for a brothel. The aromas and the offerings were staggering. Round, oval, cylindrical, squared off, flat, thin, medium, thick, extra thick, squishy inside, squishy outside, hardened inside, hardened outside, with green olives, with black olives, with black and green olives, without olives, salted, unsalted, warmed or cooled, white or wheat. When the sweet young girl behind the counter greeted us with a *"Buona sera. Dica!"* I reached into my head to pull out the two Italian sentences I had already mastered. Where is the toilet? and My name is Jo. Max stepped forward to order a round, squishy inside, hardened outside, without olives, unsalted and cooled white loaf before I was responsible for leading us to a back room that housed one of Europe's more interesting flushes-of-choice.

The second stop was the *pasta* shop--a small, square *negozio* (store) whose interior was as sanitary as a research hospital. On the left stood a silver-polished, state-of-the-art machine that welcomed flour and water in the front door and escorted *fettuccini* and *linguini* out the back, as they were cooled by a built-in fan, cut at scientifically-determined lengths and caught with the skill of a doctor at a delivery involving multiple births. On the right stood the display counter guarded by four attendants dressed in long, white coats and plastic gloves who looked over their offspring with pride. We lingered and watched them make fresh *pasta* for quite awhile. I was amazed, almost awed, by the artistry and amazed, almost awed, by what passes for entertainment when I have time to enjoy life. *Linguini, fettuccini, spaghetti, penne* and *rigatoni*--all testaments to what a serious commitment and hundreds of years of perfecting a craft can do. We selected *linguini* to make *alla panna* (in white sauce) and vowed to return, which we did, every, single week for four straight months.

Then we were off to what would become my favorite fixation. A cheese and meat paradise near the top of a steeply-sloped, cobblestone street in the center of Perugia. Hanging from the rafters in a beautifully intricate display were hundreds of uniquely sculpted cheeses and meats. *Salame* and *prosciutto* and *mortadella* and dozens of others and then, on the side walls, Nutella and fruit juices and *pasta* and breads and crackers and olive oils. Rows and rows of olive oils. Tall olive oils, small olive oils, round olive oils, aromatic olive oils, olive oils with floating seasonings and olive oils that were virgin, extra virgin, extra extra virgin!! Before I read all the labels and made note of their various sexual exploits, or lack thereof, Max had placed an order with the three identically tall and identically professional gentlemen behind the counter for some *mortadella, salame, prosciutto, mozzarella, parmigiano* and *schamorza*, the last of which was molded in such a way that it formed the outline of a tiny little human, with a tiny little head and a protruding belly. It was heretofore known, in our small circle, as the fetus cheese.

The liquor store was next. No Ripple or Mateus to pick from. Instead, for scarily reasonable prices, was a remarkable array of the region's finest wines, all arranged and stacked in perfection. All glittering with colorful wraps to protect the corks and labels that marked the history of the grapes' evolution. Their birth. Their adolescence. Their sprint to adulthood. And their death. And, of course, their afterlife, in the bottles in the lands across the globe. Their journey confirmed the presence of hereafter--a hereafter that cemented our notions of the pleasantries of heaven and of the recycling of the spirits. Max selected two bottles of Galestro, and we headed for the *pasticceria.*

Over the course of the shopping excursion, my nose had been taken on a Hedonistic ride of breads and *pasta* and cheeses and meats. I was not prepared, however, for the smells of the *pasticceria*--smells that first greeted me on the Perugian streets and then lured me inside past an artistic window display of tortes, tarts, cakes, pies, elephant ears, donuts, *cannoli* and *profitterò*--the last of which begin with a cream-filled center, surrounded by a moist, sweet cake encased in a chocolate glaze. The *pasticceria* sold them in three sizes--groups of three, groups of eight and groups of 20. Max bought the 20. Apparently, there'd be other guests.

Our last stop, mercifully, was at a fruit and vegetable store, a store that announced itself not with neon lights and blinking bulbs but with rough crates tilted at 45 degree angles that held the richest, reddest tomatoes and the largest, greenest grapes and the sweetest, yellowest peppers on the planet. Vegetables that cracked with freshness as water spilled over my lips, making me realize that I had lived my life with their impostors. Or, at best, their underachieving siblings. Max selected a few tomatoes and some green, red and yellow peppers for our *antipasto* dish and then some oranges and grapes to clean the palate--selections made not by touching them himself, but by calling the balding storekeeper to the crates with a flick of his finger. The proprietor moved from offering to offering, hand-picking the best and placing each kind in its own private, brown bag, which got weighed on a white-coated scale and marked with the price he added in his head. No pictures of different fruits on his cash register to guide the calculations. When the tallying was over, he shuffled to another crate, which we had insensitively bypassed, and threw in a dozen fresh figs. For free. As if he knew that the meal would fall short without them.

Finally, we were finished and just a few meters from Max's apartment, which was a blessing since, at that point, we had enough bags with enough food to recreate The Last Supper. And, it almost was. Death by overeating.

Max certainly knew how to live, and he immediately proceeded to open my eyes to the finer things in life, as well as reinforce several of The Seven Deadly Sins. Starring gluttony and sloth. Two post-college sports that worked themselves into my adult existence at random junctures.

As soon as we entered his apartment, an Italian aria from his stereo filled the room. He brought matches to the candles, and the table was being set as I stripped the purple plastic off of my first bottle of Galestro and freed the wine within. Our first toast with our first glasses marked the beginning of what would become a long and wonderful friendship.

The wine and the food flowed heavily that night. The two bottles were steadily but deliciously emptied as were the plates and plates of delicacies that reached the table--the meats, cheeses, fresh figs, peppers, bread, wine and *linguini*. Each item that entered my mouth slapped my tongue silly. Gave it life. Awakened the insides of my cheeks and the back of my throat.

With each nibble, it was more and more clear that a tiny sampling of each was insufficient. Woefully inadequate. It took three or four or five tastes to satisfy the early cravings. And then there was the increasing internal panic. The Torture Of Finite. Only one kilo of Parmesan. Only one tiny fetus cheese. Only half a pound of *mortadella* and *prosciutto*. Only 12 figs. I needed to keep pace with Max. If I didn't, he'd press on, innocently eating up my share or even, God forbid, moving the plate beyond my arm's reach. My behavior, my obsession, had already reached sickening proportions, only 10 hours after meeting my host.

As the evening wore on, I yearned for a pair of bloomers or a broken-in pair of sweats. I could feel my stomach pressing tighter and tighter against my already too-small jeans. And it's a very sad commentary when underpants restrict freedom of movement. Just when I thought it couldn't get any worse, it happened. The ultimate act of extreme gorging. I look back on it with confusion, disbelief, disgust. With revulsion, repulsion, expulsion. And, somewhere in the sick recesses of my mind, with utter satiation and joy.

As Max rose from the table one last time, having cleared away all of the incriminating evidence, I was aware of my purgatory status, trapped between heaven and hell. The heaven of absolute euphoria. The hell of absolute pain. I slouched down in my chair, trying to unbutton my pants from under my already untucked shirt, and wished I knew Max a lot better because, at that moment, I would have liked to remove my pants and unleash the flesh. Instead, I caught a glimpse of an object moving through the air to rest under my nose. Unrecognizable at first, much like the luggage carousel tampons, the scent brought them into clearer focus. Twenty *profitterò*. Twenty.

What could I say? What could I do? Would declining them be rude? Would he never invite me there again? He seemed poised to dig in, but I knew he'd politely offer me one first and then watch as his choice pleased me. So, I took one, and then he took one. And then I took one. And then he took one. Like a clumsily choreographed scene in a bad Broadway show, we reached for the chocolate balls. Jo. Max. Jo. Max. And, like the luggage carousel dance at

Ciampino Airport, it repeated itself 10 times. Ten pressings of the flesh. Ten scurryings. Ten forced consumptions of food.

Finally, as the hour neared midnight, we removed our napkins from our laps, we wiped our mouths, we ate no more. Instead, the two of us, stuffed like Thanksgiving turkeys primed for the holiday celebration, waddled away from the table--gobbling, cackling, waiting, waiting, praying to be shot...

Chapter Four
Petra Spots The Ass Of Orca

U nfortunately for Max and me, the Italians do not celebrate Thanksgiving. Thus, the shooting never took place. Getting home, then, in a mildly inebriated and near paralyzed state of obesity remained an issue. The first challenge, of course, was gaining some form of mobility without my unbuttoned pants dropping to the ground. Never a bridge to be crossed, however, since the waist of my unbuttoned trousers was firmly grounded in the irregular trench marks that flanked my bellybutton. Sweet Jesus.

We decided we'd walk back to my home instead of taking his car. Never testing the theory that his four cylinder VW Golf actually could have hauled our load. Besides, we thought that the three kilometer hike up and down the hills and stairways of Perugia would burn off at least two of the *profitterò*.

The decision was a painful one from the very start. Each step making us regret that one extra slice of Parmesan or *mortadella* or chocolate-casing. That final sip of Galestro or the juicy pepper. Each step striking a knife into our hearts and sides, a metaphorical slicing off of flesh that I had come to wish were literal. And final. Slow, anguished, labored forward and sometimes lateral progress. Up, up, up the sharply-sloped streets, past the stores, then shadowed in darkness, that brought us our joy and then our pain. Then hiding the foods that put us over the edge. Not speaking. Just struggling to breathe. To stay mobile. To hide our obvious embarrassment over our obvious gluttony. Caught up in a vanity that had excused itself, hidden itself, killed itself at the dinner table just moments before.

By the time we reached *Corso Vannucci*, the summit of Perugia, Max was panting like a wild boar and I like an injured one. Sweaty. Exhausted. But the summit was the summit, and it was all downhill from there. More gravity-friendly. More enticing to the temporarily-obese. Each more carefree, less labored step loosened the constriction around my waist and laid a seed of hope that I might live to see another day. Might entertain the notion of having another spot of food some day, some week, some month from then. I had obviously forgotten about the 117 steep cement stairs that led to my floor. That loomed in the near distance. That reintroduced the havoc I had discarded on my welcomed descent.

Max reached for the big, heavy, brown, wooden door to my building and opened it for me. Then, in a gesture of self-preservation, he waved good-bye to me from the bottom of the steps and watched the widening expanse, known as my butt, wobble slowly to the top. His parting greeting suffocated by the noisy pounding of my heart.

I pushed my stubby right hand into the right pocket of my skintight pants and reached for the house key, performing gymnastics to dislodge it from the deathlike grip that had developed between my jeans and my flesh. I opened the door, closed it quietly and stumbled to my bedroom. Shuffling my way to my twin bed. Passing my little pantry with its day-old bread, tuna fish, Rice Krispies and chunks of Parmesan cheese, whose pungent, powerful smell wafted in my direction and almost put me over the edge. I turned off the light. To kill the scent. And to beach. To hide. To sleep. To dream of *profitterò* and wine and gluttony. And death.

I awoke hours later to the painfully loud voice of Susanna, an older Greek tenant and overwhelming know-it-all. She was the longest resident in the house, besides Mamma, and she assumed an air of superiority as a result. I hated assumptions, I hated airs, and I already hated Susanna.

That morning, (and, I would come to find out, every morning), as soon as Mamma left the kitchen, Susanna began ranting about her time the night before and her usual exploits with a few men. It was loud, cocky and riddled with untruths. Petra, a skinny, bleached-blonde, German roommate with almond-shaped eyes, (often offset with dark black or bright blue eyeliner), a great sense of life, a mastery of four languages and an unedited sense of humor, would politely listen and smile. Later I discovered that Petra never heard a word Susanna was saying. She was happy to position herself near the one tiny window in the old kitchen. On a stool. With a record album wrapped in aluminum foil. Trying to usurp the sickly remnants of the late-September sun. And, instead of listening, thinking about her boyfriend who lived near the Austrian border, her place of great sex and mind-altering refreshments. I loved her irreverence. And I already loved the smashing of stereotypes that was coming down all around me. Two Germans. Max and Petra. Both free-spirited and full of life. Both soaking in the pleasures of each heartbeat. Both destroying the world's image of Germans as rigid and inflexible. As unaccepting and cold. Both dismantling, in their own ways, the enormous spectacle of assumption.

I entered the kitchen only briefly that morning. I backed straight out when I heard Susanna's flappings and made my way to the bathroom, a narrow room near the end of the hallway that housed a toilet, a bidet, a sink, a shelf and an old-fashioned bathtub with a thin, see-through shower curtain. There were very strict bathroom rules that Mamma had asked Petra to translate to me on the first day of my arrival, had asked Susanna to translate later that same day and had asked both of them to translate one more time that same night.

Number One: Under no circumstances should water spill onto the floor. Not one tiny drop. In the highly unlikely event that a tenant allowed that to happen, the mess must be wiped up immediately, using her own towel. Number Two: The showers had to be quick. Although our landlady was deeply proud of the availability of cold and hot water, her tenants should never abuse that benefit. Number Three: We were to take only one shower per day. Even one, according to Mamma, was considered excessive. But she would allow it. Number Four: A broken rule, accidental or otherwise, must be reported to Mamma as soon as it happened. Period.

She, apparently, had some Hitlerian tendencies.

Seconds after I was well-ensconced inside the shower and on my way to examining the profoundly protruding stomach that had blossomed in one short, 24-hour period, Petra interrupted me in the bathroom to start performing her own ablutions. As she lowered herself onto the toilet and I bent over slightly to rinse the shampoo from my hair, there was a serious eruption of laughter just outside the tub as she observed, firsthand, the results of the previous night's culinary orgy. My larger-than-ever, pale, white bottom pressed firmly against the transparent shower curtain. One cheek. Two cheeks. Outlined and in full view. Petra spewed venom as I hastily peeled the dainty little curtain off of my *sedere* (bottom), and as I did, the curtain ripped off of its flimsy rod (relieving me of any remaining dignity or decorum) and water gushed onto the tiled floor. Obliterating, in a split second, Rule Number One.

I could feel the blood drain from my face as I climbed out of the shower and onto the soaking wet bath mat. Petra just sat on the toilet, laughing, jibing, teasing as I scurried from bidet to sink to tub. Using my towel to mop up the floor but failing in my goal to cover up the soaked mat and ripped shower curtain. So facing Mamma was inevitable--sweet, large, cheeky, stern, inevitable Mamma.

She was in her room having breakfast in her sleeveless, green muu-muu and watching a TV whose volume was set on one billion when I knocked on the door. With the exceptions of her grandson, Paolo, and Italian food, I believe that the TV provided her with more joy and company than anything else. It was always on. Dubbed cowboy movies. Old Katharine Hepburn films. Slapstick. Silly cartoons and, late at night, the striptease game show. She would sit for hours, praising John Wayne, laughing, nodding off and not even beginning to recognize or maybe recognizing but not caring about the degrading commentary against women. That morning she was watching a rerun of *One Day At A Time*. Pithy Bonnie Franklin introducing Mamma to the intricacies of the American lifestyle. I prayed for a power surge.

She called for me to come in, which I did, with the wet bath mat and ripped Saran Wrap shower curtain in my hand. Before I could speak, Mamma rose from her chair, purposefully, and made her way to me. The china trinkets jiggled as she approached. I jiggled as she approached. She jiggled as she approached. And, in one sweeping movement, she grabbed the evidence from my hands and, without speaking, maneuvered past me to the kitchen.

When I arrived behind her, I saw that Petra and Susanna had secured front row seats for the scene. Petra was back to her sunning stool pretending, that time, to tune out. Susanna was at the far end of the kitchen table with her eyes on Mamma, and then on me, and then on Mamma, again. Eyes grinding, peering and with a hint of glee. Lips curved upward. Suppressing a smile. Maybe even a laugh. Borderline psychotic.

Mamma shook by both of them without looking up, without dignifying their nosiness and morbid curiosity. She threw the bath mat in the washer and the shower curtain in the trash and brushed by me as she headed for the spare curtains in the hall closet. Within seconds, she was back in the kitchen and reaching for my trembling hand, pulling me forward, back toward her TV room and to her seat, where she placed her big, hammock arm around my shoulder and a morning *espresso* in my hand. It was there that I waited, eyes opened onto the TV, and prepared to laugh hysterically at the next insipid sitcom retort. No matter how intolerable. How repulsive.

When minutes ticked by and I was slowly assured that my execution had been averted, two things came to mind. First, maybe Bonnie Franklin wasn't so bad after all. And second, there must have been an unspoken amendment to the Bathroom Constitution, always implemented but never acknowledged. Number Five: If you have some genuine Italian blood coursing through your veins, ignore Rules 1-4. That, apparently, can make all the difference.

When *One Day At A Time* was over, I pried myself away from the confines of Mamma's cocoon to head for school. Each day was the same routine. Grammar classes from 8:00 A.M.--noon. Lunch at the *mensa.* Culture classes from 2:00--5:00 P.M. And then freedom. I ran into Max as soon as I got to school, and we replayed the evening before. Little did we know, then, that that night was the first of what would be dozens of meals together and that we, in our adult lives, would never be as thin again as we were the day we met. We always wished we had taken a photo of ourselves that night for a future and frightening "Before and After" comparison. The pre- and post-double chin eras. Max asked if I would be interested in an overnight trip to Florence over the weekend. I was.

School that day brought John into my life. A classical pianist from New Zealand who, in some ways, but not all ways, ended up making my life in Perugia easier. It was a treat to be able to speak English without carefully selecting my words, repeating phrases, gesticulating with great energy and scream-talking. That got to be very taxing. And, of course, I was a spoiled brat, unwilling to acknowledge the wonder of nearly the entire international student population of Perugia speaking some English. I wanted them, you see, to speak *perfect* English, as I did the night 10 of us went out to dinner at an underground bar in the center of Perugia. Eight Germans, one Greek and I. If German is a cousin to English, it has to be an ostracized one, because there was not one syllable that seemed remotely related. So I was left to speak with the Greek woman whose command of English was poor but much better than my command of Greek, which was nonexistent. Our conversation consisted of "Do you like Italy?" and "Where are you from in Greece/U.S.?" and "Where do you live in Perugia?" and then, again, "Do you like Italy?" I was bored out of my mind. Occasionally Max would turn to me to check in on how I was doing as his cohorts and he sipped the wine they opted for over beer. I just ordered another draft that night as my brain waves abandoned their search for stimulation.

My English worsened more each day. I slowed my speech, chose simple vocabulary words and sounded impaired, as in the time I told John that at Christmas I was flying home to The United States on a charter flight. Then I went on to add, very, very, slowly, "You see, (pause) a charter flight (pause) is a flight (pause) that costs a lot (pause) less (pause) money. I am going to (pause)..." John abruptly interrupted and reminded me that he, too, was a native English speaker and that he, too, had a working definition of "charter." Right.

I noticed John the moment he entered the classroom. He had thinning brown, coarse hair, a day-old beard, large, worn hands, skinny lips to match his skinny legs and was dressed in narrow-waisted jeans and a cotton, ribbed sweater. And he reeked of cigarettes. So friendship was fine, but anything else was highly unlikely. I just couldn't stand the smell up close and personal. But it wasn't just that that would prevent any kind of intimacy. It was his hurtful, anti-American positions--which didn't take long to emerge.

He sat next to me, and I quickly was enamored of his accent and his personality. John was a bit of free spirit, not governed by traditional rules or pressures. Not overly compelled to master the language. Not overly compelled to butcher it either. He did, though. Weeks and weeks after class had begun, John's only complete and correct sentence was, *"Mi chiamo Gianni."* (My name is John.) He thought I was a linguistic genius when I remembered to pluralize *cappuccino* to *cappuccini* when I was ordering two.

That second day of school, we hit it off. The English was so fluid. So smooth. And, I could tell, so unsettling to Max whose eyes and ears were pretending to be focused somewhere else but were lingering on our every move and word from across the aisle. I wasn't sure why he was having such a reaction. First, our relationship was hardly defined well enough to start constructing impenetrable barriers. Second, I hadn't traveled thousands of miles to limit my relationships. And third, my God, it was only the second day of school.

Our teacher entered the room about five minutes late in a whirlwind of energy and Italian. She was speaking complete foreign sentences, but I was hearing nothing except some strategically-placed vowels and a delightful tune. We cracked open our textbooks and started on page one. A directive which was made clear to us not by her words but by her stepping to the front of her desk, pointing to her book and gesturing for us to open it together. As they used to do on *Romper Room*.

Within the hour, in the mother of all miracles, some of us were actually speaking Italian, with book in hand, examining the sketches of the characters who were trying to guide us to fluency. I was stunned when I heard myself making a reservation for a room in a hotel and asking for cheese in a store. I was thrilled when I could count to 20, say my colors and recite the days of the week. And almost blown away when I understood the gist of what she said when she told us to go get another *espresso* in the midmorning break. I felt bilingual. Give me *L'Inferno* today, and I'll have it translated tomorrow. It was the same kind of feeling I have when I muster one good morning of dieting and expect to be 15 pounds lighter that night.

I chugged back my *espresso* with a professional wrist-snap and welcomed our return to the classroom. The rest of the morning passed much the same way. More reservations, more orders at the cheese and meat store, more reciting of the days and months and numbers. Each minute, each word, each sentence was laying the groundwork that would lead to a house that I couldn't wait to build. That would hold the memories I'd been stripped of sharing. So by the time John leaned over to me to ask if I'd like to have some tea at his apartment during the break between our grammar and culture classes, I was on Cloud *Nove*. Max joined the three Mexican students for lunch at the *mensa* when he saw me gather my books and head out the door with John. It was only for tea, but the look on his face suggested he thought otherwise. He was wrong.

John had rented an apartment just around the corner from my house. He shared the flat with a woman with dual citizenship (German and Australian) and a man from Scotland. Each person had her or his own bedroom and a small kitchen and bathroom in common. The apartment was stark in its decorations, and it paled in comparison to Mamma's place. Still, it offered the pleasures of independence.

John set two places at the kitchen table that had three chairs with the stuffing oozing out of all corners. He used the same chipped, white plates that dozens of other renting students had used before him but went into his own room to bring back two teacups and a teapot he had bought on a visit to Australia. The cups were in perfect condition. Stenciled with scenes of the hunt--horses and dogs and men with guns painted on the sides. He led me through his tea-making ritual with almost laughable seriousness and shared the rules that were, like Mamma's Bathroom Rules, very strict.

Rarely wash the teapot. The stained buildup of tea adds a seasoned flavor to the drink. Warm the empty pot first with boiling hot water. Let the tea leaves soak a bit in a modest amount of fresh hot water before filling the pot. Steep for roughly five minutes but no more. Put the milk in the bottom of the teacup first. And then pour. Always serve a little sweet and, above all, just take a break from the day and talk.

Over our months together in Perugia, John and I did our share of talking over tea, but the conversation that day, our first day, was more unpredictable than I would have liked. It was sweet and polite and then direct and harsh. And never void of honesty and bluntness. He was steadfastly anti-American. Vietnam. ("Why didn't you ever take responsibility for your failure?") Economic sanctions. Nuclear power. ("Egos before safety.") American ethnocentricity. Even my presence in Perugia, in his language class, reeked of our butting our noses into everyone's business. ("I wish this place had fewer Americans, you know? They're everywhere.")

He was impatient and intolerant. And the mood was, at times, in sharp contrast to my perceptions of afternoon teas and classical pianists. I was confused by his invitation. It seemed he had invited me over to scare me away. And assumed he was winning as I took the hits and sipped my tea. Until finally, finally, he paused. Long enough to read my reaction. Long enough to see that I neither lashed out to defend and deny nor stepped forward to accept unequivocal responsibility.

And then I left. To go to culture class. Alone.

Along the way, my body did what my words did not when my half-eaten scone from John's biased pantry was crushed into tiny crumbs by my angry American foot. Spreading more of us along the Perugian streets. To spite him. And then I smirked, with gratitude, for a Boston Tea Party that buried that British tradition in my country's watery grave. Never to surface in our list of more happy rituals.

Chapter Five
The Day Michelangelo Was Outed

The alarm clock went off at 5:30 A.M. that coming Saturday. I quietly scooted into the shower, careful not to plaster the curtain against my breasts, stomach or rear end, careful not to allow Petra into the bathroom while I was taking a shower, careful not to spill a drop of water on the tile and careful to be in and out of the trough in minutes. For Max and I were headed for Florence.

The house was dead quiet, except for the slow but painstakingly steady snoring of my landlady. She produced extraordinary noises while sleeping, and I had been there long enough that I just had to take a look, especially since the door was already slightly ajar.

Mamma was wearing the nighttime version of the daytime muu-muu. She was curiously sprawled on her sleeper couch in her room. Backside down. Head deeply embedded in her pillow. Back arched excruciatingly upward. Arms stretched out to the sides conjuring up, again, The Stations Of The Cross. Her chest was thrust upward, and one leg was bent at the knee. The other straight out.

Every six seconds, as reliable as a metronome, Mamma inhaled deeply, gutturally through her nose and open mouth. After a one-to-two second pause, she slapped her mouth shut, leaving just a small hole on the left-hand side of her lips. Then, like a radiator, forced air pushed through, vibrating her lips and thrusting her breasts further upward, only to be lowered in the two-second interval during which the dance was set up to begin anew. Extraordinary. Frightening. The objects were closer than they should have appeared.

I slowly closed the door and made my way to the kitchen. A quick bowl of Rice Krispies, a glass of Orangina and back to my bedroom to get dressed. My favorite part of the morning and evening routines was opening and closing the blinds. No screens. No panes of glass. Just large, green, wooden blinds tightly secured by an antique brass latch that helped to block out all evidence of life outside my tomb.

I threw open the blinds and glanced down to see if Max had arrived. Not yet, but the sun had, and it was going to be a perfect day.

I threw on a sample of my newly-purchased courageous European clothing. Some black pants, a white, cotton, long-sleeved shirt, some sandals and an enormous red belt. I thought I was stylish and cool. Now I look at old photos and think I could have doubled as an employee of Allied Van Lines. I threw some things into an overnight bag, grabbed my camera and a fresh roll of film and made my way down the 117 steps to wait for Max outside. We would be driving to Florence. But first we'd head toward Siena and visit the wine country that was nestled in-between those two great Italian cities. It should take us the better part of the morning and into the afternoon to get to our final destination, particularly if we stopped along the way.

Max pulled up shortly. On time, tall, polite, well-dressed. That day he had on a blue-black pair of crushed linen/silk trousers that easily covered his large frame, an equally baggy, light, silk shirt, a smooth black belt and butter soft, leather, tasseled shoes to match. And white socks. We later discussed that in America, white socks would have spelled a major fashion disaster, items that would have evoked a "Dorks Are Us" response--but in Europe, he said, they were a claim to style, elegance and even, depending on the socks, wealth. In any event, Max was a walking advertisement for his family's stores. An ambulatory tax write-off.

Despite the handsome appearance and flashy lifestyle, there was absolutely no sexual tension between us. It was nice, actually, as it relieved some of the pressure. Allowing more of me to emerge and then more of us to emerge. More easily. More fluidly. Which can, of course, create sexual tension. We'd see. But for then, when I climbed into the car and kissed him quickly but sincerely on the cheek, it didn't seem as if there were a snowball's chance in anywhere that there would be more lip-to-body part connection beyond the one that just transpired. Except that we were headed to Florence, Italy. Where anything was possible.

We made a quick stop in Perugia for a shot of *espresso*, juice and fresh pastry for Max and then headed for the highway--a scene of confusion and chaos and even life-threatening choices. There were signs that pointed to Rome in four different directions, speeds that passed 150 km per hour in a blink and twists and turns that made the

LA freeway look like a country path. Furthermore, it was hotter than hell. Max's VW did not have air-conditioning, and I, overlooking practicality for style, was dressed for winter. In a flurry of pre-menopausal hot flashes and sweats, I reached for the window to roll it down, but Max insisted that open windows would let in too much noise on the highway and that we would be equally refreshed by opening the sunroof. A gesture which, of course, was refreshing for Max, 6'5" tall, whose head nearly stuck out the roof of the car, but not, however, refreshing for me, 5'4" tall, whose head barely made it above the glove compartment. I was dying, and I couldn't get out.

By the time we got off the highway, I was drenched. My white, cotton shirt was plastered to my body, and my black hair fit me more like a football helmet or a liver slab. Whatever stylishness and coolness had been present at 6:30 A.M., minimal as it was, was long gone. Max, on the other hand, remained well-dressed, well-cooled and tall. I knew then that the next time we would take the train, or the next time I would take a pillow, or the next time I would take John. At least his anti-American stance was more forthright and less subversive. That, on the other hand, was subtle, underhanded, slow. That was death by asphyxiation.

Off the highway meant down with the windows. It also meant heading into Chianti country or Chiantishire, as the locals call it, due to the British presence. Rolling green hills, perfectly sculpted plots of farmland, olive trees, grapevines and big skies. A luscious checkerboard. The landscape, the pace, the everything had a way of simultaneously awakening and deadening the senses. I was awake. Very awake. And then I was relaxed. Very relaxed. Only to be sharply but joyously awakened again. It's hard to describe. It's just Italy.

The early October countryside rushed past us, and I stretched to take it all in. The cypress trees, often aligned in columns leading to mansions and villas and castles and kingdoms and heaven. The sky, so big and blue and cloudy and pressing down on the land, flattening it in most places and trying to flatten it in others. The road, winding and wending and heading to more farmland and olive groves and vineyards--alternating from light green blocks to tan to brown to dark green and back again. The New England observations my father would bore me with back home were running wild in my head. The ones he would go on and on about as we were wedged in the family Skylark--I in the front seat between my parents, my sister in the back seat with my brothers. Siblings who had the luxury of sleeping out from under Dad's watchful eye. "Well, I'll be darned. That must have been a rock bridge at one time... Hey, there's a Dutch Elm. You don't see many of those back home anymore. 'Tis a shame (always saving a "tis" for those moments)... Well, look at that, those sheep are clustered near the apex of that hill. There must be something in the grass that's drawing them there... Geez, kids, those are cranberry bogs. Incredible. Just incredible... And this is called the barrens. Did you know that over 90% of all blueberry production in The United States comes from this area?"

Back then I wondered if I would ever graduate to the back seat. But there, miles away from the quaintly steepled New England towns, the rolling hills and coastal wonders of Down East, Maine, Osterville, Massachusetts or Narragansett, Rhode Island, I was finally getting it. There is something about nature that amazes--that makes us either want to narrate the scene piece-by-piece because we can't control ourselves or take it all in quietly, quietly, because words fall short or we're too overwhelmed to speak. Either way, in Max's car, I was glad to be up front.

Max was talking incessantly, remarking on each plot, each hill, each type of tree, but I could barely hear his muted words, partly by my willing him to silence. The earth, the vineyards and the grapes were speaking, and I wanted to get up close and hear everything. Everything. I refocused on Max, waited for a pause and jumped in to ask if he would pull over. When he did, I left the car and headed straight for the nearest grape. I was a virgin vineyarder. Never having observed a grape at home, just hanging there, for dear life, but held so gently, so surely by its protectors, as it soaked up the sun and rocked in the wind and avoided a fall to earth. More inspiring, in some ways, than the *Arche de Triomphe* or The Statue of Liberty or the Colosseum, because of our powerlessness to create them. Build them. Something else or someone else has to do it for us. Something else or someone else has the master plan.

Despite the strength of the urge, I resisted the temptation to peel one off the vine. It would have been too much of an invasion, a violation, like painting over a masterpiece or interrupting a friend.

Instead, I took a picture, hoping to catch some fragment of the joy. Max had an emotional geyser for a traveling companion, a perfect counterpart and balance to the personality and demeanor I already knew he felt his history and culture compelled him to assume. We were a good team.

Back to the car and more rubbernecking. Older men walking their fields while using stripped, smooth sticks as pointers and walking canes. Children on rusted bicycles in groups of two or three or solo laughing and avoiding the potholes that tractors and cars and trucks and donkeys create. Mothers hanging bleached-white towels and sheets out of their windows, presenting a stark contrast to the darkened facades and black shutters. And the earth, in geometrically preserved patterns, a visual for how we live--in squared-off plots of different colors that we're careful not to cross.

Our next stop was at a roadside winery, a small stone home with window boxes and tangled ivy. Max and I headed in and were offered sips of wine by two men who were waiting behind the mahogany bar. One was so remarkably handsome--a middle-aged man with thick, wavy, black and silver hair, inviting blue eyes, perfectly sculpted high cheekbones and teeth that were so straight and so white they could have provided light during a power outage. My mouth was wide open when we shook hands and introduced ourselves. Still, the more intriguing one was the older man to his left. His face told a story that could hold people captive for hours. The devilish blue-green eyes surrounded by waves of worn and stretched skin. His skinny lips and pencil-thin mustache that partially covered a tiny scar right under his long, straight, Roman nose. And the same perfectly sculpted high cheekbones that shone on the man whose arm rested across what must have been his father's shoulders. I wanted to touch his face. Losing my fingers in his years. In his stories. And wondered if he had grandchildren who were grateful for his time on earth.

I am sure he was well into his 80s and had probably inherited the vineyards and the winery from his father who had inherited them from his father who had inherited them from his father. My thoughts were pleasantly interrupted when the charismatic gentleman opened his mouth to share with us, according to his son, the secrets of wine-drinking. He spoke only in Italian. But it was as if he were singing.

Opera. Taking center stage at *La Scala* of Milano. Capturing us with his own private, personal serenade. It felt as if we could understand every word he sang, though we certainly could not, after only four days of language instruction. Still, between the voice and the body movements, we were with him step for step. Sip for sip.

After the perfunctory swirling while holding the bottom of the glass--smelling the drink and examining its legs--we gently tipped our hands until wine flowed into our mouths. We let it sit there, cupped in the bottom, and breathed air slowly and delicately through our slightly opened lips. Then we chewed the wine, letting it coat our teeth and tongues and, eventually, amazingly, the roofs and sides of our mouths. And swallowed. And grew aware. We took a pause in life to enjoy life. Not a gulping, slurping, gagging, swallow into altered consciousness, but a leisured, cultured, passionate, embracing of the same.

Within seconds of our third and fourth sips, the conflicting reactions surfaced again. Very awake. Very relaxed. The wine was potent, and my tongue was leaping as father and son looked on with puffed up chests and reddened cheeks. We sampled that wine and two others before we headed back to the car, eager to resume our road trip but sad to say good-bye to the pair that embodied so much of what Italy stands for. Family. Grace. Wine. History. Patience. And living in the moment.

Max and I stopped at one more winery on the way to Florence. He suggested that only I sample the drink, or as he put it, only I connect the winery dots, because he was driving. Good thing, for if I had been forced to color in the picture while behind the wheel, I would have taken us way outside the lines, threatening both my anal tendencies and the points on my international license. And while part of it was due to the influence of the wine, the more significant part was due to the power of the time. To the power of the surroundings and to the spirit of the old man we had met a few kilometers down the road.

When we finally got to Florence, we parked the car near the train station, bought two liters of *acqua naturale* and started to walk toward our destination, *Il Duomo*--the cathedral, the main symbol of Florence, the image that enters the brain when the city's jewels are conjured up. New York's Statue of Liberty, San Francisco's Golden Gate Bridge, Paris' Eiffel Tower. And our first meeting was only minutes away after having waited years to catch a glimpse.

Down the Renaissance streets and toward the place that will forever entertain, allure and attract worshipers to its steps. Wide, stone thoroughfares near the station leading to more narrow streets as we moved away. Designer windows, scrawny dogs, pizza shops, pastry stores, Medici mementos, symmetrical architecture, fashionably dressed children, a smattering of Japanese tourists and hundreds of *vespe* (mini-motorcycles) made the streets and our lives seem much smaller. Without thinking, we got onboard and rode the wave to our destination, bumping and swerving and blindly navigating our course. Caught between the smells of olive oil and storefront artistry and the ancient place of worship that was waiting. Stalled between the laughter and music of their language and the bell that was ringing just meters away. Struggling with how to live in the moment when there are so many moments worth living in. There. In Florence. In Italy.

And then, without enough warning, we rounded a corner where my imagination was annihilated by my reality. Utter magnificence. *La Piazza del Duomo. Santa Maria del Fiore. Il Battistero. Il Campanile.* Bursting up and up and up in varying degrees of height and width and splendor. Some simple. Some elaborate. All pushing the boundaries of art and architecture from way back then to now to forever without missing a beat. The dome. The *piazza*. The exterior carvings. The green and white marble and touches of rose striations. I wished that I looked as wondrous in horizontal stripes.

I lost my footing and composure as tears raced down my cheeks. I could barely breathe. So alive, so awake, so appreciative. So complete. My body and soul pushing against the confinements of my flesh. Fighting to be freed to mingle. To linger with the understanding that there would never be a first glimpse again. It was then. Only then. The poor grapes were crushed by the enormity of the time. But they politely stepped aside. They knew, after all, that there was only one *Duomo*. And I was standing in front of it. Dwarfed by its brilliance. Its grace and its patience for having waited. For us. For me.

After several minutes of lingering, mouths agape, tears waltzing down our cheeks, Max and I moved toward *La Piazza del Duomo.* Toward the white marble from Carrara, the red from Maremma and the green from Prato. Toward the baptistery with its bronze doors, the oldest of the old in Firenze. Toward the looming bell tower, offering a tall, thin complement to its partners of beauty. It grew more overwhelming with every step. Not just the architecture, the whole scene. Postcards and painters and hippies and Gypsies and tourists. Vendors and pigeons and flags and coffees and cameras.

A brisk walk through the cathedral's relatively barren interior, hordes of visitors excluded, led us to the dome's stairs near the rear of the cathedral. We stepped in and up and were quickly moved from stairs to ramps to an interior encircling of the dome to a tiny, narrow staircase on a curved slant up to the outside. From there we could view the whole city from each of the 360 degrees. Each turn brought into view the copper-colored, clay, curved rooftops of the past invaded by the hundreds of silver-colored, steel, erect antennae of the present--a simultaneous confusion of old and new. A flourishing of mixed messages. Such as the man in Rome visiting the catacombs with a cellular phone in his hand. The woman in a 500 year-old office building in Perugia sending a fax to The United States. The *ragazzo* (boy) in Siena using the ancient Latin *salve* greeting while sporting an Air Jordan Nike t-shirt. I never got used to it. There was ancient Italy--moving through the millennium with the rest of us.

Max and I sat at the top for a long, long time--watching the sun's colors dance through the spectrum and the bell tower follow its lead. With the changes in sun came the changes in everything. The buildings. The mood. The passage of time. My indebtedness to Max for having introduced me to that world. Even my commitment to religion--moving from atheistic tendencies to spirituality to religious fervor within the hour. It had to do with the climb to the heavens, step-by-step, as I passed the saintly murals and the Latin inscriptions and the plethora of mini-altars. And it had to do with our existence up in the clouds from the highest point that the *Duomo* allows. I promised commitment and sacrifices and sizable weekly donations. I was moved. I was moved. Sweet, sweet Jesus, I was moved. If only for a moment, for when we reversed our route, I reversed my inspiration. My reaction halted when my toes touched bottom. Saving me from some heavy blue eye shadow, foot-long eyelashes and sweet Tammy Fayes. I blamed it on the thin air.

After the descent, Max and I quietly explored each of the main sights--first the cathedral and later the baptistery and the bell tower. We walked side-by-side in mutual silence, overwhelmed and grateful for everything--except for the piercing insights of my English-speaking compatriots, whom I liked to pretend were Canadian.

Yes, as my eyes settled on the stunning ceiling mosaics, black and white marble and Roman columns in the baptistery and the crowds hovered around the intricately carved bronze doors of Ghiberti and Pisano and lay people contemplated the wonder of Brunelleschi's dome, the utter weight of which seemed to contradict the laws of physics, and the bell tower stretched boldly, steadfastly, assuredly to a god, the words of my fellow Americans entered the scene. "What's so great about these doors? When are we gonna go eat? How come they don't put butter on their bread? And why don't they serve ice cubes? Don't they know about air-conditioning? They should have more people who speak English here. Everything is so old and rundown. Why isn't their spaghetti sauce thick like ours? I can't believe that our hotel doesn't have a video game hookup. Why is their coffee so small? I wish I could find a bagel in this country." Blah. Blah. Blah.

At those moments, and they were plentiful, I wished Max didn't speak English so that my countrymen and countrywomen would go unnoticed. In a gesture of true friendship, he always claimed that the German-speaking tourists were saying the same kinds of things. Max was a liar.

After vowing to return in the early morning hours to silence and peace and elbow room, the two of us headed to a small café on a side street down from the *Duomo*. In the middle of another shot of *espresso*, we realized that we hadn't eaten a thing since breakfast. Just wine and water and coffee. Our own version of the liquid diet. As we stood to begin our search for a tempting dinner option, I spotted, across the way, two obvious Americans (chino shorts, brand name sneakers, horn rimmed glasses, a baseball cap, a camera, a t-shirt, a guidebook) and braced myself for another bout with humiliation. "Gee, Marge, I can't believe they close down in the afternoon." Instead, we heard them talking about the baptistery doors. The intricately carved bronze and the mastery of perspective. Not once did I hear the words butter or ice cube or video game. No bagel or air-conditioning requests. No need for me to implement John's offensive characterizations of my own people.

We moved to introduce ourselves (Kal and Finley, both from New England) and learned that they were headed to the *Galleria dell'Accademia* where Michelangelo's *David* is housed. We post-poned our dinner plans in an instant and were rewarded by the sites that were visited on us with each step. The *campanile* floating in the late-afternoon sky. The chatter of bartering at the open-air markets. The quiet conversations that emanated from street-level kitchens. The physical proximity of different genders or same genders who were more focused on the friendship than on the sexuality. And the palpable nature of a circus atmosphere. Though void of ticket booths, amusement rides, concessions and neon-flashers. But filled with tourists who did their best to look like the biggest eyesores in town.

When we arrived, the long museum lines that the guidebooks had warned about were nonexistent. We were aware of our better *very* late than never luck as we walked right in and purchased four tickets, each decorated with the kind of aesthetic detail that underscored Italy's obsession with beauty. The museum opened up into a room that is largely ignored on the path to *David*--due to the long, narrow corridor of heaven that rests next door. With *David* keeping watch.

Flanking our passage to the main event were the impassioned *Schiavi* (Slaves) of Michelangelo. Each a prisoner in his own marble. Torsos mobile. Strong and agile. Legs locked. Twisted and trapped. For forever, we thought, as we examined their faces. Except we felt a glimmer of hope for their freedom. When they could run. When no one was watching. To become what they were meant to be.

We pushed on--ourselves prisoners of the clock.

It was over a growling stomach and a spinning head that I looked up. Way up. And at the end of the passageway, I caught my first glimpse. Of him. Of *David*. His body was an extension of the light that poured in from the opening above his head. The same light that danced across our faces and souls at the *Duomo*. Except his light brought life to stillness. I froze in front of him, wanting to examine each fragment of his body from that angle and, then, from every other angle. Slowly. Carefully. Painstakingly. His hair, his lips, his ears, his eyes and nose, his hands, his torso, his genitalia, his legs and feet. How could an inanimate object evoke such passion, such emotion?

I stood. And stood. And stood. And couldn't move. I needed no chair. No rest. No dinner. No new American friends. I needed nothing. I don't know how much time had passed when I finally moved to speak--and only because a guard had come up on my right-hand side to usher me to the exit. The doors were closing, and I was the only one left inside. Besides *David*. Besides the guard. What could I ask to prolong my stay? What could I ask that would prove I wasn't one of those tourists who breezes in and breezes out with little regard for the miracle of the marble? For the patience of the master? For the story of the subject? With my steadily improving Italian, I forged ahead.

"Signore, capisco che il soggetto, David, è il figlio di Michelangelo. Vero?" (I understand that the subject, *David,* is Michelangelo's son. True?)

Then with enough twitching to crack the several hundred year-old marble and enough reddening of the cheeks to restrict the supply of blood to all other body parts, he uttered a sentence. *"Signorina, scusa, non c'è prova, ma si dice che Michelangelo era un'uomosessuale."* (Miss, there is no proof, but some say that Michelangelo was a homosexual.)

It was barely audible. *"Ancora?"* I said as I leaned toward the guard, assuming that distance had something to do with comprehension.

And so he removed his spectacles, rubbed the heel of his hand into his right eye after scratching it through his thick, wavy brown hair, and repeated, *"Signorina, scusa, ma Michelangelo era un'uomosessuale."*

A little louder but still unintelligible to me. Buoyed by the time I was buying for some last second glimpses, I spoke again. *"Come?"*

He placed his glasses back on his nose and surrounded my left hand with both of his hands. And he spoke again. Tapping my knuckles with his strong fingers as he pressed out each syllable of his message. One tap for each. *"U-O-MO-SES-SU-A-LE."*

"Oh," I mustered, as I tipped my head back and tapped his knuckles with my strong fingers. *"Ho capito."*

Michelangelo was outed.

And while academicians across the earth will line up on both sides of that claim forever, some insisting that Michelangelo's love of the male form confirms the guard's decree, others insisting that Michelangelo's love of the male form only confirms his love of the human form and offers proof of nothing else, I thought I knew one thing for sure. That Michelangelo had shared his thoughts with his nearby *Schiavi* a long time before the rest of the world was left to speculate. Leaving the slaves to decide for him and many others--as their heads and feet remained privy to such different embraces. Their minds aware of the tasks their feet could not perform. Their feet tormented by the dreams they could not accommodate. The slaves. Left to decide.

Stay in? Come out? And who, by the way, holds the chisel?

Chapter Six
Uncle Sam--We Aren't In Kansas Anymore

When I got outside the museum, Max, Kal and Finley were waiting. And debating whether or not homosexuality was more accepted in the 1500s than it was right then. The speculation about Michelangelo was, obviously, not hidden from the masses, and my awareness of the depth of my ignorance was growing with each moment. Everyone should travel.

We all admitted that we were, by that time, starving. Max recommended one of Florence's greatest treasures for dinner. *Latini*. Rustic, casual, not too pricey, delicious regional cuisine. Somewhat near the train station and our car. When we arrived at its front door on *Via Palchetti,* the 100 other visitors that spilled off the curb and down the small alleyway confirmed the quality of his choice. So we waited--to join in on the experience--a decision whose value was confirmed within seconds of climbing through the narrow doorway.

A casually dressed international crowd filled the small space with sounds peculiar to themselves. A wait staff juggled the details of orders, deliveries and unintelligible Italian with patience and humor and frenetic energy. Long, old, scratched wooden tables and chairs whose proximity tested the demands of personal boundaries. Hanging meats and cheeses suspended by knotted pieces of twine adorned the peeling ceilings. An adornment that was solely responsible for the chill down my spine--the spine of the Parmesan Princess, the Baroness of Blockage. All of which inspired a happy recollection of the day's events. Maneuvering on the highway, up-close spying of grapes on the vine, mastering the art of wine-chewing, breathing in *La Piazza del Duomo*, scrutinizing *David* and then, cholesterol heaven.

Kal, Finley, Max and I were ushered to seats near utter strangers, not that the four of us were all that familiar anyway. On one side, two Italian men. Romolo and Amadeo. On the other side, two Canadian women. Carey and Leigh. Nearly everything was shared.

The conversation, the bread, the salad, the water, Romolo's warm embraces and the wine. The homemade wine--that came in straw baskets and, at first taste, was fairly typical. But at second taste and third taste, as the wine grew comfortable in my skin, turned anything but typical.

We placed our orders as fast as we could. *Pasta e fagioli* (soup with beans), a cut of roast beef and roasted potatoes. And more *vino*. Within a few moments, the soup arrived as had the new bottle of wine and then, the rest of the meal. The soup--incredibly hearty and thick with *pasta* noodles and softened beans. The beef--tender and perfectly seasoned and as juicy as anything I'd ever tasted. The roasted potatoes--cubed and individually bathed in olive oil, garlic, freshly-grated pepper, oregano, basil and the juices of the meat. The hunger and aromas forced a trip down Asocial Lane. Grabbing. Talking with my mouth filled with food. Asking relative strangers for their scraps. Slapping the solids back with liquids. Homemade liquids. Licking my fingers. Wiping my plate with my bread. Whatever sense of dignity I had had with Max and the Americans was gone. And rapidly made worse by the wine that had set up camp in my brain.

It began with a head sway and dizziness. Signs that were delight-fully ignored as my tongue grew fatter, my lips got numb, and I started to talk just a little more loudly. I was aware of a progression, a gentle progression, until gentility made the leap to volume and ignorance and cluelessness. At that stage, I was naive enough to think that I could stop the onslaught if I sopped it all up with some bread. One loaf later, stuffed with crusts and crumbs and yeast, the speech disorders arrived. "*Pasta*" became "pathta." "Max" became "Math." And worst of all, in our discussion of horseback riding in the Chianti region, just at the peak of my stroll through decibel hell, "trot" became "twat." It was loud, emphatic and jugular and the word, in isolation, brought on a crowd of international lechers. But it wasn't until a dignified British man made his way through the crowd to offer an explanation for the lecher festival that I completely under-stood--an explanation that placed my use of the word "twat" far above (or below) my fellow Americans' ice cube and bagel com-ments at the *Duomo*. I watched as the British gentleman walked away--shaking his head and, perhaps, thinking about reinstating King

George III as a national treasure. For letting the colony slip away. Far, far away.

We left the restaurant.

Kal and Finley found a reason to leave early but Romolo convinced the rest of us to stick together and head across the Arno River to hang out at an outdoor bar. The walk took us over a bridge, down the *lungarno* (the passageway that borders the river) and along some side streets to the Pitti Palace. Then down an alleyway toward *Piazza Santo Spirito*. After what seemed like a stupor eternity, we arrived, swaying not one bit less.

Sambuca and kahlua were our drinks of choice in *Piazza Santo Spirito*. First separately and then together. It was a delicious and dangerous concoction that evoked a delicious and dangerous reaction. Equivalent to smoking a weed the size of a weeping willow and leaving me unprepared for what came next. From Amadeo. The affable Italian who, up to that point, had been charming but then, as he leaned back in his chair and folded his arms around his chest, was nothing less than aggressive. As he offered up his snide understanding of American culture in English and Italian spurts. All American cities are dangerous. All American young people use drugs. All Americans are fat, loud and stupid. All American girls get pregnant. America doesn't have any culture. "Just last week we read about a teenager in Chicago who was killed in the streets for his sneakers. You are too rich to let that happen. What does that tell you about America?"

I was already annoyed by the patterns of the attacks. First tea with John. And then some not-so-subtle eye-rolls in the student *mensa* when we talked about the American influence on the music culture. And then the disbelief at the student cafè when I proclaimed my disdain for most of Reagan's policies. "Right. Like there's anyone in America who doesn't love Ronald Reagan. Please." And I was dismissed. Summarily. As if not there. And then Amadeo. Four episodes in one week. Some actively aggressive. Some passively aggressive. It wasn't that I necessarily disagreed with their observations. It was that I disagreed with the outright blind assumption that all of us were exactly the same. Everyone. Everywhere. So they knew how to respond to me before they knew me. It wasn't right. So I half-listened and half-prepared a linguistic retort. In Italian. Poor

Italian. Struggling to find the right words to challenge his assumptions. Some of which were based on biased media and biased journalism and The Ewing Family of *Dallas* fame.

"So, what specific mechanisms have you utilized, Amadeo, to gather your seemingly indisputable data? What sorts of conversations have you had with dozens and dozens of Americans that have confirmed your crystal clear conclusions?" Those were the questions I had wanted to utter--in perfect Italian and with perfect condescension. Instead, I'm sure the following flowed from my angry lips. "Do you already be in The United States, Amadeo? Do you thinks you is to know all of the Americans because you looks at our television?" Though, at the time, the wine created a personal misperception of fluency. A misperception which, by itself, solidified my embarrassing entrenchment in the world of Category Four. One subset of the categorization of the human species that is based not on profession or social class or beauty or sexuality or intelligence or religion or ethnicity--but on coolness. It is at the root of all relationships.

Type One: cool people who seem to know they're cool. These people I like. It's their style and confidence, their smile and eccentricities, their gestures and mannerisms. It's Gilda Radner. Type Two: cool people who don't necessarily seem to know they're cool. While still cool, they seem modest and a bit unaware of their impact on others. They are not inclined to be self-absorbed because it's not clear that they think they're particularly worth absorbing. Meryl Streep. Type Three: people who, in my opinion, seem to sense their absence of coolness. They read themselves well and avoid embarrassing miscategorizations. No attempts to be a part of the cool crowd. No misguided dreams. They know who they are, and they don't pretend to be anything else. Radar on MASH. Type Four: members of this group stand apart. They are people who, in my opinion, are not cool but seem to remain rooted in the notion that they are. They are categorically, unequivocally, unwaveringly, my least favorite people in the world. Misguided. Misdirected. Misinformed. Mistaken. Mister Tesh.

In hindsight, that was one of the things that was so upsetting to me that night in *Piazza Santo Spirito*. With a drink in my hand, slurred speech, a headache and the weight of defending the entire United States on my shoulders, I was the Queen of Category Four.

The observer of coolness from a remote point--pretending to be a bilingual, intellectual American who was compelled to enlighten her neighbors to the north and her distant kin to the distant east. I was a Raging Four. A Tesher. And there was no turning back.

So as "Do you already be in The United States, Amadeo?" echoed against the storefronts of *Piazza Santo Spirito*, Max was silent. Stunned, perhaps. He had already been with me in Perugia during the student cafè incident earlier that first week. He knew how hurt I got and how sad I was about how people saw me not as Jo, *an* American, but as Jo, *America*. Still, he didn't know what to say. Instead, he just nudged his chair a little closer to mine and put his arm around the back of my seat, lightly touching my tense, burning shoulder and half-smiling/half-grimacing in my direction as I prepared for my defense. My grammatically poor defense in Italian.

"Do you already be in The United States, Amadeo?"

"No, I have never visited."

"Then why you is to think that all Americans is with drugs?"

"Because we see it all the time on the news."

"But that is not America. The news are not all America! It is some America. Do you like Americans to think that Italians is all *pasta* and Mafia?"

"That's what Americans do think. That we all have dark, black hair with big noses and are members of the Mafia who eat *pasta* and pizza all day."

"Not all Americans thinks that. A lot do. But, Americans who thinks and go in Italy and reads, they do not thinks it. And, you are the same. You are like this Americans. You makes the same ideas about us. Drugs and guns."

I grew more exhausted as the conversation spiraled downward. Downward. And was embellished with stereotypes. And news out-takes. And aberrant presidential behavior. Amadeo was joined by his Italian and Canadian cohorts--who agreed to load up and take shots at their neighbor to the south. Max remained quiet. Perhaps experienced in the art of taking cross-cultural slams. But I refused to remain quiet. A strategy I'd employed ever since I was old enough to feel the pain of ignorance. About my heritage. My Italian heritage. A heritage I defended as steadfastly as my *nonno* did. Whose unconditional respect and fondness for his Italian roots were unparalleled. And whose granddaughter followed his lead. His genes, his passions, his commitments had made their way to me. And I refused to let his death silence his core. So I just did what I always do. Speak out.

Though that defense was different. Different from chastising people's assumptions about my Sicilian grandfather--membership in the Mafia, hot-headed temper, poor education. Different from striking out against characterizations of Italians on TV and in movies as uncultured or hoodlums or both with nothing in-between. For there I was, in the country and with the people to whom I had felt so connected, whom I had steadfastly defended throughout my life, and one of them was attacking me. I wondered how he could have surfaced as my enemy when he was inside of me. It was not within the context of my dream. And I struggled with how to move forward to repair my lifetime image. My lifetime definition.

But I did step forward. With a plan. Explain the richness and diversity of America. Counter the American images on the news and silly sitcoms. Connect with him on the Italian front and get him to see my love for his country and the people and their way of seeing the world and living the life. Get him to acknowledge that he was as judgmental about Americans and America as those who watch *The Godfather* and then think they have an intimate knowledge of Italians and Italy. Talk about Americans like Malcolm X and John Havlicek and Eleanor Roosevelt and Neil Armstrong and Alice Walker and Georgia O'Keeffe and convince him that there is no one typical American. That there was no way to say that we are all this way or that way or that we all even have anything in common besides our title as Americans.

But the plan was lost within the confines of my hurt and anger. And my discomfort with the language. And their sarcastic assault. Their sarcastic group assault. Which peaked when Amadeo and the Canadians grabbed hands and rocked back in forth, venomously, as they changed the lyrics of *Bye, Bye Miss American Pie* to *Cry, Cry Miss American Pie*. A bitter, arrogant rendition that was intended to scar.

And so I just ended up shaking my head and swallowing hard and ultimately yelling until Max took my hand and led me away. From the signs in the Land of Love about the World of Hate. My dreams of Italy and my own country were being shattered each day, and I was wishing that I was still hidden from the reality. Under the sand. Buried. But then I'd never have touched his German hand. A hand that, on that night, intervened to help repair my soul.

Max held my hand throughout the streets of Florence. Over the *Ponte Vecchio*. Down *Via de' Tornabuoni*. Through *Piazza della Repubblica* and down a back alley to the hotel he had booked earlier in the week. My mood was improving with every step. It was hard for me to stay agitated while walking through Florence, Italy and while Max's affection for me became more obvious. The hand in my hand. The arm around my shoulder. The suggestion that I not let strangers rule my world and that I practice uttering a simple, sing-songy expletive under my breath before I unload.

When we climbed into bed later that night, after Max dropped to his boxers and I slipped on the bottoms of some pajamas and a Bryn Mawr College t-shirt, Max spoke quietly. "I wish I could defend my country as openly as you defend yours. As a German, I just can't. Not yet."

I reached for his hand and tried to offer him the kind of solace he had offered me earlier that evening. And right then, with my wounded heart only inches from his, the evening's future and our relationship's future seemed obvious to both of us. Friendship. Nothing more. Nothing less. We were with each other to help each other. To push each other. To comfort each other. To find each other. And to find ourselves.

And on that evening, two hands met again across the great chasm to let us know that the journey wouldn't be as lonely as we had thought. And with that in our heads and tears in our eyes, we fell into deep sleeps.

Chapter Seven
Mourning The Death Of Naivete´

I was different when we got back to Perugia. I had been in Italy only one week and already I was different. Homesick. Sad. Broadsided. My identity as an American was taking a big hit, and I was confused by the series of exchanges that the first few days had introduced. I was only one American. And one who was trying to live in another culture, learn another language and educate myself. Why not go hunt down the Americans who sing "Love It or Leave It" or who support the Nazi regime or who categorically can't stand the foreign-born employees in drive-thru coffee shops? Why me?

I was way too competitive to give up, so going home was not an option. Not that it hadn't seriously crossed my mind. I still had a lot of choices. Try to master Italian. Develop my friendships with Max, John and Petra. Think about getting involved with someone. Learn how to cook Italian as well as I could eat Italian. Try to fit in more by investing in more European clothing. Take more day trips. Invite my sister and a friend or two to come and visit. Get a dramatic new haircut. Try out the facial place on the street to the university. Visit the local museums as well as the Perugina chocolate company. Think about fasting once a week. The list seemed endless, and the main goal of each was to take my mind off of the personal work I had ahead of me. Whatever that was.

Along with mastering Italian and deepening my friendships with Max, John and Petra, getting involved with someone surfaced as a top priority. It was stunningly easy. And fascinating. A multicultural sampler--such as the two Greek boys, one of whom offered to carry my books home from school, moaned about the price of bread in Italy and, on a daily basis, hammered home the Greeks' role in the beginning of civilization. Or Kahmel, the Palestinian, who offered to help me conjugate verbs and seemed to think that the third person singular for the irregular verb *correre* could be found deep in my throat if he used his tongue as a flashlight. And Abdul, who tried to coax me to dinner by first presenting me with a rose and then inviting me to the finest restaurant in Perugia. Or Marco, who approached me on the steps of the local cathedral to ask me to translate Land Rover for him and glittered when I smiled broadly in response to hearing he was Sicilian. Like my grandfather.

As early fall turned to mid-fall and days of self-pitying sensitivity toward my American culture turned to weeks of the same, (despite a decent facial, coups in Italian class, a half-day of fasting followed by *carpaccio* with almond-slivered Parmesan and asparagus at Max's, day-trips, Umbrian strolls and letters from home), I decided to accept Abdul's invitation to dinner. We settled on a Saturday night.

When he came to my door to pick me up, he was dressed impeccably. Beautiful black, pleated pants and a crisply pressed shirt of a slightly lighter shade than his trousers paralleled the colors of his rich black hair and his swarthy face. A tie brought life to the monochrome. My look matched his. Black Capri pants, black flats and a stark-white, long-sleeved cotton shirt with silver button covers from Cody, Wyoming. A perfect complement to my dangling silver earrings.

We walked slowly through the streets of Perugia to a *ristorante* relatively near the university. Enormous windows flanked the entrance which was delicately decorated with the name of the restaurant. We gently pushed on the gold-plated handle and were greeted by a slight, dark-haired Italian man who had a waist I would kill for. With my eyes riveted on his tightly wound cummerbund, he wiggled his way to our table, in the back, in the corner, near a window that overlooked Umbria. To snow-white, starched and pressed tablecloths, linen napkins, polished silverware, fine wine glasses and a professional wait staff. A collection of sights and interactions that reinforced what the world already knew. In Italy, food is a member of the ruling class--where its preparation and the reaction to the consumption to follow is about honor. And reputation. And life.

The central role of food was never more evident to me than on a trip I took to Bacoli, Italy years later at the invitation of some friends--Lidia and Gian-Antonio Falzone. We gathered at the home of Lidia's relatives for an early lunch. Twelve noon.

Sparing all of the culinary, gastronomic and gastrointestinal details, I must state that it was an eating event. A consumption triathlon. A major opportunity for Lidia's niece to prove that she was, in fact, the Queen of All Food Stuffs and Food Stuffed. Our ascension from the *lunch* table at 5:45 P.M. spoke volumes of her Queendom, as did the fact that I packed my bags that night and headed for Pompeii early the next morning. It was the only thing I could think of to avoid another full-court press by another relative the next day.

Midway through the Bacoli lunch, Lidia and an aging in-law started a stern discussion at my end of the table. The local dialect was raging so I had to focus, instead, on their hands, mouths, eyes and blood vessels to try to make sense of the debate. Whatever was going on, it escalated rapidly. Fists were pounding, feet were stomping, and eyeballs were as wide as *due piccoli piatti* (two small plates). I reacted by growing ever more interested in my soup while surreptitiously sliding my eyes to the opposite end of the table to get a sense of the other guests' reactions to the obviously tense, embarrassing moment. There was none. Unless eating soup, naming the sea urchins that were floating in their bowls just centimeters away and scooping up all lingering remnants with some homemade bread is a reaction.

By the time I looked back, the antics at my end had degenerated more. One or the other or both were primed for a heart attack while their loved ones at the other end pulled antennae from their teeth. I moved my chair ever so slightly away from all parties in order to create some distance between them and me, but my friend dragged me into the melee by grabbing for my right arm and bringing her reddened face within centimeters of mine. As she spewed dialectical venom and tried to explain the gist of their argument and the obvious idiocy of her in-law's remarks. A few head taps--her hand to her own forehead, her hand to my forehead, her hand to his forehead--didn't bring any rapid peace. Certainly not from my perspective.

Then, five minutes later, as quickly as it started, it ended. Lidia put her tight-fisted hand in front of her face, the backside to her eyes, the fingers to his, and in one sweeping, emphatic gesture, straightened out her arm in his direction and thrust open her fingers leaving her palm exposed and halted within a hair of her enemy's face.

Banishing him. Snake. Devil. Out, out, out of the Garden of Feedin'. And then, in muffled anger and broken English I heard her say, "He don't know *nothing* if he thinks fish should be cooked that way."

Abdul and I ordered everything from soup to nuts, *zuppa* to *tiramisu*. Unlike the portions at Max's house, they were more controlled. Actually quite dainty. Probably the way human beings were meant to eat in the post hunter-gatherer era. The feeling at the end of the meal was perfect. Not too filled and not the least bit wanting, for anything. The conversation over dinner was equally satisfying. I got a lesson about The Middle East, the basics of which I absolutely should have known, while Abdul dismissed his need for an abridged American education. The world's focus on our political inclinations and our trendy lifestyles and our sports superstars painted a clear enough picture for him. Through newspapers and television and not through personal contact. I was beginning to piece together some order and pattern to the perceptions. But like a song with an erratic syncopation, it was too unpredictable to dance to.

Yet.

The after-dinner plans were to go to a local disco--a disquieting holdover from the 1970s with a spinning, silver ball and an owner with a large, gold cross snuggled in his chest hair. Madonna's *Get Into The Groove* was raging in the small disco as we made our way to the parquet dance floor and liberated the rhythms within. Just the right stomp, the right spin, the right pump. I simply have moments when I think I rule. It was the full-length mirrors surrounding the dance floor that obliterated that notion in no time. And for the second time in a handful of weeks, I was raging in Category Four. An emerging pattern of personal fourness was beginning to scare me to death.

After an hour, Abdul asked if I would be interested in going back to his dorm room at one of the university branches in town. I wasn't overly open to the idea since I still didn't know him very well. But after his emphatic assurances that we would go there just to talk, and nothing else, I agreed. I couldn't have been more clear. He couldn't have been more clear.

Midway through the walk to his room, I thought that maybe I had been too worried. Too careful. Too uptight. The night, after all, had been fun, and he had been nothing less than respectful. I was saddened by my cynicism and gave in, letting go, a bit, as our conversation shifted to personal stories, most embarrassing moments, family and dreams. Our more relaxed clothes, a little more wrinkled, a little more untucked, reflected the increasingly lighter mood and my decrease in self-consciousness. In caution. In fear.

We arrived before too long and climbed the echoing dormitory stairs to his floor. Down the long, narrow corridor to his room. Abdul's chivalrous gesture had me pass through first and head straight across to the other side. To see what kind of view was illuminated by the clouded moon. And to press the window to the top--to inhale the cool, Perugian air from my newest spot. It was then, only then, that I heard the large, steel door slam behind me. And the large, steel lock turn, again and again, to fulfill its mission. And to signal my distress.

It was only after a second or two of glancing out the window, feigning a sense of calm, that I turned to find Abdul. Naked. His back to the locked door, arms across his chest, blocking my passage to the outside.

"What are you doing?"

"What?"

"Abdul, what the hell do you think you're doing?"

Which was met with the same response.

He moved toward me then, grazing his disgusting arm against my cheek and shaking shoulder. Slowly. With his hateful lips just inches from my ear. Whispering in his native tongue. Pausing long enough to make me sick. To make me want to kill. Then he moved past me to the window. To shut out the evening's air and the cold that was filling up his space.

With his hands against the window, I ran to the door and turned the latch. And yanked the door as far as it could go. Only to meet Abdul's bare foot against the bottom. And his hot breath against my sweaty neck. So I pulled harder, trapping his toes between the door and the floor. Jamming his toes under the steel border and ramming it against his flesh. Past his toes. To the middle of his foot. With hopes of smashing up against his ankle. And his ugly face.

And then I slid out. Down the hall of the dorm. Down the steps. Out the back door. Past the partially open window and the calls from him for me to stop. But I ran. And ran. And ran. Up hundreds of tiny steps and cobblestones and steep hills.

My ankles giving way.

My chest cramping.

My lungs inhaling fire.

I tried to figure out the most direct route from his place as I was racing through the city. Knowing he would know the most direct route, having walked the path earlier in the evening when he picked me up. He might reach my home before I did. So, I went up and beyond my street to John's flat and hid in his doorway before venturing up the hill and around the corner to look down on my own house. To find him there. In front. Waiting. Staring at the door. I pulled my body back sharply and returned to John's front door with a hard knock. A yanking. Until I squatted in the doorway to collect my thoughts. My head felt heavy in my hands. My knees felt bony against my cheeks. My thighs felt weary from the pounding. And so did I. There was no answer.

When I returned to the top of the hill, Abdul had left. And there I froze, with my stomach in my throat, until I made my way down the street in the dark and mist. My head jerked from side-to-side with each labored, weakened step. Watching for every shadow. Listening for every noise. Smelling for every bead of sweat that would have collected on each of us.

The key shook in my right hand before I steadied it with my left. And then it went in smoothly. When I pushed the door closed behind me, my body slapped back against the wood and heaved itself against the splinters. My eyes flooded my lips with salt and left unfocused the images, images in a darkened space that were lit up only by the tiny light that marked the switch. I moved for that. Feeling watched. I pressed my hesitant finger on the switch and turned slowly as the entryway was illuminated.

I was alone.

As I moved to the bottom step, someone pushed hard on the locked brown door, rattling it back and forth, trying to force it open by pressing on the handle. From outside, Abdul's English had returned. "Jo. Jo. Come out. What happened? I want to talk to you. Come out."

One by one I climbed the steps to the top and, on each step, I cursed myself for my stupidity. The victim victimizing herself. Questioning why she had questioned her questions. Continuing the work that Abdul had merely begun. When I got to my room, I looked out through the tiny slats of my green shutters. Out there in the street, soaked from the new cries of the sky, Abdul waited. And called my name.

How swift and abrupt and unpredictable is the death of naivete´. How permanent and irreversible.

Chapter Eight
The Recipe Card Club
Membership Is Now Closed

He had restricted my freedoms--inside and outside my head. On the streets, when dusk settled in. In the *mensa*, as I scanned the student crowd. Just inside the brown door, near Mamma's arm-of-safety. Down the slopes to Max's home, when I heard footsteps just behind me. In bed, as I fought the urge to understand and envision what I had been lucky enough to escape. In my journal, which protected my private thoughts. In my ability to experience unedited happiness, unrestricted laughter, unabashed living. Outside my window. Inside my eyelids.

Perugia turned gray. And cold. And limiting. Everything I had envisioned Italy not to be. The attempt at a personal advance was met with a personal retreat. Max was the first to notice the change but not the first to learn the reason. I didn't want to disappoint him as I had disappointed myself. Irrational. And all too common a reaction for the victim--a result of society's warnings and expectations for those who trust. For women who trust.

I had risked too much--my soul, my identity, my sensitivities. It was time to return to things I knew best, that were safest in a place thousands of miles away from home. Friends and food. And school. Always a haven. Always a place to shine, to steady myself, to prove that I was good, again, and deserving, again. Always a place to rest inside the lines. Protected.

In some ways, school was getting better every day. By November, changing singulars to plurals was becoming automatic. Words were starting to emerge in clusters, stepping away from their Morse Code past. The double-r rolls were more easily distinguished from the single-r skip. The translation of my instructors' questions was taken in wholes and not in pieces. Max and I even started to speak in Italian when he couldn't find the right word in English.

At the same time, we were pleasantly inundated with Italian culture--enjoying group visits to museums, five-course potluck meals at our classmates' homes and learning about the more egalitarian Etruscan society. A society where men and women were more valued for their individual and unique contributions and not strictly for the qualities modern society has embraced--such as strength and competition.

The only sticking point in the classroom setting was my grammar teacher. Francesca. Or, as she was fondly referred to, The Whore of Babylon. She was obsessed with the young men, and each day it was the same routine. Every few minutes, Francesca would break to ask the Greek boy or the German boy or the Australian boy or the Mexican boy how to translate the Italian phrase she had just uttered into Greek or German or English or Spanish. She would rest her high-heeled shoe on a front-row desk, flutter her eyelashes, lean forward and ask the Athenian, *"Come si dice in Greco?"* He would also lean forward and flutter and respond with pride under his rich, curly, dark hair in whose locks our teacher was metaphorically rolling.

As fascinating as I find language and communication and rolling, I had not signed up for an Italian class in Perugia to learn how to make a reservation in Greek. And I particularly did not want to learn it with a coquettish flair. The males loved her, and the females with a brain were determined to learn in spite of her. Still, her flirtatiousness, combined with her episodic bellowing to return chaos to calm, made the decision to move out of her section a simple one.

My roommate, Petra, had raved from day one about her language instructor. Signora Gala was a no-nonsense woman. She was about 5'8" tall, wore dark dresses with high collars, never smiled just to be polite, but did smile when the situation truly warranted it. During one mid-morning break, I spoke to *la professoressa* about wanting to switch to her class, approaching her with the same caution Dorothy had exhibited when she first inched closer to the Wizard's curtain. She loomed large and important and bold. I loomed infinitesimally small and then, even smaller, when she abruptly asked why. Without a smile. Without emotion. Unless stone is an emotion.

I pulled together enough Italian to tell her I had heard good things about her teaching from her students and that I was looking for a classroom with a serious environment and that there was somewhat of an urgency about my need to learn Italian well. I hesitated to say more because I didn't know if Signora Gala and the WOB were friends. Whatever I said was temporarily good enough because she granted me an audition on the following Monday--in front of her other students. And so I scurried away after I genuflected and smiled and thanked her enough times to confirm, to a fault, my appreciation and nervousness.

A nervousness which was augmented by Petra, who brought up Giustino, the one who was no longer with us, who ventured into class for his entry test with too much confidence, too much swagger and not enough fear. He was summarily dismissed, exactly 12 seconds into it, right then and there, in front of everyone, when he made *one* error during the inquisition. When he confused the masculine and feminine agreement on one past tense verb and had to gather his books and leave.

I was good. But I wasn't that good.

Over the course of the weekend, I pretended I wasn't thinking about it that much. It wasn't that big a deal, I told myself, and if I didn't get into her class, I would try to get into another or even sign up for some private tutoring. I was simply committed to lasting in there for more than 12 seconds. Like at a rodeo. To try to stay on the buckin' bronco the longest and win some kind of dignity as my face lay in ground dirt and horse dung. But Mamma made it clear that she would not settle for anything less than success. "I can't have any half-Italian daughter of mine failing in what could have been her native tongue. No I can't." And then she grabbed my cheeks and led me to her couch, where we sat for four straight hours and rehearsed the likely scene. My errors were greeted with a clicking sound and a shake of the head. And then a hand to my shoulder as the explanation was granted. "The noun must end with an 'i' since it is plural. The past tense of *morire* is *morto* not morito. *La gente* takes a singular verb." My correct exchanges were greeted with a smile and red cheeks. Proud red cheeks. And some squinty eyes.

We finished the evening with dinner for two. First, *pastina*. A broth with the tiniest Italian *pasta* of all. The same broth my *nonna* made for my *nonno* every single week. Which earned her a tasteful little pat on her side with his gentle hand. And a grateful smile. And then we had bread, a slice of chicken, tomatoes dressed with olive oil and some lettuce. And a spot of wine. By the end of the evening, I was speaking with relative ease. And Mamma took full responsibility for the progress. As she should have. Without her, the goal of dung might have faded far away.

When Monday came, Petra and I walked to school speaking Italian. She was interested in Mamma's and my dinner--a visit she could enjoy only through me since she'd never been invited in for such an event. It was Mamma's one overt bias. Though relatively harmless. As long as I was on the receiving end.

I eliminated any swagger when we entered the classroom--thinking that might have been partly responsible for Giustino's demise. She was a no-swagger kind of gal. Petra and I took seats next to each other and quietly waited for Her to arrive--to a scene that was so very different from Babylon down the hall, where people would already be talking too loudly, writing on the blackboard and disrupting the well-conceived arrangement of chairs. Signora Gala, on the other hand, commanded attention when she wasn't even in the room. Like Big Brother. Big Sister. Or maybe even Big Mother.

When *la professoressa* walked in, whatever noise there had been was immediately silenced. And quickly it started. All Italian. No Greek. No fluttering. No English. All class. Not one break. Not one deviation from the ultimate goal--to have each of her students leave her classroom, at the end of 12 weeks, with a more-than-acceptable level of fluency. From the sounds of the opening exchanges, they were well on their way. It felt fluid. And serious. And good.

I, however, felt unqualified. Like the one who had gotten called up to substitute into a varsity basketball game during the regional tournament finals. The one who had to be ready to be put into the contest in place of the normal high scorer. The one who was expected to know all the plays, have mastered all the skills and perform without error in front of a very demanding, feared and revered coach. It was a tense picture, even for someone who knew how to play the game.

Big Mother was good enough to let me warm-up before entering the fray. So I was on the court but no one was passing me the ball. But soon enough it started. The onslaught. All in Italian.

"Gio, welcome to class."

"Thank you, Signora Gala."

"Where are you from?"

"I'm from The United States."

"Tell me. Why do want to study Italian? And why did you come so far?"

"I want to learn Italian because my grandparents are from Italy. They were born here."

"Where?"

"My grandfather was from Sicilia and my grandmother was from Abruzzi."

"What do they think of you for wanting to do this?"

"Both of my grandparents are not living, Signora. In fact, my grandfather died before I was born. I wanted to come here to get to know him better and to understand more about what his life was like in Italy before he came to The United States at the age of 14."

"How will you learn that here?"

"I have relatives in Sicilia. The wife of my grandfather's brother is still alive, and my mother has cousins there, too. I want to learn the language well enough to go meet them and talk with them."

"When do you think you will go visit?"

"Well, it depends on how well I learn Italian. They don't speak English."

She folded her arms across her chest and looked down at the floor as she walked slowly to my desk. Deliberately kicking her toes forward, as if skimming stones along the sand. Her thick, wide heels causing an echo that permeated the new silence. When her black, pleated skirt swept its way onto my bolted-down desk and rested on a corner of my opened grammar notebook, she unfolded her arms and placed her pointer finger on the corner of a page that spelled out the conjugation of some irregular verbs.

My heart pounded, and my mind considered the significance of her finger resting on irregularity. Abnormality. But then I looked up at her from my little desk to find one of those minimalistic smiles. And a pointer finger that was pulled back into her fist to open up into a shake. A strong shake. With my hand--which was sweaty and cold. But firm.

"Gio, that was very, very well done. No errors. I wish you good luck with this dream and, from what I hear, I think you could meet them very soon. Now I'll ask the rest of the students to welcome you to this class."

With that, thunderous applause spontaneously erupted, made even more dramatic by the acoustics in that old schoolhouse, which drowned out the sound of her heels as she moved back to her desk. Arms still by her side. Skirt barely moving. Petra leaned over and patted my right shoulder, and held it there, and said that I hadn't missed a beat. Not one beat. I leaned into her, and tears welled up in my eyes. Evidence of the most accepted feeling I had had since my arrival on that foreign land. As I had been taken in--not as an American, but as a student and as a granddaughter and as me. Jo. Gio.

When the local bell tower sounded, marking the end of the morning session, I gathered my notebooks, let my energy be the sign that my soul was reemerging, and paused at her desk to thank her on the way out. I hoped my smile would tell her I had placed my fragile and injured ego in her seasoned hands and that she had held me well. And pushed me well. And shook me well. My brain, my heart, my courage and her Italian powers. She stepped out from behind her curtain to show me what always rested within. Within me.

As I passed the fig tree behind the small stone wall bordering the school, I stepped high onto the old stones, reached well into the branches and pulled down a handful of fresh figs. I peeled back the green skin, popped one into my mouth and started to skip, almost unaware that the juices of Italy were spilling down my chin and coating me again.

And I skipped my way home. To tell Mamma of her daughter. And her happy, happy day.

It was comforting, on some level, to have returned to school for solace. Among other people and places, I thank college for that-- where balancing the brutal intensity of the academic program, along with varsity basketball, admissions and student internships, made me start to think I could do it all. That was what was pulling me through in Italy, at least in school. So with the academic scene quickly and successfully rerouted, I could return to my list of other familiar things, such as food, Max and John. And, as is often the case, I started with food.

Over the years, I have come to realize that most of my food fixations center around two major categories. Potatoes and salt. When asked about which 10 things I would take with me to a deserted island, after the obvious water, matches and transportation, I always move to food products that almost exclusively fall into those two categories and am then faced with the demoralizing task of having to downsize the list. Homefries. Potato chips. Baked potatoes. Potato skins. Aunt Jo's mashed potatoes. And French fries--with the subcategories of McDonald's fries and curly fries and, in a pinch, steak fries. And then the salt, with potato chips and French fries, of course, straddling both categories. But then popcorn, tortilla chips, crackers, peanuts and cashews. My mother's suggestion when we were little that "a nice carrot stick" or "a nice celery stick" would do the trick to cut our hunger reflected her profound misunderstanding of our family-wide obsessions. Or, maybe she was just plain afraid of the force.

The force that makes me calculate the number of fat grams in a whole bag of Doritos before I start to eat them. Or the force that makes me follow a bowl of crackers and dip around the room at a party or peel open a bag of Cape Cod Chips in Aisle Four of the Super Stop & Shop to eat vociferously as I wend my way through the remaining aisles. Ultimately leaving the flattened bag on the electric counter for the cashier to ring up.

It was in Italy that another food made its way into my Deserted Island Survival Kit. The addition--*pesto*. I vividly remember where I was when we were first introduced, much as we remember where we were during periods of national crisis. I was in my room looking over some verb conjugations when a smell from Mamma's kitchen wafted into my space, right through the closed door. The verbs turned past tense in exchange for a trip to the stove--where I found Mamma preparing lunch for her grandson, Paolo. The sauce had already been fixed and was the obvious source of the aroma. I asked Mamma if I could come in and see what she was cooking. Since the artistry was winding down, it was, apparently, a good time.

The color of the sauce was a vibrant green, green, green--like Mamma's green muu-muu, except not as large. It was a surprising complement to the traditional red and white sauces. The fervent Italian nationalism eradicated the notion that the trio was a mere coincidence. Just as the tomato (red), *mozzarella* (white) and basil (green) *caprese* dish was conceived with the banner in mind.

Mamma ripped off a piece of bread from the circular loaf that was resting on the kitchen table and waved me to dip it into the sauce. Pavlov would have had a field day with my anticipated and then actual response to succulence. A borderline sexual experience. Verging on tears.

Mamma was obviously satisfied with my reaction and decided to rip off another piece of bread for me to dip with unabated glee. As I popped the soaked bread into my mouth, it was never more clear what culinary fans of Italy had been saying for years. That their mouths are never more alive than when they're in Italy. That while others go to Italy for the art, the architecture and the velvet land-scapes, they go to Italy to eat. To return to familiar restaurants and shops that feature foods they can never find back home. To bite into an incredibly fresh tomato or 100 varieties of olives or perfectly prepared *prosciutto* and feel their taste buds skip. Finally, I under-stood.

The utopian mood was invaded by a knock on the door, and Mamma prepared to bound from the kitchen to greet the soul that gave her life meaning. But before she did, she grabbed my cheeks with her strong right hand and invited me back the next morning--to show me how to make the sauce myself. I was weakened at the thought of having a private cooking class with her, a 5'9", 250-pound, 69 year-old, silver-haired grandmother with whom I had just fallen in love. Muu-muu and all. The next morning couldn't come fast enough.

I was into the kitchen very early that next day but was disappointed to find it occupied by only Susanna and Petra. Mamma was in her room watching TV. When I heard the Italian voice-over for Bonnie Franklin float our way, I knew why Mamma was absent. It was her *One Day At A Time* time. So Susanna, Petra and I sipped some *espresso* while Petra expressed her horror at my plans to miss grammar class. Her reaction made me a little nervous but not enough to reject Mamma's invitation. I trusted that Big Mother would understand.

Susanna, too, was visibly shaken--not by my truancy, but by Mamma's invitation to me. Susanna was a competitive, threatened woman who liked to claim our landlady as her own. Her misguided obsession made me want to alter my Four Types of People Categorizations to be based on Perceptions of Reality instead of Perceptions of Coolness. What Susanna didn't know is that Petra and I knew how much Mamma was bothered by Susanna. So conversations with Susanna, Petra and me were often a little uncomfortable. It's hard for three people to talk with ease when two of the three people know something the third person might also know but doesn't necessarily know the first two know. In any event, Mamma liked to rule the roost, and she didn't like anyone insinuating her way into her realm. Susanna tended to do that. A woman without one ounce of Italian blood fabricating her membership in the ruling party of our tiny dominion. Mamma obviously weighed the benefits of continuing to accrue Susanna's monthly rent versus booting her out. Apparently, at that point, the steady income was more important.

As the music for *One Day At A Time* signaled the end of the show, Susanna and Petra left for school *in fretta* (in a hurry). Susanna was enrolled at the local university--studying other areas of academia in the Italian tongue. I was capable of far less and all with an accent that many described as non-American but also non-Italian. Even so, it represented a marked improvement over a few weeks ago when I left New York City with a fluent command of every Italian word that should never be uttered in good company. Still, I was distressed by what was left to accomplish.

As soon as the door closed behind Susanna and Petra, Mamma made her way into the kitchen. The silencing of the TV was a sign of the seriousness of the moment. We were going to cook, and there would be no distractions.

I had come to the kitchen equipped with some paper and a pencil. Eager to copy the recipe step-by-step or even to have Mamma copy it. In her own handwriting. Like my mother's recipe cards in her own handwriting. How I will touch, smell, read and cook from my own mother's recipe cards after she's gone. Knowing she had once touched them, written them and nurtured my own family from them.

Her bran muffins. Her lasagna. Her *pasta* sauce. Her Chicken Cordon Bleu. Her hamburger and bean casserole with cheese and Pillsbury biscuits on top or her tuna casserole with potato chips. Occasionally, a recipe from my aunt would have danced in. Her brownies or mashed potatoes or her own lasagna. Finding those was like finding an extra Christmas present under the tree after all the used wrapping paper had been jammed into garbage bags, and the last bit of eggnog had been drunk. And finding them together, my mother's and aunt's recipes, felt like a poignant reuniting of two people who had shared 50 years of living and cooking and child-rearing and friendship. The recipe cards. They'll bring back some of the things I will miss when they are gone, or when she is gone, now that one already is.

Mamma laughed out loud when I asked her to copy the recipe onto the piece of paper that covered her table. "There wasn't a written recipe," she hooted. "You just have to read the moment. Try to *feel* how much basil and Parmesan should go into the mix. Try to *feel* how much salt and parsley and oil." But as a sufferer of Emotional Culinary Disorder, with no Ritalin to turn to for help, I couldn't even feel how much mayonnaise should go into a tuna sandwich. I decided to write down every move and try to feel later.

The first thing Mamma did was get a bottle of red wine out of the cabinet. It was early morning so I knew it wouldn't be for us to drink. But when two tiny glasses appeared, reminiscent of *The Flintstone* glasses that housed grape jelly, I discovered I was wrong. Mamma poured a small portion of red table wine into the glasses. No more than an inch high. We swirled a bit and swallowed a bit and, in an instant, she made the cooking process profoundly less stressful. I felt confident that if forced to make a pattymelt right then, that the mayonnaise decision would not have been a big one.

Step One: Drink.

Then the real work began. Mamma pulled out a huge bundle of fresh basil whose smell absolutely permeated and cleansed the senses. She gestured for me to help remove the stems and any browned areas, which I did, with minimal confidence and maximum trepidation. Easing the tension slightly by convincing myself that it wasn't bypass surgery. She packed the leaves down into a large measuring cup, firmly, since basil seemed to be key. And then, surprisingly, threw the leaves into a Cuisinart. I had half expected to see some machinery from the prehistoric age appear. A big rock and a small rock. Some pottery shards and obsidian. A femur and a scapula. From there, she moved to the garlic. Again. Fresh. She selected two large cloves and tossed them in with the basil. And then *pignoli*. Pine nuts. She mentioned that some people substitute other kinds of nuts for the *pignoli* but that she never does. Couldn't imagine it. She was heading down the path of the fish discussion at the Bacoli luncheon but, without a fluent partner, the flame wasn't fueled. The fish wasn't fried.

The pine nuts were joined in the Cuisinart by nearly a cup of packed fresh parsley. That, she said, was optional. I was writing feverishly. What was negotiable. What wasn't negotiable. And was starting to stress a bit. A mood which Mamma sensed. She nudged the Pebbles glass in my direction.

Then she got out a huge chunk of Parmesan cheese. She had bought the best. Straight from Parma. The cheese was softer and more textured. Mountainous-looking but flaky. And the smells were attacking. She reached for a cheese grater that was exactly like Nonna's. Thin silver metal. Four different kinds of serrated edges. Worn from use. She started to rub the Parmesan up and down one specific side of the grater reaffirming, again, how the most simple acts in life make me the happiest. As the cheese easily slivered off of the chunk, it fell into the interior of the grater, which Mamma had rested on a plate. In an instant, she had freshly ground Parmesan cheese all neatly collected in a delicate mound. Looking, smelling and feeling like nothing I had ever known. She grated and grated until it *felt* right and then threw it into the mix joining the basil leaves, garlic, pine nuts and parsley.

Just as our mouths needed a little moisture before we began, the *pesto* concoction needed some, too. So, on came the jar of olive oil, opened and turned down onto the mix for three full seconds. Again, no skimping. And no measuring. Just seasoned guesswork. And then a small amount of melted butter and a pinch of salt. Mamma turned on the Cuisinart and made sure that the Parmesan met all the edges of the bowl to diminish the chances of inconsistencies in the greenery. And then, presto. *Pesto*.

She poured the sauce into a few thin but relatively tall jars. Whatever distance there was between the top of the *pesto* and the top of the jar she narrowed with olive oil. In the most tender gesture of all, however, she got a small piece of tape, wrote "Gio" on it and waited for the containers to cool before she placed the tape on the jar that had the most *pesto* inside. While we polished off our drops of wine, Mamma filled in the remaining details about how to cook the *pasta* and how to do last-minute preparations on the *pesto* before placing it on the spaghetti.

As she spoke, I put the finishing touches on my notes and delicately placed a drop of red wine and a drop of green *pesto* on each of the four corners of the white piece of paper. And while that made for a banner recipe sheet, I knew that, ultimately, I wanted it to be rewritten in Mamma's own handwriting. After a morning of feeling and being and warmth, she deserved to be the one to raise the Recipe Card Club membership to three. Mamma--who gave me her cooking secrets, my aunt--who gave me her name, and my mother--who gave me her roots. And, after that, membership would be closed. Forever.

The Making Pesto With Feeling
(And A Little Wine)
Recipe Card

Step One:
Drink. (A tiny bit.) Pour yourself a small glass of red wine. Sip it to start and then as need arises.

Step Two:
Combine all of the following ingredients in a Cuisinart:

~ about three cups of tightly packed, fresh basil leaves with brown leaves and all stems removed
~ two huge cloves of garlic
~ a good handful of pine nuts--do not anger Mamma with poor substitutions
~ parsley--a little more than the pine nuts but not a lot more--optional
~ freshly grated Parmesan cheese--build a mound that looks a bit smaller than one cup--use one of Nonna's cheese graters
~ olive oil--open up the jar, and pour for about three seconds--if forced to guess, about ½ cup
~ melted butter--about half the quantity of the olive oil
~ a pinch of salt

Step Three:
Flip the switch on the Cuisinart, and let it mix for awhile--until all of the ingredients are blended to avoid dark and light patches of greenery.

Step Four:
Pour the *pesto* into small jars. (Leave a little out for Step Five.) Add olive oil to cover the distance between the top of the *pesto* and the top of the jar. If desired, label the jars with the names of those you love.

Step Five:
Put a small drop of *pesto* and red wine on each corner of the recipe card. It'll help you remember the first time you made this and how good life can be.

Step Six:
If you make this with a mother or an aunt or someone else you love, make sure she writes the recipe in her own handwriting and puts it in a safe place. There shouldn't be any need to ask why.

Chapter Nine
High Anxiety
Cyclopes, Lions And Plaster-Of-Paris

I am always amazed by how quickly things can change in life and what it is that is responsible for making that happen. My intense feelings of despair after my struggles with and attacks by Amadeo and Abdul were miraculously dissipated by a grammar teacher who helped to instill some confidence and a cooking teacher who helped to instill some love. Two very sweet encounters with two Italian women who helped me see that I had relinquished way too much power, too much emotional power, to those who challenged my core.

I had allowed Amadeo to speak for all Italians in Florence and to convince me that my lifelong defense had been unjustified, misdirected and even a waste of time. But he didn't speak for Signora Gala. She was able to take one American at a time and react to one American at a time. And not just one American. One human being. Signora Gala had a class filled with foreign students--Germans and Swiss and Dutch and Mexicans and Americans--and she met each on her or his own level. "Look, if I handle you firmly but carefully, can you cut it in this class?" It had to do mostly with intellectual competence and not national origin. And Mamma's household was a study in that. Except her cutoff had to do with respect. Both combined to match the qualities of my *nonna*--whose openness to and acceptance of the wonders of diversity were anachronistic. Way ahead of her time. Together, they made me wake up to the lessons I was learning outside of the subjunctive tenses and the Etruscan arches. Wake up to my own strokes of choice in a pool of diversity, the likes of which I had never seen before. Backstroke. Freestyle. Float. Tread. Drown.

Just at the end of that complexity of emotions, that slapping between respect and assumption, between love and abuse, I ran into one of the most tender moments of my life. Max's late-November tribute to my 27 years of living. The details were flawless. A seven course menu hand-written on European block paper with a black fountain pen. A bottle of wine that he found in a dusty, Florentine store. Which waited to be opened and to breathe since the year I was born. And champagne. Fresh bread. And dish after dish of colors and spices and textures and flavors that spoke of affection and planning and friendship. He ushered me into his bedroom while he prepared the final touches. While he readied me for the birthday entrance. But I could never have been readied enough. A melodic Italian aria politely echoing off of his apartment walls. One hundred votive candles flickering in the winter breezes. A stack of presents to commemorate our months together. Framed photos. Garden books. Journals with shared memories. Sweet kisses on my cheeks. Left and then right and then left again. And a perfect rendition of *Happy Birthday*, in English-with-a-German accent, that took away all sadness of my first birthday separation. I never knew that friendship could be so generous.

His well-planned, well-executed, filled-with-love celebration made it harder to make sense of the range of acceptance. There didn't seem to be a pattern to people's love and hate. To people's inclusion or exclusion. Some Italians counted me in. Some Italians counted me out. Some men lived to violate. Some men lived to respect. Some women emerged confident and strong. Others emerged threatened and weak. Some knew how to explore the layers of my character. Others thought they know the deepest depths without the slightest clue.

At the end of my most special birthday evening, when Max gave me one more set of birthday kisses outside the door to my flat, 27 rounds and one more for good luck, he jump-started the kind of reflection that later invaded my dreams. About how I maneuvered with the waves and made sense of the chaos and unpredictability. Saw others in their own stereotypes the way I was seen in mine. Category One or Category Four.

I knew I had just received the best birthday present of all. A glimpse of Italy's mission for me. To define myself. To know my important pieces. And to know the ones that overlapped with others and the ones that were completely different. And to notice the differences. And wonder--about other people's personal journeys and personal attacks. And the spectra of respect and assumption. Of love and abuse.

* * *

The younger students in class were already getting worked up about the pre-Christmas exam--even though it was three weeks away. I was not. Maybe it was a sign that I was calming down or just acknowledging that there were other things to get worked up about. Or maybe it was a sign that I was getting old.

Not that there hadn't been others. Like not being able to get in shape in a week. Realizing that I no longer knew most of the songs and bands in the Top 10. Ripping a gray hair from my eyebrow. Finding myself on a small town street in front of a pack of cars and remaining determined to follow the 20 mph speed limit while cursing "those kids" for being in a hurry. Responding to the "Do you like Meat Loaf?" question from one of my students with "Only when my mother makes it," when the student was, in fact, referring to the singer.

My mother monitors her passing through the years with the Skin Bounce Back Check. Pulling up the skin on her hand and counting how long it takes to fall back into place. It wasn't all that long ago, she says, that the transition was uncountable. Now she could do a load of wash and vacuum the whole house during the time it takes to fall back. She often wonders what she was doing when it moved from unclockable to clockable. Probably doing loads of wash and vacuuming the house.

In any event, the exam sparked little interest for me. If I did well, I'd get a certificate. If I didn't do well, I wouldn't get a certificate. I feared no one. I was a rock. I was an island. She-rah was in the house.

My unparalleled and overt glee over ignoring the exam was an obvious sign that it was still way too important to me. I was officially old enough to acknowledge the pathology of my own delusions, to see my own smears on my own windows and to strive to erase them. I had things to see and places to go. And one of those places was Rome. So while kids seven years my junior were buying extra grammar guides and forming buddy-studies and drilling themselves on the 500 Italian synonyms for beautiful, John and I made plans to go to Rome. He was an obvious target for a travel partner given his outright commitment to non-communicative bliss. As dedicated to wallowing in ignorance as Dante was to figuring out our destinies, as Michelangelo was to that finger, as da Vinci was to the smile and as the Pope is to rhythm. Though not the kind on *American Bandstand.*

A bus left for the capital from Perugia nearly every day at 6:30 A.M. Despite the time, it was convenient. Door-to-door service from *Corso Vannucci* to *Piazza della Repubblica* in Rome. John and I arranged to meet at the top of our streets, the very point from which I had looked to see if Abdul had left my front door. And although I never laid eyes on Abdul again, he was always at that corner. On that hill. In those shadows. Lurking. Calling.

We agreed to meet there by 6:10 A.M., at least 20 minutes before the bus would leave. That would have given us plenty of time to walk the steep, winding streets to the summit and then to the end of *Corso Vannucci.* To the public gardens. Where Garibaldi was glorified in a small statue and where Max and I would have one of our many conversations about German pride and his mistrust of it.

It got to be 6:10 A.M., and John was late. As always. I should have gone to his house. I didn't want to miss the bus or have to run to make it and end up sweating all the way to Rome, making my own contribution to the already ripe ambiance of the bus-world. Just as I was about to work myself up into a lather, John rounded the corner. Smiling. Spry. Cigarette in hand. I wondered if the light-up of his butt had made him late. Clearly his razor hadn't. Not that it mattered. I loved his smile, and his bounce and his lateness were early enough that we didn't need to run. So, instead, we strolled.

The bus ride to Rome was a wonderful one, despite the pounding headache from *espresso* withdrawal that I had as we passed Todi. Instead of moaning about the hour of the day and what I had to go through to be ready to leave by 6:30 A.M., the sun helped me see that it was truly wonderful to be up so early. It had a way of changing the look of things as it moved across the sky. The early morning sun brought an essence to the countryside that was different from late morning. Different from early afternoon. Different still from sundown. It made me wish I had some semblance of artistic ability. Just an ounce. So that I could throw up an easel and paint the same scene at four different times of day. A pleasant reminder of the passage of time. One day at a time. Each filled with its own colors and tones and subtleties.

Throwing up an easel, however, was not an option for me. My history in the arts was less than stellar. Less than exemplary. It began in first grade on the first day of school. A near nervous breakdown brought Miss Hurbaugh running to my side to discover the source of my anguish. Utter certainty that I would flunk her class, have to stay back or even be demoted to kindergarten for having colored outside the lines on my triangle. There it was. In full view. A green crayon stroke obviously outside the barrier. The green line nestling up close to the black one and then forcing its way through to the other side. Inviting itself over. Playing on the grass, the driveway, the slide, the bike. Without permission. Bold. Wrong. Crude. Such anal neurosis did not bode well for creativity, for exploration, for blowing the doors off of preconceived boundaries. My early signs were unmistakable. And reeked of an artistic dead-end. A creative cul-de-sac.

I loved paint-by-numbers and connect the dots. Starting with Number 1 and plodding along. Two next. And then three, obviously. I thought the kids who skipped around were demented. Unstable. Like the ones who disregarded the carefully labeled order of the encyclopedia. Or a deck of cards. I sometimes wondered where they were now. Probably not teaching math. Probably living with a disorderly desk and underwear that aren't folded. Wrinkled sheets and misfiled addresses. Unmatched socks and pencils behind the bed.

After first grade, the art phobia snowballed. There was the class I sat in on during my second year of teaching. Things were going well while we worked with inanimate objects. The L.L. Bean Blucher. The corner of my office. The pencil sharpener. But as soon as the objects lived, my artistic side died. The first victim was my own face.

My teacher, Ms. Gayle, bless her, assured me that the realistic self-portrait was largely mathematical. Measure the distance from ear-to-ear. Measure the distance from nose bridge-to-chin. Measure the distance from eye-to-eye. Then methodically transfer the details to paper. We were to draw what we saw and use our rulers as guides.

The mixture of mathematics and art was devastatingly upsetting to me. I was afraid that the science would get tainted. That the art would spoil its purity. I had a similar confusion of feelings the first time I heard German spoken in northern Italy, saw *Wiener Schnitzel* on the menu in Bolzano or noticed *Lederhosen* for sale in Caldaro. They just didn't go. And they just did not go. My self-portrait was frightening. A nose like an anteater's and an overtly Cyclopic tone. Meanwhile, the 16 year-olds who were flanking me were producing masterpieces. Things I would frame and put on my wall. Mine was destined for a kitty litter.

After years of waiting, I tried again. An oil stick class at the local adult-ed. I scrutinized the class description. For beginners. Beginners. O-n-l-y beginners. I told few friends about the sign-up. Even they had specific rules. Praise me for my courage. Do not ever ask how the class was going. If I don't talk about it for awhile, do not ask me if I have quit.

I got the list of items I needed to buy and went shopping. That felt good. Even cool. Leaving the art store--feeling like an artist. Hoping I'd run into someone I knew. Someone who would see me carrying my odorless turpentine, my black and white oil sticks, my new paint brush and an old cloth that I casually picked up off the counter at the checkout stand. Real casual. Like an experienced creator.

I had to miss the first class. Class two, I slithered in. Some funky people were already there. Men with ponytails and beards and women with wild hair and 60s jumpers. They knew how to set up their easels. They had classical music going and were focused on the subject. Mercifully, a subject that was not breathing. I was relieved to think I could avoid, for at least one more week, another Cyclopean trauma. There was a bronze statue, about 18" high, with some flowers, a small box and three tennis balls surrounding it. Before everyone else arrived, I clarified the class level.

"This is for beginners, right?"

"Yes. What level are you?"

"I am in the level before beginner. I have not had an art class for years. Years. Not since I was five."

I lied. But after seeing my work, I knew she would fall for it. She seemed nice enough. She seemed to understand my anxiety, and, if nothing else, she was very aware of it. And so, I set up my easel--

with difficulty. Got a stool. Took out my oil sticks and brush. Got a can for my turpentine. Proudly displayed my old cloth and immediately got a raging headache, worse than the one I got as we raced past Todi. The turpentine, not so odorless. Within seconds, I was blinded from the toxins, my back was killing me, and the all-consuming anxiety made my first grade incident look like a walk in the park.

The hardest part was making the first mark on the paper. One little speck. And then another. I was pressing for exactitude. Held in accuracy bondage. Just as I couldn't feel how much Parmesan to grate for the *pesto*, I couldn't feel the strokes. The passion. The shadows of the objects. Oh, for God's sake, I writhed in silence, it was a bunch of tennis balls, a box and a bronze statue. What was there to feel?

It didn't take long before my teacher found her way to my easel. She yanked my black oil stick out of my hand to *show* me how to feel. She started by getting the oil stick slick and ripe and then peeled back its wrapping a little more, dipped it in the turpentine and made two dark, bold scratches on the upper left-hand portion of the paper. Apart from the real work. Scribbles. Nothing more. Then she moved front and center. Five minutes later *her* painting was on my paper. Not *my* painting on my paper. I couldn't even find my opening marks.

So I just stood there and watched her draw. She had wanted me to feel, and I was feeling alright, but I knew it wasn't the kind of feeling she was after. She finally handed me back my black stick and walked around to invade someone else's work. When she got to the guy next to me, she started slobbering all over herself. Raving about his style and mastery. His observance of the musculature in the bronze. When she held it up for all to see, I wanted to die. His work was amazing. I wanted it. I was sure he'd be famous one day, while I wallowed in infamy. Real fodder for the artsy-fartsy-friends' laugh-fest. Any coolness I had felt at the art store was gone.

I panicked and realized that I just couldn't risk it. I was too afraid she would show mine. That she would try to make a disabled artist feel welcomed. Try to inspire some hope and camaraderie. I decided to leave early. So 15 minutes before class was scheduled to end, with my head and lower back still throbbing, I packed up my things at earth-shatteringly fast speeds. When I walked over to her to thank her for her attention, she took my pad from my hand, opened up to the first sheet and showed the woman she was currently working with my pathetic attempt--which had worsened since she left the scene of my easel. And then, in the most emphatic blow to my artistic ego ever, ever, she praised me for the two bold, black marks that appeared in the upper left-hand corner of the paper. She praised me for the feeling. For the free-spiritedness. "Those are the best signs of hope," she said. "The most alluring part of the work," she said. The very two damn marks that she, herself, had made when she peeled back the paper, did a turpentine dip and loosened up the oil from the stick. She proclaimed *her* careless, thoughtless scribbles as *my* finest work!

The next steps were clear. 1) Never go back. 2) Get art therapy. 3) Never, ever again think that a Cyclops can do art. And with that, I had a plan and found my comfort back inside the lines. And that is why the morning sun dance over the rolling Italian countryside would get painted only in my mind. Only for my eyes. My eye.

John and I congratulated ourselves for our bold dismissal of exam preparation and chuckled at the poor, panicked youths back in Perugia poring over reflexive verbs while we moved toward the Eternal City. I had been to Rome on only one other occasion. When I visited the Termini train station with my dismembered tampons and $11 in cash. I was looking forward to a more relaxed adventure that day--free of menstrual and exchange rate blues.

The *Piazza della Repubblica* fountain, which spewed refreshing water, beautiful forms and wish-filled *lire* by the thousands, cooled our wrists before we found a nearby tourist office that would spare a decent map. John and I settled in at an outdoor cafè, ordered an *espresso* and an elephant ear pastry, spread the map out over the small, white, round table and with the help of an 8,000 pound guidebook I had lugged over from The States, started to plan the day.

Some sites were mutually nonnegotiable. The Colosseum. The Pantheon. The Fountain of Trevi. The Spanish Steps. Vatican City. A good lunch. And *Piazza Navona*. While Rome wasn't built in a day, we were going to visit it in one. And as anxiety started to set in about what we had to accomplish in so little time, we realized it would probably not crumble in one either. So, the nonnegotiables became negotiables. We decided to start with the Colosseum, not be consumed by the suggestions in the guide and see where our whims took us. We embraced a Throw Caution To The Wind mentality--with caution being a relative term.

For mostly financial reasons, John and I decided to walk everywhere in Rome in order to avoid the taxi, subway and bus scenes. We had both gotten used to watching our *lire* and getting the most out of our cash. While the times I spent with Max seemed almost celebrity-like, of other worlds and more elegant circles, the times I spent with John were what I knew best, of this world and more simple circles. I was content with each. One for its difference. One for its sameness.

John and I did our best bit of skimping when we did day-trips and when we ate together. Back in Perugia, we traded in our empty wine bottles for 200 *lire* each (about 10 cents then) to offset the cost of dinner--to buy some *tortellini*, Parmesan cheese, peas, fresh sausage, *panna* and $1.50 bottles of wine. So, walking in Rome was a given, even though we could have gotten away with a free bus ride. Almost nobody, nobody, nobody pays, but we didn't want to risk it. When a cheater does get caught skipping out on the fare, it is a humiliating price to pay.

The civilized and legal routine is this. You buy your bus ticket at a store that has a big blue and white T out front. The tickets are relatively inexpensive, and one will take you anywhere you want to go in the city. You climb onboard and make your way to a little machine, usually in the rear of the bus, that validates your ticket. It cuts a little corner off your stub, stamps it with the date and time and is good for anywhere from 30 to 90 minutes after you board, making transfers an easy thing. You step to the side, hold onto the railing above your head or, if you're lucky, you get a seat next to an open window, have a cordial conversation with a native and know exactly where you're supposed to get off.

The uncivilized and illegal norm is this. You do not buy a bus ticket. You squeeze your way onboard, elbowing and squirming and bumping cohorts like popcorn kernels in hot oil. Like sperm to the egg. You make your way to a seat that is reserved for veterans, the handicapped or the elderly. You do not budge when an 80-year-old, one-armed man, sporting a World War II medal gets on and expects you to vacate your seat, even though you catch him glancing at the sign that says you should and then at you and then at the sign and then at you again. You ride the bus as long as you want, making sure that the window next to you is hermetically sealed, not letting in one morsel of whatever clean air is remaining in the city. You make sure to light up at least three unfiltered cigarettes on the trip and blow the revolting smoke into the faces of the people who are millimeters away from your lips. You are not the least bit worried that you are riding the bus for free, and, in fact, you would feel absolutely indignant if an official transportation person boarded the bus and asked for your stamped stub. Since it almost never happens, you have no reason to worry.

If it does ever happen, an exorcism unfolds. Once the bus is jammed to capacity, (it would never happen on a nearly empty bus), a uniformed person steps on and orders the doors and windows locked and, supposedly, renders the validation machines inoperable. He or she moves down the aisle of the bus asking each rider, one-by-one, for a validated stub. If the validated stub is presented, all is well. If the validated stub is not presented, all hell breaks loose.

Act I: The Validated Stub Is Not Presented. Rabid gesturing, maneuvering, shouting and sweating. Red faces. Bulging jugulars. Half of the profanity I had mastered in my youth and some I will never speak of again. More rabid gesturing and maneuvering and then, finally, the payment of the fine, freeing up the lead actor to move to the next subject. See Act II.

Act II: The Next Subject. See Act I.

The play has as many acts as the bus has people. Only each subsequent act is played out with much more heat, anxiety, impatience, antagonism and humiliation as the frustrated, non-Tony-nominated actor moves down the aisle to members of his supporting cast.

So, if we *had* ridden the bus, we would have paid. But, under the best Roman bus circumstances, a walk was preferred--particularly since all the main sites, except Vatican City, could be walked to from *Piazza della Repubblica* without much effort.

If we strolled the streets of Rome with an aim for taking everything in, we wouldn't have gotten off the first block. But we knew we needed to strive, however free-spirited we were trying to be, to keep our eyes on the goal. It was difficult, though, as the reasons for Rome's designation as an "open city" (unable to be bombed) during World War II were hammered home on every corner. With every steeple. Every bas-relief. Every camera's dream.

We could have spent a lifetime examining the ancient streets, the churches that now rest below street level, the Roman baths and the open *piazze*. We could have fed the pigeons, marveled at the fountains, paused at each altar, visited the museums and rented a *vespa* to breeze through the streets with wind blowing through our hair. We could have gotten caught up in the unparalleled bustle of the ancient capital and caught the wave of human energy, of frolicking in the present, of touching our toes down on the pulsating streets of a Roman culture that had no equals and of being sung to in the language of Italy that allures, entertains and loves with each word. Each syllable. Each vowel. Instead, we took in what we could handle and what was inevitable. Avoiding overindulgence and leaving room for the impact of the Colosseum. Like not eating too much bread before the main meal arrives.

The approach to the Colosseum is magnificent. From any angle. We happened to come at it from *Piazza Venezia* (or the Tribute to Pompous Opulence) next to which fake Ray Bans were sold for $3. We veered to the left of the white spectacle and approached the Colosseum from *Via dei Fori Imperiali*. Spied on by the hills of Rome as the bold *corso* (wide thoroughfare) steered us forward. From a distance, I saw the Colosseum and knew I would never tire of laying my eyes upon it or of conjuring up its image when I was not near. As I never tire of my first glimpse of a newborn child or a loved one's crinkly cheeks after first waking up.

The Colosseum bursts up out of the road like an enormous wedding cake at the end of a long bridal aisle. From a distance, the antics of the past are long forgotten. The massacre of wild animals and condemned criminals, the weapons of death, the 50,000 thunderous fans, salivating lions and petrified slaves, the political strong-arm and the sharp demarcation of Rome's social classes. From a distance, they are replaced with beauty. An elliptical beauty that rises up toward the skies. The clouds. The heavens. With an interplay of Ionic, Doric and Corinthian design and the remnants of arches that

moved from side to side, giving strength and wonder to the architectural marvel.

John and I walked slowly down the *corso*--surrounded by centuries
of ruin. The Roman Forum. Now toppled columns and eroded
foundations whose stillness, whose paralysis, bear witness to a time
when it breathed and sang and jumped with the events of the day.
Religion. Business. Politics. And stone trophies that documented
victorious battles and Rome's place among the leaders of the leaders.

Just as I had been struck by the modern TV antennae poking up
out of the ancient, clay roofs of Florence, trying to force the new and
the old to live together happily, I was struck by the collapsed pillars
and broken pathways living alongside speeding motor traffic, vendors
selling bottled water for exorbitant prices and men pawning cemented
replicas of the Colosseum itself, absent the tiny little lions and the
tiny little Christians, pairs whose violent cohabitation has never been
documented. If you took time to think, it was a truly scary sight.
Reinforcing the notion that the skin on the hand of Rome no longer
snapped back in unclockable speed. Rome was old, and the 20th
century additions were making it age even faster.

John and I walked hand-in-hand along the modern stone wall that
bordered the ruins. First I'd walk on top, spying the hundreds of cats
that had found a home under and around the debris. Or the tiny spot
of cloud that hovered over the Roman Forum. Or the colorful feather
that was wedged in the stone wall's otherwise gray facade. And then
John would climb up and bring my attention to some detail that had
skipped my eyes. The tiny Italian flag flapping in the apartment
window. The young father singing to his baby twins. The four young
girls swaying down a narrow path with their arms linked in friendship. We loved sharing our lines of vision.

The sharing of sight was never more vibrant than the time I took
a trip to Sicily, many years later, with an artist friend. As the two of
us sat on a small hilltop in Segesta, overlooking the craggy hillside,
bringing into focus one of the most well-preserved Greek temples in
the world, Vincent commented on the shifting hues and diverse colors
that came to life on the temple as the sun moved across the sky or as
the clouds invaded its path to the pediment. I, instead, was struck by
the symmetry of the place of adoration. The methodically-spaced
columns, the sense of order and balance. It seemed to represent an

attempt at calm given the chaos of living. Together, we helped to complete a fuller picture, a picture that would have been very different if one of us had been absent or if more of us had been present. Life.

I couldn't wait any longer. I wanted to get there. So I tugged on John's hand, pulling him off the stone wall and across the street to where the Colosseum rested. We slithered by the horse-and-buggies, the manageable crowds and the hunched over, sleeping old man who was trying to sell not only upgraded plaster-of-Paris replicas of the Colosseum but of The Leaning Tower of Pisa, The Vatican and The Pantheon, too, making anxious tourists out of those who were irrevocably allergic to chintz.

It was hard not to realize, as our feet crossed the threshold from the outside to the inside, that we were walking the same ground that thousands had walked before us. Thousands who had climbed the now long-gone wooden planks to their proper social tiers. Women and slaves to the fourth level, more than 150 feet above, to stand or sit on hard benches. Men and members of the upper class to the lower levels, resting comfortably on chairs that brought them closer to the show. Gladiators and animals trapped below the wooden flooring, waiting for their chances to fight for their lives.

We walked as far as we could and let our eyes imagine as we strained to the left and then to the right, penned in by the solid walls that limited our mobility and freedom. Even as a woman in the modern era, I laughed to myself, the Colosseum won't let me go where I want to.

John and I picked a spot to sit down, first to read the guide and then to close our eyes to continue to let the horrid scenes of the past come to rest, however briefly, in the present. We thought it was the least we could do to pay tribute to those who died in the sculpted astrodome of gore. An ancient boxing site--with man and beast in the corners and 50,000 hungry, cheering, morbidly-inclined, Don King think-alikes watching from the sidelines.

As I battled the tension of my imagination, the roar of the crowds, the nets and spears and tridents being hurled through the thickened, noisy air, I took solace in knowing that amidst the miniature Vatican Cities and Leaning Towers and *Davids* that were being pawned outside the antiquated, elliptical boxing ring, that Don King's plaster-of-Paris hair was not yet up for grabs. A gesture that was *almost* enough to make me forgive the travesties of centuries ago.

Chapter Ten
Drove My Chevy To The Trevi
But The Trevi Was Dry

The growl that jolted us awake, minutes later, in the heart of the Colosseum, had more to do with hunger than with lions. It was already past noon, and the elephant ear from breakfast had lost its hold. John and I decided on a picnic, somewhere near our next stop, which we hadn't figured out yet. Like Gidget and Moondoggy. Two free-spirits on the street-beaches of Rome. But with the Hawaiian men's bathing suit and the maximum bust-projection pink bikini trapped in a movie set foot locker in Hollywood.

We took our time wandering, meandering and popping into three or four different stores to collect the pieces of our lunch. Bread. Tomatoes. A chunk of Parmesan, for me. *Mozzarella*. Olives. (I had grown to like them.) A little *mortadella*. Two bubbly waters, two Peroni beers and two bananas for dessert. Nearly everything had its own brown wrapper, a smoother version of grammar school bathroom paper towels, and was then tucked inside one large plastic bag.

John and I headed toward The Pantheon without talking about it and slithered down a side street to lean up against someone's home to eat lunch. Looming above us were some potted plants that were battling November's march toward cold, some bleached-white, tank-top undershirts and a couple of Italian women who were commenting on the weather, dinner and where we were probably from. Spain and Germany, I heard them say. Wrong. I liked that.

My mind was on the food, even though the bones of my rear end were being sharpened on the cool steps of Rome. I wasn't in the mood for my beer, which John drank, but I was in the mood for polishing off the Parmesan before he could get even the skinniest slice off the corner. Not that he would have wanted it. While most people seem willing to acquire a taste for things like beer, caviar and initially-repulsive seafood, very few seem interested in committing the same patience to developing the buds that are welcoming to my Parmesan. That serves me well--for just as the poor images of New Jersey keep more vacationers off its beautiful shores, the misconceptions about Parmesan leave more of it hanging in hundreds of cheese stores across the land. Domestic and international. More for me. Unwitting slobs.

John and I finished up quickly, somewhat aware of the time and of our need to catch an early evening bus to Perugia. I was already feeling sad about that, already preparing for our departure while we were in the middle of the day. That was something I learned from my family. Anticipation of the future while ignoring the present. Let's talk about dinner while we eat lunch. I was the only one in that Dysfunctional Club on that trip. John never thought about anything but the present. Sometimes to incredible extremes. Like the day his father wired him money because John had signaled that he needed cash for shelter and food. As soon as he got it, John went straight out and bought a hunter green, wool sweater and a rich, dark, cotton umbrella with a mahogany handle. Within hours of filling his empty wallet, he was left with a few thousand *lire* and something to use if Perugia got pelted by frigid rain. The likelihood was small, but the choices made him happy. And, he said, that was the point. I thought resisting death was the point.

We followed the large, golden-colored signs to The Pantheon and were led to the impressive entrance of the enormous temple. An entrance that was decorated with incomprehensibly large pillars whose circumference could not begin to be hugged by one person, pillars that had a way of dwarfing their visitors' egos and setting the scene for an appropriate, respectful passage to the inside.

We were thrilled when we entered to find only two other people, a security guard and another tourist, the former standing watch near a small wooden table with a large, pink Italian newspaper and the latter standing right in the center of The Pantheon--looking up and at the dome and then beyond it through the hole at the top. John and I took seats and opened the guidebook to discover that Pantheon means many gods, and that the walls are 25 feet thick in places, (almost as thick as my childhood home was tall), and that the dome, itself, is revolutionary in design, (with squared-off pieces carved out of it to lighten the load), and that the concave floor, with a drain in the center, catches the water that the hole in the dome lets in. A hole which, I imagine, provides a clearer, unobstructed path to the heavens and the gods and brightens up and warms up the dark, cool, but cozy inside with some natural light from above.

The other tourist strolled over just then, it was almost awkward not to, and asked if he could share our guidebook. His beautiful, dark skin, rich, brown eyes, radiant smile and American, east coast accent helped me answer his question in record-time. With widened eyes and a gaping mouth. And then we introduced ourselves. John from New Zealand. Jo from Boston. And Dana from Boston, too. I was stunned by the instant and overwhelming bliss I felt when we discovered our common roots. He was my first one. My first one since Air Gloria had carried me away from familiar accents, the North End and Cape Cod. I was relieved. And overjoyed. And half-expected and half-wanted the doors to fly open, the Bee Gees to swarm in, and Dana and me to hold hands, spin and belt out in our best warbling falsetto--*Yes, It's Nice To Be In Massachusetts*. Dana, mercifully, seemed way too cool for that and, amazingly, thank many gods, even I was.

Dana explained that his girlfriend (who had left to get a *cappuccino* because the chill inside The Pantheon had gotten to her) and he were studying in Rome. Archaeology. He asked if we wanted to meet her when we were done inside, which we did, but only after we went in three different directions before exiting The Pantheon's doors. I did one slow, full circle, pausing at every crevice, every word, every detail in the rounded temple, unequivocally aware of the power that was all around me. Maybe it had to do with the sheer size. Maybe it had to do with the interplay of darkness and lightness. Maybe it had to do with the presence of not just one God--but many gods. I couldn't say. But I could say that I would be back, eager to be squashed by a building that breathes antiquity and makes us realize that some of the pains of our present are just specks in time. Droplets in a river. Grains of sand on a beach. Contributing to the outcome-- but not directing the outcome. At times, I liked that obscurity. And, at other times, I was tortured by it.

We crossed a courtyard, happy to be back under the warmth of the Italian sun, and Dana spotted Elsie (nicknamed for her initials, L.C.)

at a cafè counter across the *piazza* from The Pantheon. He moved up behind her with a smoothness and a tenderness that made my heart ache. That made me wish I were sitting on that stool sipping the froth off of the steaming *cappuccino*. We, too, ordered coffee, and before the second drops of it coated our throats, we could see that they made a perfect couple. Perfect complements of style, of energy. Perfect blends of beauty. And more than anything, they just seemed so gentle with each other. So kind. Like two old souls who had been together for 100 years but who had the life and liveliness of teenagers.

As time ticked by, it was obvious that both John and I were enjoying their company and the smooth-flowing English. It had been months since I had been around other Americans. I felt different. More comfortable. More confident. And, oddly, more powerful. A majority feel. It was the first time in my life I even knew there was such a thing. And was uncomfortable enough with it, that feeling, that newness, to know it was something I wouldn't share with my current company--company whom, I was sure, hadn't spent their years-to-date floating effortlessly in that same bubble.

After paying, we wandered with some purpose to The Fountain of Trevi, a large, lavish expanse of godly-human forms with enormous chests, bulging biceps, long, flowing hair and faces that were halted with looks of intensity. The noise from the pulsating waters could be loud, at times, and was responsible for drawing natives and foreigners alike to the cold, white steps that partially encircled the fountain, to stare at and into the water with looks like those on the pigs' faces that hung in the meat shop windows just across the street. Frozen. Still. And eerily peaceful.

The noise from the waters competes with the noise from the crowd. The elderly gentlemen, like Nonno's drugstore cowboys, who gather straight back chairs and hold court outside the upper edge. The tiny children, the fashion princes and princesses, with wobbling legs and flailing arms, taking on the challenge of climbing over others' outstretched limbs as their laughter enhances the scene. Italian boys and girls, thin and bronzed and poster children for one kind of ultimate beauty, already skilled in the art of flirtation, in the art of romance, in the art of the seduction, holding hands or coupled in sit-spoons or running their long, thin fingers through their own and others' hair. The aging women, who forget their youth and shake their heads and try to whistle through their teeth to invade the sexy encounter. And the foreigners, lining up their cameras for one more precise shot of the fountain--while missing the lifetime of words and passion and glory that pass outside their lenses' narrow view.

The Fountain of Trevi is the sacred place of wishes requested and wishes granted. All for a few hundred *lire* tossed over our shoulders with our backs against the waters. As it quietly gathered its visitors' wealth. With no guarantees for fulfillment. So I was determined to push the fountain. To make it work for its *lire*. And played with the idea of wishing to be 5'9" tall. And 125 pounds. And a movie star.

On the count of *uno, due, tre* we threw coins in and waited. As if holding our backs to the fountain would guarantee the wish. When we got just a few feet away, Dana wanted to know what we had wished for. I volunteered that I didn't want to go back to Perugia. That I wanted to go back after we had a chance to visit Rome more. "That is exactly what I wished for," John said. "So, let's do it. We can afford it." This from the man who traded room and board for a mahogany-handled bumbershoot.

"You can stay with us at our apartment," Dana said, with the kind of openness that was common over there, where people shed the inhibitions that led to distinct, sharpened barriers back home. That led to caution. That led to paranoia. It felt freeing. "Sure," said Elsie. "We have twin beds that we normally push together and cover with a huge comforter. You can have one bed, and we'll have the other. It won't be the most comfortable thing you've ever slept in, but it won't cost you anything."

It made me wonder about John's Trevi wish as he looked over at me for some kind of sign. Apparently, the raising of my eyebrows and the tilting of my head, just as a dog does when its owner inserts a vocabulary word that doesn't go with dinner, treat or outside, was exactly the sign John needed. We were going to stay, he had decided, however hygienically-unprepared we would be. And with that, Dana and he began to map out our immediate future.

Now John was the kind of guy who could brush his teeth with cold water and his pointer finger and turn his underpants onto the other side to get two days' use out of them. I was not that kind of person. But if I were given a long-reach, medium bristle toothbrush with brand name toothpaste and a pair of fresh, clean underpants, I could cope with the rest. I wondered if Elsie would get it. That was answered soon enough when she leaned over and said, "As we keep walking around, we'll keep an eye out for a Standa. We can buy a new pair of underpants and anything else you need. You can use all our other stuff if you want. Toothpaste, soap, you know."

And so I loved her--both for her overt sensitivity to parts specifically unnamed and her subtle inference that while the guys thought they were planning the rest of our day, we were going to have at least some say about our direction. I was wishing I had known her for years. I had a sense of time wasted.

Elsie and I reentered Dana's and John's conversation to hear them talking about The Spanish Steps, *Piazza Navona*, a nice dinner near the hotel and St. Peter's and The Vatican Museum the next day. Sunday. I was glad we had left the details to them. When I looked back at Elsie, our barely perceptible smirks hid our antagonism over their assumed control of the situation and reflected our understanding that they had planned exactly what we had wanted anyway, absent the underpants.

Our first stop after the detour to Standa was The Spanish Steps. I don't know what I was expecting, but I was disappointed. No flowers. No sunbathers at that time of year. Though in some ways the barrenness offered a much needed reprieve. I was already numbed by the magnificence of everything. Or maybe it was just that our arrival there had come too soon after having purchased a new three-pack of cotton, Hipster Jockeys and a Colgate toothbrush.

After walking up and skipping down and inhaling the view from above The Spanish Steps, there was plenty of window-shopping and candle-lighting in neighborhood churches and getting lost in the loops and curves of Rome. There were speeding motorcycles carrying meticulously appointed boys and girls primed for their Saturday evening dates, *espresso* smells visiting the streets and mothers opting for lungs over telephones in tracking down their vagabond children. There were violinists under the outdoor restaurants' tents and flowers posing as centerpieces and fresh garlic being peeled and crushed and finely diced.

Along the way, down every street, at every bend, with every wish that accompanied every candle, with every smell and every note and every mother's cry, Dana, Elsie and I reverted. We named our homesickness and our New England withdrawal symptoms and talked about Larry Bird and The Kennedy Family and Cliff on *Cheers* as if they were classmates at our old high schools. And we did so without interruption. And without John. And with total ease. As if we were completely aware of how wonderful it felt to feel connected. To have to explain less and less instead of more and more.

And then, as if all of that were not enough, in the middle of some reminiscence or some local joke or some exclusive memory, a Boston accent would slip in, without warning, and be welcomed. An accent I was forced to expunge in college when "bubbla" had to become "bubbler" which had to become "water fountain" which was less colorful and less original and less me. Without interruption. Without John. Without making sure he knew about The Curse of The Bambino or Radcliffe College as we traipsed across Rome. Without making sure he knew about how our accents return when we are feeling most comfortable, most accepted, most connected. Most most. And we did so without interruption. And without John. And with total ease.

He was out of it, and I watched as he retreated. Little by little. Alone. Silenced. Void of jibes. Small. And I did not stop. On purpose. It was about getting back at him, in whatever way possible, for the pain he had caused me. His personal, arrogant criticism at a *Corso Vannucci* cafè for our sanctions against New Zealand for differing stances on nuclear power. The relentless attack on me during our Gubbio day-trip for his concerns about the direction of civil rights. The argument during a culture class break because of his sweeping generalization of and characterization of every single citizen from Savannah, Georgia to Dell, Montana. Week after week. Against me. Because I was American.

But at that very moment, I was no longer alone. I was with Americans. Numbers. And it was about more than just numbers. I stepped aside enough to acknowledge that and to see that Abdul and Amadeo were in my head. Invading me, again. Joining me, again. But I didn't step aside enough. And that should have directed me better. Should have steered me away from wanting to impose on someone else the kind of isolation I had suffered since I had been away from home, away from the things I knew best, the people I knew best. I was in a position to impose or prevent, and I leaned toward impose. And kept on walking. Feeling buoyed by the numbers. By the imbalance. By the power.

When we finally arrived at *Piazza Navona*, at the end of thousands of footsteps and leather shoe window displays and domed cathedrals, I passed through it more fixated on the controlled conversation than on the scene. The glorious fountains, dozens of pigeons, natives reading poetry out of small, black books, artists battling the chills to sketch portraits and caricatures and tourist restaurants that rest on the rectangle's borders were lost on my spite.

We showered back at Dana's and Elsie's flat, and John and I got as dressed up for dinner as we could. He was quiet. Barely present. Far less arrogant and center stage than I had seen. I opened my new Jockeys without the kind of celebratory gesture I had imagined and put on the same clothes I had had on since 5:30 that morning. And wished that I were small enough to fit into Elsie's clothes. But since she hovered around a Size 2, I knew I'd look more like a sausage link than a human being.

A restored, ancient bath restaurant was located just at the end of the street and a little towards *Piazza della Repubblica*. We entered in the lower level and were greeted by a man whose hair was so dark it looked blue. It was hard to resist swooshing my hand through it as I walked past. It was only my recollection of strangers doing that to me when I was young that made me resist the temptation with him as he led us up the stairs, through one main dining room and to a rooftop terrace with dozens of browning cacti and other plants along the perimeter. I was disappointed by the long table of Japanese tourists that had already settled in--preferring places that were frequented by only the locals or Italians on holiday. Our two tables yelled "Tourist Trap." A label whose significance didn't take long to play out.

Three middle-aged men in black pants, black cummerbunds, white, pleated shirts and sparkling, sequined vests. One with a cordless mike, one with a violin and one with an accordion. I always thought there needed to be a Vocational Training Certificate for that type of entertainer. The cornerstone class would be called "Read The Moment"--whose primary message would be, "If the diners do not make eye contact with you or dip their faces downward putting one hand almost salute-like over their eyebrows or work vociferously to maintain the conversation that had already begun at the table, the entertainers should move on, without smiling, without asking for requests, without dreaming about luring precious çoins to the silver collection plate."

My family members could be the sole architects, teachers and assessors of that course. We are the masters of feeling embarrassment and could help those accordion players and roaming microphonists recognize the painful signs. One brother fleeing the room during a *My Three Sons* episode when there was an awkward sexual moment between Fred MacMurray's character and the woman who tried to replace his sons' mother. Or more of us grabbing the nearest pillow and squeezing it into our eyes as Dennis The Menace uttered one more "Gee, Mr. Wilson" or sang *Oh Holy Night* during the holidays while his insipid face was wedged between the wooden slats of his banister.

The most extreme example of our inclination toward instant embarrassment was the Christmas caroler. We dread it as the season comes upon us. It's cold. Snowy. The tree is up, and the lights are in the windows. We are in our den watching *Rudolph, The Red-Nosed Reindeer* or *Frosty, The Snowman* or *It's A Wonderful Life*. And then, without warning, there is a knock. An unexpected visitor. Someone reluctantly gets up from the floor or couch to peek out the window to find a massive collection of people outside our door. Wearing winter jackets. Hats. Some even sporting muffs. Carrying music sheets and candles. And all obviously wearing the kind of boot that allows them to sneak up ever-so-quietly on innocent families. The lookout drops to his knees, scrambles across the floor and out the den door, and others follow--leaving one poor sap to respond. Usually, the most slow-footed. Usually the most innocent. Usually, me.

I drag myself to the door and open it and, as is the common denominator with all those embarrassing moments, the main question is, where do you look? At the singers? At the ground? At the next door neighbor's glowing TV where Rudolph can be seen flying for the first time? Do you smile? Do you do it in the middle of *Good King Wenceslas*, at the end of *Silent Night* or when the whole blessed set is finally over? And then, do you give them something? Do you make a donation? Do you offer a cookie and hot chocolate? Do you compliment? Or do you let them know that they just sang over the first of Frosty's meltdowns or the spotting of Zuzu's petals in Jimmy Stewart's trousers? Far too many decisions for the youngest member of the family--a family that is linked, like no other family is linked, by the thread of Disorder of Instantaneous Embarrassment. DIE.

The most fun part of the caroling, for more than one reason, is when they finally leave. On the most recent debacle, I found my family pressed into the bathtub of the upstairs bathroom. Laughing hysterically at having fooled them again. Like the carolers would've thought to serenade them next to the family toilet. The crowning glory that year was when my mother proclaimed, "We are a very odd family." An emphasis that made me proud.

So, there I was in Rome and was, in essence, surrounded by a Latin brand of carolers, wearing no earmuffs but carrying an enormous hand piano. My company had not yet begun a conversation. Nor were they skilled in the art of the head-dip or the hand-salute. So we were locked into one more round of *Volare* or *When The Moon Hits Your Eye*. I could barely resist the temptation to see if the restaurant had a tub that was big enough for four.

What seemed like hours later, they finally stopped playing and singing. I left the acknowledgment to my dinner partners, relieving me of the pressures my family would have forced me to assume. The waiter came over to take our drink order, and while the other three chose beer, I ordered a glass of red wine. He brought a bottle instead.

I was seated next to John and was hoping to start repairing any damage I had done earlier in the day. He was cautious, as I would have been, but also surprisingly forgiving. By the time I reached for my wine to pose a toast to friendship, new and not-as-new, we cracked glasses with some sense of restoration.

They had two beers each, and I had two glasses of wine before they switched over and ordered another bottle of red. When it came time to order dinner, I was forced into a culinary *faux-pas*, which instantly repulsed the Italian wait-staff. Red wine with seafood *pasta*. I wanted seafood, and a switch to white wine was heartily discouraged. I was not prepared to duplicate the night of a friend's cotillion when the consumption of red wine, followed by white wine, followed by red and white wine in the same glass, led to a straddling of a Ms. Pac Man table at a local bar for a rematch of an earlier romp against the new debutante, while her broken dress hoop dangled messily over the back of her head. Nor did I want to duplicate the night I witnessed in Perugia when another dining travesty was committed by an uninformed American who opted for Parmesan cheese on her seafood dish--a decision that rendered the dish, according to the waiter, inedible and rendered the consumer, according to the waiter, a glaring example of how our two countries are separated by a hell of a lot more than just water.

I was fortunate that our waiter, though repulsed, was not eager to instigate an international incident. We were merely labeled, *en masse*, The Ignorant English Speakers. And I saw the trade as this. You press sparkling sequins in my face and force me to listen to *Three Coins In A Fountain*, I ignore culinary protocol and send dead fish to acclimate themselves to a red sea.

Hours and hours passed in those ancient baths as our words covered everything from the inane to the incredible. We started with a sharing of our backgrounds--beyond our current country labels. A ritual that was curious to John who didn't grow up with the same kind of mix. Dana. African-American. Elsie. Portuguese-American and African-American. Jo. Italian-American and Scottish-American. Taking note of our different histories despite our common labels and our common histories despite our different labels. And John listened.

From there we moved to a discussion of archaeology to The Sistine Chapel to classical music to the native Maori of New Zealand to the wide variety of toilet-flushing methods in Europe--the pedal, the handle, the chain, the button, the occasional hole--and the angst we all felt as we searched for the method-of-the-moment. And then to the wonders of Italy. Its people, culture, art, architecture, food, wine and fascination with the pleasures of today. For a country who gave rebirth to the world in the 1400s and 1500s, it still romped, at times, like a young mother, thrilled with the realities of now and dreaming only with hope about the possibilities of the future.

The Japanese table had long since cleared as had every other table on the terrace. The four of us remained (with four empty bottles of Antinori) as the clock moved well after midnight, and the waiters didn't move at all, giving us the impression that they weren't in the slightest hurry for us to leave. One, in fact, who spoke a little English, settled into a chair to join us, but never uttered a word, as I shifted the conversation away from the chain-string flush and the good old days of Rico Petrocelli toward the fact that John and I never got to hear Dana's and Elsie's wishes from The Fountain of Trevi.

"Well?"

Elsie shifted her rear end on the wooden, straight back chair and reached for another sip of the red wine that lingered in her glass. Kicking it back with a thrust, skipping the smelling, swirling and chewing phases and going right to the swallow. Dana picked that moment to glance at the dying plants that decorated the balcony and to comment on the long drop from the terrace to the trash cans that rested below.

"If you share your wishes, they don't come true," Elsie finally said--with a tone that was stark in its contrast to what had gone on before. Like lightheartedness. Laughter. Silent connections. So I backed off, out of self-preservation and out of my desire to read boundaries and adhere to them. Even when I was confused by them.

So I shifted the conversation again and turned to John, where the boundaries were less defined, and rehashed in my head the day's events. And my treatment of him. A long-delayed exchange for his treatment of me. When I spoke, after revisiting every scene, every barb, every attempt to dismiss him, it seemed disconnected to that gathering. Out of the blue. But not to me.

"John, I'm sorry if I made you feel bad today. I apologize."

He was shocked. I could tell. Not only because apologies just weren't part of our relationship, but because the conversations that I was orchestrating (or killing) were taking unpredictable turns. John accepted the apology and dismissed it as nothing. Gesturing it away with a flip of his hand. But I asked to keep going. To explain my behavior. To justify me.

Encouraged by their nods and sincerity, I began nervously, anxiously, my voice high-pitched and halting. Early stages of tears forced their way through my exhaustion to coat the eyes that couldn't look anyone in the face. I was worn out by the food and wine. And by the unnamed tension. Worn out by living through what I was about to describe. And surprised by my willingness to cast privacy rules to the wind with my new friends. However cautiously.

I started slowly, weaving my fingers in and out of the candle that flickered on the table. Drawing attention away from my open wounds and embarrassing pain and toward the flame. Faster and faster. Suddenly aware of the space I was occupying as I placed pieces of the past on the table.

Overt, unedited, inaccurate, painful, sweeping anti-Americanism.

Presidential policies, the Vietnam War, loud tourists, our stance on nuclear power and our gaudy distribution of wealth. The Cold War, water pollution, energy consumption, tyrannical rule and the violent, drug-addicted behavior that, apparently without exception, runs irreversibly rampant in every corner of American turf from east to west.

Attacked by assumption and group-association. The victim of their narrowness. The victim of my naivete´. And isolation. Accusations and criticism piled up as I did my best to survive and thrive in a foreign country, with a different tongue, a different history, a different future, a different sight. As the spears came from all directions. Personal. Political. Spiritual. International. Irrational. As I seemed to stand alone in my culture. In my label.

And then I sipped some wine. And passed over Abdul. Reattaching myself to my rules in the wind.

And gulped some water. And took a breath.

And held my finger over the flame until it stung. As I wondered and then asked, slowly, quietly, with a hint of permission, if it were too much to be seen as just me--one American. Not me--all Americans. Someone unique who has been influenced by her culture. Not some inevitable caricature of the worst of her culture.

And then I stopped. With the last syllables drifting off. Over and onto and into those who chose to catch my words and carry them. With the wick between my fingers. Bringing dark as I thought I brought light. Leaving me scared and relieved and nervous. And as exposed as I had been.

The Italian waiter who had joined us climbed out of his chair and started to clear the remaining plates. I looked at Dana and Elsie at the instant their faces were focused on each other. For a silent and seemingly familiar message between friends.

It was enough to move my attention from me to them. And open my eyes. A little. And then a little more. Until the nature of my remarks begin to take shape in my head. And elbow. And swing about. And pound. Until a volume got turned up when Dana leaned in to scream. Or speak. Or whisper. Or say nothing at all.

Over the course of the day, I had noticed Dana's socks and haircut. Elsie's rings and wire-rimmed glasses. I had noticed his soulful voice and her classic style. Their silver necklaces. Her sharp wit. I had noticed that they were quiet, at times, and spontaneous, at times. And I had noticed their black faces in that sea of whiteness-- but never more than at that very moment.

From their faces, from their silence, right then, I awoke to read the moment. Understand the moment. And the variety and degrees of pain at our small table. The theory became the practice. The page became a person. A voice. A tip of the head. A face across the table.

There was no screaming. No speaking. No whispering.

Words muted in their throats. Unuttered. Unwished.

Later that night, as I stood in front of the old, rusted mirror in Dana's and Elsie's flat, a distorted picture of me was cast up on the tiny surface--taking away the image of the person I always thought I was. As I splashed water on her, the Trevi wishes jumped back to haunt and question just under the layers of her stinging eyes. Who shares? And who doesn't?

I wondered what that meant, if anything, and I wondered about patterns, and I wondered what they were thinking, and I wondered if I had found the answer in their voicelessness. And I wondered who I was to think I had found anything.

I couldn't even find myself in that mirror.

Chapter Eleven
At Whom Is He Pointing, Anyway?

Any expected tension about the sleeping situation was null and void. We got into bed and slept. Or tried to. I kept thinking back to the questions and challenges I had presented to myself after Amadeo and Abdul had invaded my sense of me. *A glimpse of Italy's mission for me. To define myself. To know my important pieces. And to know the ones that overlapped with others and the ones that were completely different. And to notice the differences. And wonder--about other people's personal journeys and personal attacks. And the spectra of respect and assumption. Of love and abuse.*

Around 5:00 A.M., I rolled over to find John staring right at me, his face lit up by the remnants of the moon and the earliest stages of daylight. From the glossy look of his eyes, I knew it had been a rough night for both of us. We spoke at the same time. "I'm sorry." He pulled me closer to him, and I found a spot for my face right between his cheek and his shoulder. And that was all that we said before we closed our eyes and tried to salvage some rest from our endless night.

The *cafè* at the end of *Principe Amadeo* happily filled our orders of *cappuccini* and cream-filled donuts early that next morning. The four of us chose a window table in the sun's path and sat down--to an awkward beginning. Quiet. Stumbling. The silence forced me to wonder more about what is left unsaid in conversations than what is actually said. And wonder how much I know about anything outside of my own world.

A minute after the coffee and donuts had made it to the table, I decided to invade the awkward emptiness a little. I looked at Dana and Elsie and said two things. "First," with glistening eyes and a fluttering that lodged itself in my throat, "thank you." When Elsie greeted my pool with a pool of her own, I knew she knew exactly what I meant. I was saved from having to explain, and I was grateful.

And then, after another minute of less awkward silence, I spoke again. "Your wishes...."

Elsie reached across the table with both of her hands, searching for and finding both of mine. Her fingers tangled in mine and covered mine and patted mine. With grace. And dignity. I took a deep breath. And we smiled at each other, as John bit into his *bombolone* and Dana reached his hand to the back of Elsie's neck and massaged the tension that rested at the base of her hairline. Right at the border. And we nodded a little. And smiled a little. Dana and Elsie and I. And reached for sips of the *cappuccini* that were waiting.

We took the subway to Vatican City. It was a long ride from *Piazza della Repubblica* to the stop closest to St. Peter's and then a long walk after that. It just forced us to prolong the ecstasy that was waiting. I thought it had something to do with resisting temptation and a modern-day penance. Instead of one *Our Father* and three *Hail Marys*, it was one long subway ride and three long blocks. Amen.

Like every other architectural wonder in Rome, the approach to Vatican City is impressive. We are Dorothy, without the poppies, as we dance down the streets to the Oz that awaits. Bigger than life. The largest of its kind. The best that humans can do to pay tribute to God himself.

At first, the eyes catch on the circular colonnade that encloses the enormous *piazza*, eternally filled with tourists and priests and colorfully jacketed Vatican guards and old women in black-hooded coats offering seeds to the hordes of Catholic pigeons that call Vatican City their home. Then the eyes wander to the cathedral itself, set at the back of the *piazza* and resting on dozens of tiny steps that welcome the masses each day. Sparkling. Ornate but not gaudy. Symmetrical with asymmetrical features. Bright but subdued. Peaks, like the fingers on The Sistine Chapel, stretching upward to touch the hand of God. And then the eyes move in one large circle. Resting on the apostles, in statuary splendor, keeping watch over the religious center. And toward the window from which the Pope emerges to address his followers and to address those who get caught up in the intrigue of religion and devotion and faith and to address those who have to wonder what they're missing as they stand in that sea of dedication.

I felt small. Dwarfed. A droplet in a river. A grain of sand on a beach. As I stood tall, a fraction of a shadow in the surrounding colonnade. There's No Place Like Rome.

Since it was a Sunday, the Vatican Museum hours were a little shortened. So we decided to go there first and visit the cathedral after. Hurrying along the enormous wall to our left, passing a supply of t-shirt booths (price of one shirt permanently fixed at 5,000 *lire*, as steady as its neighbor's stance on female priests) that was as endless as the walk was, and finally arriving at the entrance to the museum. We flashed our student ID cards, got a small price reduction and headed up the set of interlocking staircases that, by themselves, could have held our attention for several minutes. When we got up to the real entrance, we were inundated with options. Audio cassette. Guidebook. And one of five paths that all led to The Sistine Chapel. Routes A, B, C, D and E. We opted for Route A, no cassette and no guidebook and started down what looked like, to the novice, us, a much prettier version of Interstate 95.

The main challenge in the Vatican Museums was crowd control. Skilled drivers were the best traveling partners in that setting. They knew when to go with the flow, when to pass on the left and when to head into the breakdown lane to pass on the right. They knew when to signal when shifting lanes and when to go for it, abandoning the rules of the road. They even knew when to stop and enjoy the view or when to backtrack to ask for directions. That day I was fortunate to be with three other very good drivers. Aggressive when necessary. And mellow when necessary.

Calmer tendencies were called for in, among others, the Raphael room, the map section, the tapestry area and, of course, The Sistine Chapel. Aggressive tendencies were called for in the extensive and unlabeled bust section, the We Cover Up Body Parts With Leaves Because We're Repressed area and the busy, overdone rooms where paint was slapped up on every available corner. My driving partners that day agreed on the Three Ps. Pass the privates, pause at Raphael, and proceed to the ceiling quickly.

The route to The Sistine Chapel is long and windy, through dozens of large rooms and cordoned-off smaller rooms and narrow staircases with concave steps from years of weighty visitors. Any of our preconceived intentions about how to "do" the Vatican Museum eroded instantly. The people, the architecture, the entrance of brightness through the tall windows and the aged skylights and the artistic smorgasbord were the causes of the internal conflicts that urged us to see as much as possible without seeing too much. But how were we to choose between masterpieces and masters? Between *The School of Athens* and the ancient maps? The polished marble and religious triptychs. The historic portraits and archaeological nuggets. There *was* no choosing, so blinders went on until something slipped in through the sides and enticed us to gaze. Which we did. Gladly. But ever aware of the chapel at the end of the road.

When we finally made it to the chapel, a 20th-century voice boomed out to warn us that it was, in fact, a chapel and that people needed to respect it as such. I liked to think that people wouldn't need a reminder--which, of course, they did. Every 60 seconds from the moment the chapel opened its doors in the morning until the last person was ushered out at closing time.

The process of restoring the ceiling and The Sistine Chapel had just barely begun. So, for the time-being, the colors remained less lively, more soiled and earthy. Not that I would have known. When I don't know what something can be, I can't be disappointed if it doesn't live up. But restoration or no restoration, the ceiling lived up. It lived way up.

I instantly developed a strategy to view the works completely and, in my opinion, properly--barring the unfortunate absence of the earplug. That facet was needed to avoid overhearing the comment that destroyed the euphoria of my first glimpse of splendor. "Yah, yah, darlin'. Ah saw this vary ceilin' in a movie oncest. What was it? The Agony and The Defeat?" It took all of my strength to avoid injecting, "Yes, yes, sir, this is an actual Hollywood movie set. But the movie you're thinking of is *The Agony and The Ecstasy*, not the opening script to *Wide World of Sports*. Welcome to Universal Studios, ignoramus." Clear evidence that at times I harbored as much disdain for Americans as others harbored for me. Though my disgust, I liked to think, was based on personal experience and not distant perception. But maybe they thought that, too. In any event, the resonating warnings about respecting the sacred place held me back from a Sistine first, a Sistine brawl, a Sistine civil war.

So, instead, I walked to the center of the chapel and looked straight up. Then slowly, carefully, with back arched and neck and eyes straining, I moved my sight all the way from one end to the other end with my feet planted. I lingered. And tried to notice the nooks and crannies of the work--the flow of the beard, the shape of the ark, the curve of the sun, the softened oranges and reds competing with the blacks and browns. And I tried to make sense of the wonder of the feat. Arms over the artist's head. Body balanced on rickety scaffolding. Mastering proportion and emotion and spirit from dizzying heights.

Then, finally, after minutes and minutes of scrutiny, I wrenched my feet from the cemented grip and moved toward *The Last Judgment.* Putting my back to it and scanning the entire length of the room. Again. Slowly. Carefully. Noting how that beard, that ark, that sun all looked a little different from that vantage point. Moving. Shifting. Challenging the eye.

Then I glided to the side, staked out a seat on the benches and sat. With binoculars, I repeated the end-to-end routine and then brought myself back to the beginning to try to recall or imagine, one-by-one, the significance of each of the scenes. I was appalled by my ignorance. My Baptism, Confirmation, mandated Sundays, Christian Education classes and memories of mantillas offered no hope for the shallowness of my knowledge.

Then my eyes were drawn to the famous painting of God stretching toward Adam's hand. *The Creation.* The finger of God to touch the finger of man. The stretch that is replicated thousands of times on the $2.50 t-shirts that were found several hundred yards away. But whose touch was never actualized. Maybe God wasn't actually creating Adam. Maybe He was pointing at something else. Someone else. In the wake of last night's self-centeredness, it crossed my mind that He might have even been pointing at me. "Search, search, search for years and years, dear God, for the American woman in the dirty corduroys and ripe turtleneck. And when you find her, point to her. Point to her, dear Lord. She will know what you mean." Yes, she knew what you meant. She's insane.

Despite the obvious paranoia, my emotional reaction to the ceiling did not compare with my reaction to *The Last Judgment.* For that scene, I remained seated, refocused my binoculars and leaned back against the wall. First randomly scanning the whole image. And then trying to go about it more methodically. Starting in the upper left corner and moving across and then back to the left and across again and again. Until my eyes got caught on one face that leads to one arm that leads to one body that is trying to climb up from purgatory or is getting pushed down into hell. Hell, there, is scary. Skulls and horror and gray-skinned devils and snakes and darkness. And hovering about it all, there looms God, making decisions. Thumbs up, thumbs down or thumbs sideways. " I'm gonna put you on hold. I've got to make a few calls, and I'll get back to you in, perhaps, eternity."

As a young girl, the image of hell loomed loudly in my bed at night and in my Wednesday afternoon, Christian Education classes. "You will burn forever, and you will feel it, and you will never, ever, ever, be allowed to leave." It haunted me that I was so mean to Stephen Morton in Grade 8 Geology, loudly accusing him of picking his nose and wiping it on his pants, right in front of his classmates. Or that in our front driveway basketball court, I let fly three swears in perfect syncopation when I couldn't sink 10 baskets in-a-row from the right elbow. I worried that if I died before confession that I would go straight to hell. All because of some poor follow-through and a shaky backspin.

I like to think that I walked away from that version of hell in high school, after my French V teacher had us read *Huis Clos* (No Exit) by Sartre. The story of three people trapped in their own personal hells, each person's hell made that way by the two other people with whom he or she would share eternity. I redesigned the fire and brimstone version to fit more of Sartre's design. My personal hell would be to get stuck in a space, for eternity, with two people who jingle their pocket coins incessantly, stop in front of the toll basket to examine their change while the line of cars stretches endlessly, leave their blinkers on for miles on the highway when there isn't a snowball's chance in hell of taking a turn and talk with their mouths filled with already well-chewed food and in-between swallows whistle fanciful, warbling, childhood tunes, like *Michael Rows The Boat Ashore,* with pursed, wimpy lips and a tedious grin.

But then, as I sat or stood in front of *The Last Judgment*, it occurred to me that the painting is basically about two main things.

First, morbid curiosity, like rubbernecking at a car wreck. Second, being able to walk away, as an adult, from hell, particularly now that I know it's been relegated to a big wall in a beautiful chapel, far, far away in Rome, safe and sound.

So with the various levels of neurosis and adolescent torture behind me, *The Last Judgment* affects me a bit like excellent writing does--pulling me in and making me aware of a depth that I can't fully comprehend the first time. That that one carefully chosen stroke (or word) in one corner is meant to be very carefully linked to that one carefully chosen stroke (or word) in another. I want to look at it again, read it again, sing it, again and again, paying more attention to all of it, not just those corners, so that I pick up things that I was too immature, too flippant or too dense to have picked up just then. I want to dig a little deeper, see a little more, know a little more and take one more teeny step toward understanding, as much as I can, more of the messages, more of the images, more, I hope, of the creator--knowing that the teeny steps will never ever get me there, to a Michelangelo, to a Toni Morrison, to a Gabriel García Márquez, to the exact experiences, their exact experiences. Like standing in front of a distant point and stepping half of the distance to that point, half again, half again. Never, ever wholly reaching it or touching it or feeling it. But waving to it from an ever-shortening distance, knowing I can make it a life's mission to get as close as I possibly can. To their words and ideals, of course. But not to hell. No, don't take me there.

The immediate plan was to get back to Perugia and that meant saying good-bye to Dana and Elsie. I was surprised by how quickly I had come to like them and would come to miss them. I knew that it was partly about them--their personalities, their styles, their perspectives. But I knew that it was also partly about me--my isolation, my loneliness, my need to feel part of a group. A welcoming group.

Dana and Elsie went with us to our bus stop. When the big blue vehicle got started and we knew we had to get on, we hugged and offered, again, the invitation to come visit us in Perugia. I didn't want to let go. I didn't know if I'd ever see them again, and yet I knew I would always see them again.

As John stepped onto the bus and tugged on the back of my shirt, pulling me away from the intensely long hug that I was getting from and giving to Elsie, she whispered in my ear. "Thanks for hearing what I didn't have to say."

So, sobbing and smiling and looking like a walking oxymoron, I backed onto the first step of the bus and saw Dana and Elsie holding onto each other and heading into a pale sea in their colorful canoe. From the bus I was squinting and straining, hoping to find someone who might just know if and when to offer them a paddle and who might know if and when to get on in for the ride. Not that I could tell from a distance. But maybe I could tell at half the distance and half again and half again. Never getting there--but waving to it from an ever-shortening place. As close as possible. Like the two fingers on The Sistine Chapel.

God.

Maybe He was pointing at me after all.

Chapter Twelve
Nonno And Signora Gala
The Human Cheat-Sheets

I t was an awkward time in Perugia as the end of my course and December break nudged closer. The local veterinary and medical students faded away as they stressed about their upcoming exams. The international students were combining that with travel plans, and the colder weather was forcing people inside. In the lulls between insanity and solitude, I set my mind to a few disparate tasks--anything from making plans to go home for Christmas via Belgrade, Yugoslavia to sending some Italian holiday cards to reviewing the subjunctive tense to taking black and white photos of Perugia in winter. I also made a major decision about the hair on my legs--in the name of fitting in more with the local crowd. I let the hairs grow wild, unchecked, unworried about and uncombed.

I wasn't at all like my sister--who could let the hair grow for weeks only to have her legs look like a newborn's *sedere* (bottom). I was Jo, The Hair Monger. My dad used to appease me by telling me that dark hair on a body is a sign of strength. I liked knowing that although my best friend in grammar school was much taller than I, she had to have been much weaker given the minimal presence of wimpy, blonde hair on all appendages. So, in Perugia, as each dark hair emerged longer and longer, bolder and bolder, I felt that my international cohorts were thinking to themselves and maybe even saying to each other, "Gee, that Gio must be strong. Very strong." So despite the first few days of itchiness, I realized, again, that those Italians were onto something.

The real truth is that I was growing it for one main reason--to add another tradition to the annual Christmas festivities. I knew it would be a memorable family moment when I rolled up the pant leg of my flannel pajamas to expose the human shag. No rusty, orange twill. Just the rich, dark black variety. But one week before I left for home, I succumbed to some kind of pressure, some kind of half-pressure, and shaved. One leg. Just the left one. Leaving the other to my family. A sort of Christmas Will. The asymmetry had its benefits. When I needed to catch a glimpse of the American custom, I looked west. When I needed to feel connected to the European way, I'd look east. On my path to bilingualism, I made a stop at bilegualism first.

Once the hair-growing episode was on automatic-pilot, I had other things to turn to for entertainment. For starters, it was just plain wonderful to be in Italy around Christmastime. The country goes all out for the holiday. *Panettone*, a six-story high pastry, makes a seasonal appearance there as it did on my own family's Christmas table. Spectacular white lights adorn the city streets in intricate designs. Ornaments glitter on small trees outside the town shops, and music bellows out from strategically-placed speakers. And no carolers. Italians just bathe in their bathtubs during the festive season. They don't use them as holding pens for the impaired.

In the midst of those activities, some seasonal, some uncharted, Max's parents and sister came to visit. We jetted around Umbria, from Todi to Lake Trasimeno to Assisi, in their enormous, black Mercedes Benz, and I was treated to some of the best Italian meals and wines I had ever had. When I ordered fish near the lake one evening, in a small *ristorante* that held four elegantly appointed tables with silver candlesticks in the center, and neglected to order wine to go with it, Max's dad invoked, "But, Gio! The fish must swim!" So, I acquiesced--enthralled by the image of my stomach as a fishbowl.

It was during that same period that I also spent some time updating my journal. A worn and tattered book that was made in Germany and held, on its blocked pages, my high and low points from college and beyond. I always searched for a prime location to scratch my memories inside. On the cathedral steps. Propped up in bed. In the park at the end of *Corso Vannucci*. In the *panino* cafè. And I would always use my *nonno's* fountain pen--an heirloom that passed from his hands to my mother's to mine. A Wahl Eversharp 14K Gold Seal Signature with marbleized casing. Now filled with black ink. Not the blue ink that was left in it when he died. Years after he had made his last notation as an insurance inspector. Long after he had signed my parents' wedding card. And my siblings' birth cards.

The first time I decided to move the pen out of my printer's rack and into use on my journal entries, I was saddened that the tip ran dry. Despite my earnest attempts to bring his pen to life. Yet one more obstacle between him and me. One more twist of fate. It was only after I bathed the pen in warm water that it gave in. Allowing me to twist it apart and tempt the bag that held the aged ink. Freeing it. So that it ran wild on my counter top and memories. Spots that confirmed his presence. Since his hands had placed that ink inside. And my hands had taken it out.

When I glanced at my last entry, I realized that several weeks had passed with blank pages to show for my experiences and nothing written down to jog my memory. I wrote what I could remember and wondered what I had missed. It wasn't the big things that I worried about. It was the little things. Which often end up being my big things. Like the precious look on Max's face when I bought him two wine glasses to finish off his set or the excitement that ripped through my stomach when my sister called outside of her normal schedule or the trout that arrived at my table with its eyes still in its sockets or that I was mistaken for an Italian by an Italian even *after* I had spoken.

As I reconstructed the missing weeks, I found myself committing a lot of journal-time to the trip to Rome. To Dana and Elsie and John. Every detail. Every site. Every thought. Some parts verbatim. Some parts rewritten with *key substitutions* that the evening's deafening silence had forced me to accept. *I begged to be seen as just me. One American. Not all Americans. One Black. Not all Blacks. Someone unique who has been influenced by her culture. Not some inevitable caricature of the worst of her culture.* It was powerful. Seeing it there. In black and white.

It was during one of my journal-writing episodes in a *Corso Vannucci* cafè that I ran into Marco again, the Sicilian vet student who came onto me on the steps of the local cathedral by asking me to translate Land Rover. The one who was relieved to see my welcoming reaction to his being from Sicily, not the typical, condescending glare he gets when he says he was born outside of Palermo. As much as that look ate at my core, I knew it couldn't have compared to the depth of his reaction. There's always a pecking order, and it always seems to be from north to south. Top to bottom.

Marco joined me at my table that day. Politely. He ordered *due espressi* and asked about what I was writing. I tried to make sense of my journal entries in English and then make sense of them in Italian as he listened. Patiently. With his deep-set, near black eyes focused on my own deep-set, near black eyes. He turned the journal from my direction to his and tried to read my thoughts out loud. A Sicilian spin on my native words made them seem better. Richer. His language, his accent, invited me in.

When we stood to leave the cafè four hours later, I was very aware of his subtle good looks, receding hairline, tanned skin and strong hands. His humility and earnestness. He was different. So when he asked if I'd be willing to meet him again the next day and the next and the next, there was only one choice. And I looked forward to it. And arrived on time to enjoy another afternoon of Italian and Italians.

Marco and I passed six consecutive late afternoons in that *Corso Vannucci* cafè talking about family and vet school and the differences in our cultures and Italian pronouns and how or why people fall in love. He was patient with my Italian and tried to avoid speaking the dialect when other Sicilian friends would conspicuously find their way into the bar and over to our table. He brought pictures of his mother and brothers and younger sister, taken in front of their Sicilian hilltown and their family winery, all linked by the kinds of eyes that drew me in--deep. I brought pictures of my family and of my grandfather, including his last, with the five grandchildren he knew and not the four others he didn't. Three cousins and me. Marco seemed to be the first person ever to understand how I felt about that reality. About never having known him. About wanting to rest my eyes on his home. He said I carried Nonno's Sicilian spirit with me-- in my character, in my loyalty, in my drive to battle society's narrow views.

I was lucky that Marco was Sicilian. He was lucky that I was, too.

It was after our sixth slow, lazy afternoon at the Perugian cafè that Marco finally asked me to his apartment for dinner. I wasn't exactly sure that I had translated the invitation correctly until he pulled up later that night in front of my house in a minuscule automobile. My knees bumped up against the microscopic glove compartment, and I could touch the back windshield with a modest stretch from the front seat. It was more like a motorcycle with a roof than a car.

When we arrived at his apartment, halfway down from the city's peak, Marco went to work immediately. He pulled some home-canned tomatoes ("right from my mother's garden in Sicily") and spices from his storage area and spun magic as I sat down at his makeshift table with wobbly legs and a dented surface and sipped some homemade wine that was stored in old, glass, Coca Cola bottles. Marco cooked and talked at the same time, both slowly so that I could make sense of it all, and within minutes a light, delicious and perfectly spiced sauce for the thick spaghetti emerged as did a little bread, some more wine and a couple of candles stuck into used wine bottles. When he moved the radio dial to a station that featured Italian opera and sang along beautifully for a minute or two, word for word, I was happy. And was beginning to feel sure that what happened at Abdul's would not happen there.

During dinner and after dinner, we sat and sprawled and talked. And worked hard at understanding and at being understood. He chose his words carefully and spoke slowly. And did a good job of making me feel that I could speak the language well, even if he sounded as I did when I stuttered to John, "a charter flight (pause) is a flight (pause)..." We carried on (or tried to carry on) some lofty conversations that night. About the fact that true Italian actually originated in Sicily. About the role of women and men in The United States compared to Italy. And about love and how it, according to Marco, can transcend words. Transcend language. At the time, I thought that he was just setting the scene for sex without talking.

The ending to the night was just what I needed. An after-dinner *espresso* at the underground bar (where I ran into a surprised Max) and a warm good-bye from Marco outside the door to my home. It was as if he knew about Abdul and knew, for right then, that was enough. And I hadn't said a word.

Exam day finally arrived. Just in time. Perugia was turning into a haven for the neurotic. Everywhere I went there were study groups grilling and drilling, shaking and baking, slicing and dicing. On the post office steps, in the university lobby, in the bright yellow restaurant with the best *panini* (sandwiches) in Italy--delicious *mortadella* or *formaggio* placed simply, undecorated, unsmothered, between thick, fresh bread with heavenly ridges. My long conversations with Marco had done as much for my exam preparation as they had for my soul--so on the day before the big test, all I had to do was review some of the tenses and flip through my notes. I was slowly learning how to be in school. And in life. Learn as you go. Keep up. Think about it. Try to have it make sense. And then put it to use.

On the day of the exam we were to arrive at the university well in advance of the start. When the time was right, we were ushered, cattle-prodding style, into an enormous room with chairs that were designed for the Italians' narrow frames and not for their American cousins' expanse. I slid my body in and took out a couple of pencils. No dictionary. Just pencils and brains.

Students who had spent the last several weeks wildly exercising their first tastes of freedom out from under their parents' arms contributed to the palpable tension by feverishly flipping through their Italian-English, Italian-German, Italian-Greek dictionaries for the answers. Others were biting their fingernails and scratching their heads. Others were staring off into the distance, waiting for some kind of revelation, some kind of epiphany, some kind of miracle. And then an Italian voice echoed through the barren space. "The exam begins now."

The first part of the first part was what I had expected. Short answer questions involving articles, conjugation of verbs, different tenses and vocabulary recognition. The second part of the first part had to do with reading comprehension. The third part of the first part was a dictation. Only one word stumped me. *L'oscurità.* Darkness. It was appropriate that that was the word to trip me up--since my Italian experience was proving that I had been traveling in it for a good part of my life.

Despite that detour, I still felt confident and pleased that I hadn't wasted a lot of heartbeats on the preparation. John, on the other hand, was rattled by the breadth of the exam and was regretting not having spent less time cooking *tortellini* and drinking cheap wine and more time studying himself out of *l'oscurità*. I was shocked by his reaction and then relieved by the transient nature of the delirium. Shot back to less responsible and more reasonable reality when I asked him if he'd honestly trade the sites and lessons of Rome for a passing grade on a meaningless exam. No. He wouldn't.

After our break, we were moved into a holding cell outside the room where the aurals/orals would take place. With uncharacteristic meticulousness, we were called one-by-one to face off against the university's instructors. Ten to 15 minutes later, we would emerge, most somewhat ashen, with mouths agape. Others hysterical. No one would tell exactly what went on inside those four walls. But with each exit, one neurotic would gently press the escapee up against the wall and extract pieces. Valuable pieces. "There are three of them in there, all women, one dressed austerely, one didn't seem to know that her leg was hoisted high up on a chair, one just smiled."

The confirmation of my old grammar teacher's presence escalated my anxiety to the point where I could barely stand, where I was wishing I had taken an early vacation and gone to Germany with Max instead, in a Mercedes that was as big as Air Force One and where the fish would be swimming instead of being lodged in my esophagus, restricting the passage of air.

It was in that condition that I saw John exit the inquisition, that I barely heard him say good-bye, that I barely felt him hug me and kiss me before he raced out the door flailing and failing, that I barely recalled where his Christmas plans were taking him and for how long. My anxiety was ridiculous. And then they called my name. I leaned forward, away from the dirty, gray-plastered wall, and marched through to meet my examiners. Signora Gala, my new grammar teacher, the Whore of Babylon--Francesca Fortebraccio, my former grammar teacher, and Signora Ferrelli, my culture teacher.

Once inside, the four of us immediately began a conversation, and the beginning of that conversation, directed by Signora Gala, was nearly identical to the one we had had in her class on the very first day I switched. She was fixing the scene, giving me my own personal cheat-sheet, or at least a head start. The time passed quickly, and with each word, each sentence, each question, I knew I was nailing that test. Their head-bobs, smiles and comfort reflected it--as did their pride at my having chosen Italian and Italy to fulfill this deepest need.

At the end, I received rave reviews, even from Signora Fortebraccio, who was touched by my reasons for wanting to learn her beautiful language and for my wanting to bring my *nonno* back to life. I strolled out, grinning and unburdened and proud. And when *I* was gently pressed against the wall, by those in search of what then seemed like the most trivial of details, I was still thinking and speaking in Italian. And I looked up, way beyond the confused faces of my classmates, way beyond the confines of Perugia, and whispered to him. To Nonno. In his language. A gesture that bridged a gap. And began to paint me into a different last photo.

Chapter Thirteen
Getting Pretty Hot--Feeling Pretty Cool

T he very next day, only four days before Christmas, with a decent exam score and a little certificate that said I could move to the next course, I boarded Yugoslavian Airlines. After a night in Belgrade, under blizzard conditions and in a tiny single with no heat in order to secure a cheaper rate, we flew to Boston in the hands of an airline that served fresh shrimp to coach customers to offset the fear that flying on Air Obscuria incited.

Christmas was good. The hairy leg was a conversation starter and stopper and so were some of my details of my Italian adventure. I thought of Marco a lot at Christmas, for as people pressed me (or didn't press me) for details, words failed. A sense of separation emerged that I had never felt before. Not in a bad way. Just in a real way. A kind of awakening about how we live. About how much people know and understand of anyone other than themselves. Maybe even including themselves.

Over my month-long visit to The United States, my mother and I firmed up plans for her late spring/early summertime excursion to Italy, and my sister, Katie, and I confirmed her late winter/early spring trip. Time passed quickly in-between family dinners and hour-long phone calls and visits with friends in New York City and Boston. Before I knew it, late January found me back on Yugoslavian Airlines and trying to make sense of the conflicting emotions. Utter longing to stay on with family and friends. Utter longing to return to a culture and lifestyle I had come to embrace. I wanted everyone I knew to go to "the other side," as Nonna used to say.

A major snowstorm in Zagreb, Yugoslavia forced an eternally long layover, where I was introduced to a deicing machine. My vehicle to Italy, smothered in ice and snow, being cleaned off by a giant water pistol. I wasted some time in the airport bar drinking coffee with a native Yugoslavian who cockily testified that he was fluent in English and then went on to tell me that he had flown over to The United

States on December 37th. I didn't realize that different time zones meant extra days. I noted that in Yugoslavia I'd still be in my teens.

In time, I made it back to Rome and to Perugia safely. Max was there to greet me with his sister. I promptly went to his living room, climbed onto his couch and slept until awakening 15 hours later--to Max leaning over me, checking my pulse. The same way my mother did during my college vacations when I would sleep well past the lunch hour and into early afternoon.

I was eager to see and spend time with everyone again--Max, John, Petra, Mamma, Marco. I had missed them when I was away. Max's soul. John's spirit. Petra's life. Mamma's blend of tenderness. And Marco's everything. It felt fun to be able to fly so far away from home, to touch ground and to know people. I was an international jet-setter. "Gio Marshall--strong *and* global."

When I got back to Mamma's the next day, I discovered that she had rented out the other twin bed in my room. It had been 14 years since my sister and I had slept next to each other in twin beds, and I wasn't ready to go back. Especially since I feared that my new roommate might have made me do the things my sister did. Like get out of bed to turn off the lights, maintain a sharp line of demarcation between us and keep my paws off her records. So I made the decision to move out--making plans within a few hours with the help of a local placement agency. The hastiness of my choice obscured my anticipation of the sadness of telling Mamma the news. For both of us. Knowing we would miss reveling in our Italian roots. And our discussions about *pesto*. And our late-night sessions with dubbed Hollywood movies. My selfish explanation for the move reeked of frigidity when compared with Mamma's explanation for why I should stay. "*Sei mia figlia.*" (You're my daughter.) And to think it was all because of a rented twin. And some memories of a sister who did not respond well to a scratched 45. Still, I knew we'd keep in touch.

So in the remaining hours under Mamma's watchful arm, I made sure that I enjoyed, more than ever, the last of my minutes with Petra. Her sunning routines, our early morning conversations over *espresso*, her observations about life in the confines of our home and the glimpses of her blunt and caustic humor. "Great. Thanks for leaving me with Susanna. Maybe the aluminum foil on my record album will set her on fire."

It was never the same between Petra and me after I left. I was sad and surprised to discover that we were only situational and locational friends. I left without saying good-bye to Susanna. Neither sad nor surprised. Neither situational nor locational.

My new flat was small. One tiny kitchen. One tiny bedroom. One tiny water heater. Two tiny cots. Tiny, tiny showers from then on. But it was mine. Mine. And within hours of moving, a task which involved lugging my six pieces of luggage down the 117 cement steps of Mamma's place, out the brown door and 50 feet down one hill and up another, I realized I had made a massive compromise of comfort for independence. Not the least of which was the paucity of heat.

I spent the first few hours of freedom combing the streets of Perugia in search of *una bomba,* a medieval-looking heat contraption that was ignited with the flick of a switch. I rented the device but rarely turned it on--fearing a midnight explosion. This from the woman who was comforted by Yugoslavian shrimp over the turbulent Atlantic.

Max came over that first night with several gifts. Some wine, so I would never be thirsty, some bread, so I would never be hungry, some salt, so I would always have spice in my life, and a poster with dozens of different kinds of *pasta,* so I would always have beauty around. I loved our definition of beauty. For many people, it's a sculpture or a landscape or the magic of birth. For us, it's good looking *manicotti.*

Max and I ate at the little dining room table with the real marble top. Dinner helped to warm us and take our minds off the subzero temperatures in my new place. It was nice to have Max with me, and I am sure he knew I needed that long before he stepped inside. His presence made the strange noises and unexpected adjustments more bearable. Less unsettling. But as each minute passed at my little kitchen table, a table made littler by Max's frame, I knew eventually he would have to go, and I would be alone. In the tundra. With visible air emanating from both nostrils. With strange water faucets and a lock that felt unsafe. I kept picturing myself in the toasty comfort of Mamma's place or Max's extra bedroom. It was unproductive imaging at its best.

When Max pulled closed the downstairs door to my apartment and tested it twice, under my direction, to make sure it was locked, I brushed my teeth and washed my face quickly before the hot water ran out. I put on some long underwear, flannel pajama bottoms, a turtleneck, a sweatshirt, thick wool socks and a winter cap that came down over my ears and climbed into bed. Wrapping the blanket around me like a cocoon and smooshing my face down into the paper thin pillow--turning once just to look at *la bomba*.

It wasn't all that bad. And, it wasn't all that good.

Over the next several days, as I tried to decorate my barren abode and roamed the streets of Perugia sampling different *espressi* in different *cappuccino* bars around town, I waited for Marco to get back from his long, long Christmas visit to Sicily. And I began to count the days to my sister's arrival, marking them off my calendar with a red felt-tip pen. Ever aware that one more "X" meant one day closer to having her in my sights. I had more than a month of Xs to wade through.

I also mulled over whether to enroll in the *Corso Medio*, the next level of study, or to travel throughout Germany with Max. The *Medio* deadline was imminent, and I knew if I delayed that decision long enough that I missed a class or two, I would be irrevocably lost. I was stuck in indecision, made all the worse by John's return from his hiatus in February, on Valentine's Day, which is just one day in a week-long Italian celebration of love. The timely arrival did not go unnoticed by Max.

John had spent several weeks traveling to a non-Italian Europe and had ended up in Amsterdam for quite awhile, home of a Marijuana-By-The-Book and a portable Female-Favors-Red-Light economic system. And a very successful system at that judging by the enormous plastic bag that John let drop onto my marble table his first night back and the Mona Lisa grin that was permanently etched on his face.

Since I assumed that his time away would be incalculably more exciting and daring than mine, (10 countries in two months as opposed to the hairy leg story), he got more air time. And within that air time, the thrill of Amsterdam got the lion's share.

"Yah. Prostitutes stand in these windows on the main streets of Amsterdam. They hold these red lights and do anything to welcome you inside."

"Huh."

"Yah. And there are these other places, legal places, that sell drugs. You walk in, and there are books and books of choices, samples, descriptions. A hashish smorgasbord."

"Huh."

"Yah. And there were these prostitutes."

"Yup. You told me."

"Did I mention the books?"

"Yuh. You mentioned the books."

I was wondering if he had seen Anne Frank's hideaway or visited the Van Gogh exhibits or traveled outside of Amsterdam to the quaint Dutch suburb of Marken or climbed a windmill or read up on the tulip industry. I was also wondering what would have happened if I hadn't abandoned the hairy leg story so quickly. I could have worked on the buildup, the climax and the resolution and, at the very least, I wouldn't have repeated myself repeated myself repeated myself eight times.

In any event, the Netherlander Baggy was a spicy addition to the traditional *tortellini alla panna* with sausages and peas. The sizzling pig product on the two-plate portable burner didn't mind sampling the oregano's understudy as snorts filled the room and more *pasta* was consumed than humanly healthy. At the end of the evening, when the last pea was crushed between my fork's tines and John licked a solo drop of cheap wine from my cheap wine glasses and the spice bag lay flat and immaculate on the marble top, I boldly went over to the *bomba* and flipped the switch. Take that, I said. The bedroom was heated within 15 minutes, and when John and I climbed into the anemic twin slabs, void of most of the then unnecessary long underwear, turtleneck, sweatshirt, thick wool socks and winter cap, I didn't even notice that my breath and his breath were invisible. We just held on tight, afraid that the cots might surrender to the added weight of our lingering arctic dress, and fell asleep. Still starving. Still trying to remember if we had even eaten dinner--the 16 sausages and two kilos of *tortellini* having been relegated to figment status with one very long Dutch drag.

My friendship pattern in Italy was vastly different from that back in The United States. In Perugia I was surrounded by men. Some in friendship. Some in other roles. Despite various levels of tensions and jealousies and sleeping arrangements, Max and John remained just friends. Marco did not remain just that. It was a picture perfect Saturday when that became clear.

Marco finally returned from Sicily in early March and called as soon as he got in. He had thought hard about our first week back together and had a plan for each night, nights which came to play out with remarkable spontaneity despite the organization, despite the calculated buildup. After-dinner *passeggiate* (walks), *gelati* (ice cream), picnics, dancing, movies and a week-ending surprise. After our many, many conversations over coffee and dinner and phone calls and letters I'd received while he was away, he had eliminated any and all fears of a repeat of Abdul. He was respectful, patient and incredibly kind and helped Nonno smash the perverse stereotypes of Sicilians as, among other things, violently hot-tempered. Just by being who he was. I had come to trust him. So with each night that passed, each one more comfortable, more connected, I looked with childlike anticipation and curiosity to Saturday. The climax. I wondered what he had in mind.

Marco stopped by at around 10:00 A.M. that Saturday and was dressed, as he often was, in jeans and a thin wool shirt. He told me that I should wear something similar and that I should also wear boots, if I had them. He had brought an extra one of his wool shirts in case I was unprepared. I wore his--even though I had two of my own hanging just inches away.

I wasn't allowed to ask any questions. I just got into his car, his motorcycle with a top, and we headed down and out of Perugia. Leaving behind the Umbrian capital and its curvy roads and international crowds to arrive at a hidden paradise within a quarter-hour. An enormous, old, rustic farmhouse in the surrounding valley which, I later found out, was owned by an elderly couple who were friends with Marco's parents and with Marco. There were huge dining and kitchen areas with bricked and tiled floors, wooden-beamed ceilings, a long, battered, dining room table with barrels for chairs and a stone fireplace. Marco made a fire and within minutes the flames were warming our faces and bodies. His flannel shirt made me hot.

After Marco moved the screen in front of the raging fire, he took my hand and led me out the back of the farmhouse to a small barn where, alert and ready to go, were two beautiful horses. Large. Bright. Shining. Large. And large. All three, horse, horse and Marco, decidedly unaware of the intense, somewhat irrational and somewhat justified fear that I have of those creatures. Blame it on the family down the street from me when I was little who rented out horses for 50 cents an hour and then got them moving by smashing their rear ends with a small snow shovel. Or blame it on my jealous grammar school friend who purposely taunted one of her horses to start bucking while I was trapped in the stall. Or blame it on another friend who, thinking I was ready to ride on my own, encouraged me to trot slowly away and informed me, too late, that I should avoid pointing the horse in the direction of the barn--as the big papa horse found life in his legs and took off at 110 mph in search of dinner. The facts didn't change. Every single time I was around a horse I got brutalized. The challenge was to convey those sentiments in Italian.

But I didn't have to.

Marco turned and read my face and decided we would share a horse. So with one foot on Marco's hands and the other swinging over the rump of the horse, I was hoisted up. He climbed on behind me, wrapped his arms around my sides and reached for the reins, and then moved us slowly and gracefully away from the barn. For the first time in a long time, I was relaxed enough to start to appreciate the wonder of those beasts.

And the horse wasn't so bad either.

Marco and I rode through the worn fields. Unused and overly-ripened and damaged crops had collapsed into the paths that had separated one kind of vegetable from another. It was cold outside, but it felt good. And we knew there was a fire waiting for us. Marco stopped from time to time to check on how I was doing or to point out something I certainly would have missed. Anything from an old stone wall to the small kites on the hillside to the weathered men playing *bocce* ball in the distance. I was so focused on how much I was loving the moment that I couldn't concentrate on anything else unless it was brought to my attention. So I was grateful for the pauses.

It was on top of one of the Umbrian hills that Marco stopped the horse, had me spin a quarter of the way around, tip back slightly and look straight at him. "I know you need me to be patient. I don't know why. But I will wait." Moments like that made me wonder if I knew why. I had to move beyond Abdul. And perhaps I should right there. Right then. In the middle of the valley. On top of that stud.

We picked up the pace a little on the way back. We just bounced along. All in careful unison. Once inside the farmhouse, Marco stoked the fire, poured two glasses of wine out of a home-capped bottle and started to work in the kitchen. I offered to help, but he insisted I remain curled in front of the fire. A directive that was met with no resistance, since I had no real desire to wrench myself from absolute peace to go slice an onion or two.

I was gently awakened when Marco strolled in, at least two hours later, carrying a plate of very fresh quail surrounded by roasted potatoes, onions, peas with garlic and carrots. And on different plates a simple salad, dressed with olive oil, vinegar, salt and fresh ground pepper and a round loaf of bread that had been warming near the fire. Marco arranged the food on the table, lit up the room with more candles and came to me. Pulling me up by both hands and leading me to the head of the long wooden table. He sat next to me, just around the corner, and asked that we take a minute to appreciate each other and the fire and the food. Which we did. In silence. And then we ate. Slowly. Slowly. Well into the afternoon. Savoring each bite. Each roasted morsel. Each drop of homemade wine. And the hours passed. And our conversation brought us closer. In every possible way.

When we finally cleared the table and headed up the back staircase, warmed from the moment and the moments, I was nearly fully satiated. And hours later, when a bright, winter sunlight streamed through our thick-paned windows and stirred us into the wee hours of Sunday, wrapped up and lost in just a thick white comforter and a thin patchwork quilt, we were warmed and completely satiated.

And Abdul's memory rested under the horse's heavy hooves. Buried in the garden. Under the rotted plants and frozen earth.

Chapter Fourteen
Walls

Part of Marco's and my connection was fueled by our fondness for and appreciation of things Sicilian. It is what drew us together. It is what joined us in the world. And against the world. My awareness of that part of our relationship helped me look at its significance. Its power. The power of connections--especially cultural ones. How they gave us something to latch onto when we felt out of place or somewhere to place others when we felt threatened. In or out.

In or out. I was working to avoid that route and was trying to see the connections as being about inclusivity and real life and real things and not about exclusivity and imbalances. I wanted to wrap myself in knowing that my grandfather and Marco walked the same streets and spoke the same dialect. That they breathed the same air or might have found peace in the same vineyards. That they looked at the same moon from the same direction or dipped their toes in the same water--even though Nonno's streets and vineyards and waters were 100 years younger than Marco's. I liked dreaming of those and I wanted them, for me, for then, to be enough.

I was disappointed by my naivete´ in Rome. And my selfish reaction to my first bouts with powerlessness. The bouts that living in Italy had provided. Away from the comforts and the privileges I never knew I had--until they were stripped away. And I was forced to live without them.

At the very least, I was glad I was awake. And thinking.

Two days after we returned from the farmhouse weekend, I opted not to take the *Corso Medio*. I had missed a few days by the time I sat in on a class and was already lost. The reality of what it would take to master a foreign language had settled in, and I didn't know if I were up for the long haul. Clearly, right then, I wasn't.

So days later, when Max came over to ask me to go on vacation with him to Germany, I was available. And interested. He wanted to take me to a *Deutschland* that exists beyond the *Glockenspiel* and *Hofbräuhaus*, to move from March to April in a Bavarian village, the communistic German Democratic Republic, West Berlin (inside The Wall), East Berlin, Hamburg and Frankfurt, visiting museums and having picnics and boating on the Rhine and romping on university campuses and wrestling with the marked contrasts between freedom and imprisonment, between truth and propaganda. And then we'd pick up my sister in Munich (the destination of a much less expensive flight) for our German/Italian holiday. It was too good to be real. Jo Marshall--spanning a small circle of the globe, picking up and dropping off favorite people at their respective ends. For Max would leave for his home, Berlin, at the end of the counterclockwise German journey, and Katie would leave for home, Boston, at the end of our vertical sprint through Italy. The whole month promised to be filled with living, newness and growth, laughter and loss. And putting off some of the emotional twists.

It was when I mentioned the idea to Marco that our shared utopia was invaded. That our common pasts took a back seat. He was bothered, he said, as we sipped Campari at our cafè. He was concerned, he said, as he tipped back in his chair when I made light of his hesitation. When he questioned the existence of truly platonic friendships and the sincerity of Max's intentions, his eyes looked more angry than deep. When he questioned my commitment to our relationship and to him, his face looked more cold than warm. His reaction was not aggressive but not subtle, and it had elements of possessiveness that were unsettling. That brought up dormant memories.

So quickly and so unexpectedly, as if Marco and I had had no other kind of encounter, no other incomparable conversations, no dinners by a farmhouse fire and countryside horseback rides, I found myself hesitating, protective and cautious, and within a few days, I found myself in Max's car, escaping over the Austrian border.

Max was a very proud German. I knew that from our first few conversations. It was obvious--his ecstasy about Boris Becker's victory at Wimbledon, his excitement about the imminent World Cup and Germany's chances, his listing and description of Germany's highly successful businesses--BASF, Bayer, BMW, Mercedes Benz. ("Henry Ford did not invent the automobile. It was a German. A German.") But he always denied his pride or refused to admit it. "Pride is an American concept. An American fixation. Your fixation. I just don't have it."

Finally, after months of knowing him and talking with him and nudging him, it eked out. We were seated on park benches at the end of *Corso Vannucci*, near Garibaldi's statue and the bus stop for Rome. It came near the end of another long and intense conversation. Pushing. Pushing. He teared up when he spoke. And I cried--for the pain of his nearly disclaiming a heritage. My whole life was about embracing what he had felt driven to deny. Yet there was my closest friend on my best adventure paralyzed by a fear of national pride.

"Look what it leads to," he said. "Look what it led to. One small step. Barely recognizable at first. And then another. And another. And it *could* happen again. In Germany. Anywhere. We have to keep our pride in check, because after you admit pride, what's next? Admit it again? And again? And then every day until you find yourself chanting it on the street with a raised fist? How long until the successes of Boris Becker and the National Soccer Team lead to a conclusion of physical superiority? And then intellectual superiority? And then overall superiority?"

I couldn't completely understand nor completely stop what seemed to me like an irrational progression. But Max was more aware of things I wasn't. It *had been* an irrational progression, he would say. Profoundly irrational. And it had been rational in that it was calculated and meticulous. Rational and irrational at the same time-- and that's what scared him most.

Max mapped out each detail of the trip. Where we would stay, how we would travel, what we would see. As always, I was indebted to him for showing me a different world, a world that existed beyond the east coast, outside the Italian boot and in our intellect and our hearts. Emotions ran wild and in opposite directions, crazy and suffocating, guilty and incredibly free. Beer halls and *Lederhosen*, mountain hikes and delicious dinners, family visits and symphonies.

Bavarian jigs and sausage-eating lessons, one-act plays, fishing and marveling at the German hills and greens and blues.

It was only when we discussed Dachau, the World War II concentration camp just outside of Munich, that his mood would change dramatically. That his pride would change dramatically. That his face would turn red and then pale. And he would barely start to stutter. Still, he planned to show me all of Germany. He agreed to show me all of Germany. Not just part of Germany. And not run from the associations of the past. While his pride in himself was at an all-time low, my pride in him had never been higher.

Dachau. Max and I walked side-by-side, in deafening silence, as we saw footage of the skeletal survivors, their skin merely resting on their bones, the areas around their eyes blackened. Their eyes sunken in. Their faces void of any recognition. We remained silent as we walked by the sign on the Gate of Lies that read *Arbeit Mach Frei* (Work Makes You Free) and saw the kinds of ovens that had sent millions of Jews and homosexuals and physically disabled and Gypsies across Europe to their deaths. The only sound that broke the silence of the masses that day, the women and men and children, was the sound of paralyzing pain, of tears. The sobbing. The moaning. People wiping their soaked faces with their tired hands.

I didn't know what to say to Max. Or what to do. I knew his guilt and shame were profound. And I knew I couldn't begin to understand it--even though I felt some of it myself. I was ashamed to belong to the animal group that gave birth to Dachau. And yet my pain was nothing compared to those who had walked those grounds and walked those grounds and walked those grounds and then not walked those grounds. It was the absolute least we could do. And it was torturous.

Max and I sat on a bench. His head resting heavily on his hands. With tears streaming down his face and onto his wrists he said, "Every single German should visit this place. Every single German should be forced to come here." I came around behind him and enveloped him as much as I could. And whispered to him--to let him know I was there. And rested on him as his body wretched. As he gripped my hands with his.

We froze, silent, as visitors came and left. We froze, sick, nauseated, guilty, ashamed. Horrified, confused and angry. When we finally did leave, we both knew we would never be the same. Ever. And we both knew we would do what we could, in our own ways, to make a difference. One student at a time. One conversation at a time. Trying to put faces and stories to the staggering numbers. It started ever so slowly. And, as Max said near Garibaldi's statue in Perugia, "one small step, barely recognizable at first, and then another and another."

Segregated water fountains. Backs of buses. Separate neighborhoods. Clubs with no Jews or blacks. Internment camps. Hollywood stereotypes. Media biases. Limited opportunity. *It is what drew us together. It is what joined us in the world. And against the world. My awareness of that part of our relationship helped me look at its significance. Its power. The power of connections--especially cultural ones. How they gave us something to latch onto when we felt out of place or somewhere to place others when we felt threatened. In or out.* Little steps.

Everyone needed to visit Dachau. Because it could happen anywhere.

The capacity of human beings to move forward after witnessing trauma is a frightening one. It is hard to know if it has to do with carelessness and insensitivity or with survival. We witness a fatal car crash on the way home from work, are consumed by it for days and then find ourselves going 70 mph in a 40 mph zone or learn of a string of church-burnings across the southern states and vow to offer a donation of money or time or both to rebuild the places of worship and then find ourselves spending our cash and minutes purchasing the latest, newest version of the cordless phone.

That happened in the days following our Dachau visit. As we made our way across the East German countryside, on our way to Max's home within the Berlin Wall, or lifted our beer mugs on the *Kurfürstendamm* or raced through the city in the family Mercedes or watched a fashion show at the convention hall or tapped our feet to the jazz music that boomed throughout the Berlin clubs. We moved from an all-consuming devastation to what seemed like an ultimate return to our former selves. But, the return was not complete--for the images would pierce our experiences at the most unexpected times. In the middle of dinner. Over a toast. In our dreams. And although less and less frequent, it was clear that we would never live without them again. Never again. Never again.

Max and I took in as many sites as we could in West Berlin. We even ventured into East Berlin for the day, a visit I thought I was handling splendidly until I realized some of my money had been stolen from my pants' pocket. I then frantically realized that my day visa could have been stolen, too, which would have placed me in jail overnight, and perhaps even longer, in the German Democratic Republic. When I found the visa in the front pouch of my anorak, my relief was extreme, as was my desire to return to the free side, where The Wall was painted with bright colors and lively cartoons and hope and was not as gray as it was on the other side, to match the sky and the buildings and the spirits of the people we met.

After Berlin, Max and I did a counterclockwise tour of Germany. We ended up in Munich where we waited for my sister to arrive on a Lufthansa flight. I was out of my mind with excitement, and for good reason, for it would be one of those rare times when the expectation and the reality ran over the same route.

Chapter Fifteen
Holy Week At The Hofbräuhaus

An unspeakable relief washed over and around and inside my body when the notice on the tote board moved from On Time to Arrived. I don't remember what language the message was in. But I knew my sister had touched down in Munich safely. On Easter weekend. And that was enough.

Katie and I had come a long way since our earliest recorded encounters, such as when she asked at the dinner table, right in the middle of grace, only two days after I had added myself to the group that would then be six, "When her going back?" Or when she begged to hold me only to let both of her arms fly out to the side and watch as my tiny infant body plummeted from her grasp toward the hardwood floors that loomed below. Now when I pack my bags to head home after the kind of too-infrequent visits that hundreds of miles of separation impose, she asks, instead, "When her coming back?" as her arms fly out to the side again, but this time in a warm embrace.

Katie was wired with excitement when Max and I spotted her through the large, glass enclosure near the luggage carousels. Waving. Beaming. Jumping up and down. And so were we. She was through the various lines in no time and in Max's and my arms before I could get anxious about what was taking so long. We gripped each other and hurled ourselves up and down, like two kids on a pogo stick. Making a scene. Not a family first. Nor a family last. But possibly an airport rarity given the stiff upper lips that greeted us when we finally separated. Youthful America visited on elderly Europe. Without their permission. I got the sense that they couldn't wait for us to grow up and embrace the behavior of old age. We, for the time being, remained committed to our infancy. There were benefits to each. And drawbacks. And both were becoming more clear.

I knew Katie could and would, in an instant, eradicate all evidence of the loneliness or isolation I had visited from time to time in Italy. With one glimpse, one smile, one question, one answer, one march down hysteria lane. If nothing else, the next two weeks would bring laughter, a kind of laughter that cultural differences restrict, that acquaintances do not supply and that family ties insist upon. It began with her first words.

"I battled *Nipplus Erectus* from Boston to Munich." Not the exact kind of greeting I could ever expect from Max or John or Marco when an airplane's heating ducts weren't working. "I could have hung bath towels off of them," she said as she hoisted her luggage over her shoulder and headed for the exit with me just behind her-- picturing Mammary Towel Racks for sale in the Duty Free Shop.

Max drove us to our Bed and Breakfast just outside of central Munich. A short tram ride would get us right back into the city. We said good-bye to him for the day and agreed to meet back at the *Hofbräuhaus* at nine o'clock that night. He said he would get there a little early to grab a table and three chairs. "It could crowd up pretty quickly," he said. "Beer is a powerful force," he said. With German-brewing pride.

Katie peered from the window to watch Max's and my good-bye, to try to learn the nature of our relationship. Our hug and kiss left her confused. Short of either stripping down to diddle a little or extend-ing our hands for a curt and emotionless handshake, she was destined to be in the dark. When I got back inside, I told her we were just friends--but of a different sort. A sort no one would understand. Our shared experiences had led us into territories that were foreign to most travelers. And to each of us before we crossed in Italy. When we first waved at each other from two distant emotional points, two distant frames of reference, and decided, consciously, to meet somewhere in the middle. Where he could see me better and I could see him better. And where we could touch.

Our pre-*Hofbräuhaus* dinner in Munich was a farce. Katie and I could not decipher one item on the menu except *salat* (salad) and our waiter could not have been more pompous. Totally unwilling to help and reveling in our ignorance. He tipped his head back and slapped his order pad when we mistakenly chose from the Children's Menu and then the Lunch Menu before we, by default, landed on the right spot. So we were forced to draw on roots and words from other languages--groping for anything remotely recognizable and hoping for the best. Since it was out of our control. The privileges that come with knowledge and the helplessness of ignorance did not go unnoticed. Nor did the behavior of the waiter--who shirked his responsibility to share. It was about much more than just dinner.

We ordered something that looked like the French word for chicken, recognizing that we'd go down together. If you're ordering cow brains, I'll be there with you. If you're hovering over the toilet three hours from now, I'll be there with you. We were shocked when chicken actually arrived at the table minutes later with a succulent potato and some other vegetables, we think. We dug in and made sure, sure, sure that the waiter knew we had gotten *exactly* what we had wanted. We felt triumphant. It was a misguided euphoria that fell in the category of "I *will* kill you little mosquito buzzing in my ear even if I awaken with facial lacerations and auditory damage, or I *will* unscramble that last Jumble clue even if I have to look up every single world in the most recent *Webster's Dictionary* to do so." The path to insanity is a short one, but that night I was thrilled to have company.

So, we left the restaurant in good spirits. Ready to speak some more German in the *Hofbräuhaus*. Not even stopping to think that there wasn't even the slightest chance that the word "chicken" would be tossed back and forth in casual conversation. We were terribly drunk with power, edging toward Category Four, without one tiny sip of anything alcoholic. Just high on wait-staff spite.

We crossed the plaza that was dominated by the *Glockenspiel* and looked forward to crowding in with the international hordes the next day to watch the scene of horses and humans and spears unfold in the clock's inner-workings. Seconds later, the *Hofbräuhaus* welcomed us to an incredible atmosphere. Packed. Smoky. Raucous. Condoms for sale on the walls right inside the entrance. Elderly women biting into uncooked thighs of buffalo meat. A very drunk American stopping himself inches away from his girlfriend's breasts, as if he were trying to tune in Airwave Japan with her mammaries. Finally, we found Max, just before he reached Tokyo.

He had reserved a great table, right near the Bavarian band and in full view of the irresistibly strong German women who were capable of hoisting 14 steins (each holding about 2 to 3 beers) at once. Four steins on a lower level. Three more stacked on top. Two hands equals 14 and hero-worship. We ordered a round and started sampling as soon as the glasses hit the table. Max immediately ordered three more, assuring us that we'd finish our first round before we could find her to order another. It was a strikingly bold and brilliant move. I was proud to be with him.

The conversation between the three of us started as most do when there is an imbalance in familiarity. Polite. Restrained. Inquisitive. I saw myself in Katie as she strained to understand Max's brand of English. A brand that was then so comfortable to me. A brand that had maintained its uniqueness but lost its difference.

As soon as the steins were closer to mostly empty than mostly full, the stilted conversation changed. I glanced up to find my sister dancing a polka with a 75 year-old man and Max trying to make sense of the English that a teenage Scotsman was screaming into his left ear as I took long and flavorful drags from the cigar that had been given to me by the twin brother of the man with whom my sister was gyrating. There was a distinct difference between Max's and Katie's definition of letting loose.

Soon after the second round of beer and the order of the third round, all conversation halted. We all found ourselves intimately engaged in a European version of *The Chicken Dance* (dinner had come in handy) and belting out the phonetic versions of what we assumed were real German words. Ines. Zvy. Sofa. Our translation of *One, Two, Couch* didn't have the lusty ring we had expected. So we ignored it and just sang out, clicking glasses with our neighbors and eagerly awaiting the third round of beer.

The third round brought a new twist. My sister sported a wool hat with a long, black feather, Max smothered his well-coifed hair with my worn-out Red Sox baseball cap, and I loosened the silk ascot from Max's neck and wound it around my head, bandanna style, as we joined in robustly on the 17th round of *One, Two, Sofa*. Rocking back and forth, slapping the table and hugging the strangers who flanked us. The pictures that we took as the evening unfolded annihilated any hope we might have had of holding public office one day. Bimini or bust.

It was time to go.

When Max took us to our place and said good-bye, I didn't know when I would see him again. He was headed back to Berlin and we were headed in the opposite direction. My heart ached. And Max cried. We knew how much we had changed because of each other, and we didn't know who would pick up the slack, who would point out that choice or that fault or that perspective or use that hand to comfort that soul. Maybe we just had to do it for ourselves. The prospect was more than just a little scary. And more than just a little sad. As he pulled away in his VW, I could barely see him through the panes. And pains.

We slept much more than soundly that night but our collective dreams reeked of disturbance. Like Katie's dream that I pulled up in front of the Bed and Breakfast the next morning in a 50-foot silver canoe with my arm slung cockily over the back of the front seat, wearing an Isadora Duncan scarf, jamming to *That's The Way, Uh-Huh, Uh-Huh, I Like It, Uh-Huh, Uh-Huh* and sounding a bullhorn to get her going. "We have a long drive to Italy," I said, "and the canoe eats up a lot of gas."

My dreams featured Max and John and Marco. Together in my head. The four of us. Not that we were ever all together outside of my head. One by one, I felt them slipping away. Or being pushed away. One headed for Berlin. One headed home to New Zealand for a few weeks before returning for one last stint at the university in Perugia. And one headed, ultimately, to Sicily. The slip versus the push was a distinction that my subconscious did not help clarify.

If our mother had known how Katie and I had remembered Holy Week, we were sure she would not have hidden two Easter cards and plastic bags filled with our favorite Easter candy inside my sister's suitcase. Cadbury Eggs, malted milk balls and Hershey's Kisses. Instead, I'm sure she might have opted for other treats. Like some cloves of garlic, a silver cross and a Linda Blair doll. We apologized to her over breakfast as we made our travel plans.

It was mid-afternoon, after a morning of modest sightseeing, when we found ourselves on a half-day train ride through Austria and into Venice, Italy. We managed to get a compartment to ourselves--a large rectangular space with six cushioned chairs, a picture window on one side and a glass door on the other, and curtains to block out, if desired, both the view and the other passengers. Those impetuous people who press their faces against the window looking for spare seats. That was a real coup.

The key to compartment travel is to move quickly. The seats that face each other must be pushed down from the top to form one long couch or landing from one side to the other. All three sets must be manipulated immediately. The curtain on the passenger-side must be drawn, all inhabitants must climb on top of the cushions and then gather as many coats, hats and towels as possible to simulate sleeping conditions. When people crack the compartment door to look inside for seats, they will see one of two things--people sleeping or a collection of human pigs. Either way, they will move on, and the compartment will become private property.

That was selfish, of course, but it beat running the risk of traveling for a dozen hours with nose-pickers, loud-talkers, bad breath, strange snorers or an old man with the hairy hands of a troll. Yes, that happened once. And we knew that if it got so crowded that our seats were needed, that someone would not hesitate to climb in. Fortunately, from Munich all the way to Venice, it did not happen. It was a miracle--and a sign of things to come.

We spent the hours playing cards (mostly Hearts and Gin Rummy), reading, writing, talking, pretend-sleeping and having me play food messenger as the train wended its way through little villages and enormous mountains. When we stopped, I'd jump out, run into the station's cafè bar, anxiously check my watch for the scheduled time of the train's departure, purchase two cheese sandwiches, some Cokes and bad potato chips and sprint back to my spot before the train revved up. We didn't have a plan if it had ever pulled out before I got back on. So it was a good thing it never happened.

The time passed quickly as the world passed by with changing moods paralleling the changing climates. Mountains seemed to call for austerity and order. Sunshine seemed to call for warmth and chaos. It was in our opening moments in the Italian sunshine that it first occurred to me to speak to Katie about our heritage and its impact on who we are and what we've come to be. I stepped gingerly. As I wanted her to hold my fragile dream with the caution it required. No one in my family, not even Katie, knew. No one knew.

"Katie, do you feel some kind of a connection to our grandparents now that we're into their homeland?"

"No, not really," she said, with a tilt to her head that hinted at some respect. Some reflection.

"You're not struck by the fact that this is where it all started? That this is where our lineage began?"

"No. I just never think about that," as she placed down a trio of tens in Gin Rummy to solidify her victory.

She collected the cards and stacked them in a neat pile on the cushions. I watched in mild amazement as she nonchalantly shuffled them and prepared for another round. With her focus then mainly on the game. And my focus mainly on our very different ways of viewing our history. Hers from the seat of honor. On Nonno's lap. In that last photograph. We had an identity chasm between us that was as large as the Grand Canyon. I had to wait and hope she'd guide me to her side. And not shirk her responsibility to share her precious power.

Our arrival in Venice forced us to bid good-bye to our cozy, compartment living. We dragged our suitcases along the floor of the train station as other visitors rushed toward their jobs or hotels or first shot of *espresso* or morning newspaper and the large, shining windows that frame the splendor of Venice. I was so caught up in the wave of humanity, in the pushing and shoving and jockeying of luggage and coats and bodies, that I was unprepared for how it would take my breath and knock me back. The Grand Canal.

A wide expanse of water and waves and activity. The barbershop striped poles. Massive bridges. And myriad vessels carrying anything from bananas to wood to star struck tourists. We looked straight ahead as our feet stumbled down the steps to the water's edge. And then we moved our heads left to right. And left to right. And acknowledged the kind of unmatched joy that comes from the unexpected. Like having our adolescent stomachs jump up and around and down when our father's car swept over a hill that had come up too quickly.

The waves from the vessels slapped against the suitcases we had rested precariously close to the water's edge. Soaking up all there was to soak up. As did we. I turned to Katie who was equally stunned, caught with an innocent look on her face. A look of wonder. Disbelief. I thought that the unrestricted acceptance of beauty and the unreal had long been dead. But there it was. Alive and thriving inside and outside each of us. On the Grand Canal. In Venice, Italy.

As time passed, we lost ourselves in the alleys of Venice and were coaxed to delightful lapses on the African blankets that sprawled over the limited asphalt of Venice, in the tiny chapels that dotted the city, during read-ups on the unparalleled, masked festival that attaches itself to Lent, in front of the Byzantine art that lines the museums and with sips of *cappuccino*. At times shedding currency before it fluctuated one point, one *lira*, five one-hundredths of a dollar. As when we spotted a striking, gray-haired *gondoliere,* wearing a blue and white striped t-shirt with a short-waisted jacket, leaning up against one of the storefronts. His name was Antonio. "Like our *nonno*," I said to Katie, before we followed him through the narrow, seasoned maze to the *gondola* that was waiting. To treat us to elegance on water. Velvet-covered thrones and a private serenade. It was the first and only time that personal caroling didn't lead to excruciating embarrassment. Maybe because we were already traveling in a bathtub, of sorts. The moment felt rare despite the dozens of *gondole* that dotted the waterways and the dozens of *gondolieri* in deep voices or falsetto singing *O Solo Mio*--rendering the scene outstanding fodder for the Floating Theater of The Absurd. The Floating Theater of The Oxymoron.

Antonio dug the long pole into the depths to propel us and direct us down the city's watery streets as I told him why I was in Italy and that Katie and I were sisters and that we had grandparents who were born in his land. And without missing a beat, he compared our faces, one olive-colored and bookended with dark-black hair, the other fair skinned and surrounded by light brown locks, and replied, *"La stessa mamma. Ma un'altro padre."* (Same mother. But a different father.) When we told our mother, she said, "Oooh, no. Did you make sure he knew that wasn't true?" She didn't want some gossiping *gondoliere* in Venice, Italy thinking she was a floozy. "It could spread, you know. They talk." Right. From the canals of Venice to our local hometown diner. "Hey, did you hear what my sources picked up in Italy, Dick? Those Marshall sisters. Katie and Jo. I heard that their mother slept around." I just didn't think so.

"*Non e' Italiana*," Antonio persisted, as he pointed to my sister. And shook his head. *That one's not Italian*. The translation hurt her. I could tell by her change in mood. And the new significance of the old tune that lingered on the waters.

The days in Venice flew by. We passed our time getting lost on the hundreds of cryptic side streets, crossing at least half of the city's 400 plus bridges, visiting the Doge Palace, walking over the Bridge of Sighs and venturing to the top of the *campanile* to view the entire city. We sampled some delicious seafood dishes, had my sister's luggage repaired at a small establishment called The Dog Shop and emptied our wallets at *Piazza San Marco* when we ordered *cappuccini* and croissants at an outdoor cafè and were told that the $30 price tag was partly due to the ambiance. Ambiance this, I whispered then. But now, as I rest thousands of miles away from the sprawling rectangular *piazza*, away from the waters that took me to Torcello and Burano and Murano and Lido, the waiters who sang their greetings, the outdoor orchestras whose crisp, lively music accompanied us to sleep and the thousands of pigeons that ate croissant crumbs and coffee grinds and birdseed for free, $30 spells a bargain.

After one last day in Venice, most of which was spent at an outdoor cafè under the warm Italian sun, gazing out over the cold and dirtied waters and the boats that form a different kind of traffic jam, our schedule dictated that we press on, and we did. Reluctantly. Pausing several times in the train station to catch one more glimpse of the Grand Canal. One more glimpse of the magnificent bridge. One more glimpse of the blue and yellow and tan and red narrow, vertical homes that had nudged up to the water's edge. Until our train for Florence signaled its impatience to take us to a place where, for one of us, a tall, curly-haired male would emerge more perfect than *David* himself. And strike without a slingshot and a stone.

Chapter Sixteen
Michelangelo--Artist, Architect, Matchmaker

The time we had allotted for Florence was a minuscule fraction of what we would have liked. That was obvious on the first afternoon when the *Piazza della Signoria* held us for hours in its wicker chairs, chairs that rest in the unique shadows of the Town Hall's medieval facade. We slowly, lazily sampled four kinds of *biscotti* dipped in *Vino Santo* and mused about living in Florence one day. Surrounded by beauty, creativity, genius and power.

Our task those first few hours under the arm of the *piazza* was to plan our time well in Firenze, a task that was repeatedly invaded by human beings, Italian and otherwise, who lusted after our prime wicker real estate. Real estate that was rivaled only by the local pigeons who were free to soar over the offspring of Medici power, (cathedrals, museums and masterpieces that beckoned at every corner), land wherever they pleased and be fed well for their efforts.

Our memo pad ran out of room as the must-see sites spilled over the edges, top and bottom, side-to-side. So we dipped some more *biscotti* and savored the most important sites of all. Peace. Time. And good company.

When we blinked our eyes open the very next day, after an April night spent on our hotel terrace, gazing out over the clay sea, the battered ivy, the flower pots and the Italian faces flickering in the light of late-night television, the touring began, with each stop offering a lifetime of treasures. The Uffizi Gallery--site of what some say is the most splendid art collection in all of Italy. The cream of the cream's cream--sipped by hundreds of thousands of visitors each year, ranging in degrees of enlightenment and appreciation. And the *Ponte Vecchio*--the only bridge in Florence left unbombed during the destruction of World War II. There we lusted after the gold and silver and delicious gems that appeared out of nowhere under the chained-up wooden storefronts that line the priceless crossing. We were grateful to the shop owners who hid their cynicism about our buying power in their professionalism. And *La Chiesa di Santa Croce*--where we paid our respects to Michelangelo, da Vinci, Galileo and Dante Alighieri, whose burial tombs or tributes rest inside. We agreed that we would have liked to spend as much money on homes for our living as they spend on homes for their dead--tombs of marble adorned and plenty of unnecessary room to move around. And *Piazzale Michelangelo*--for a panoramic view of the city and an exquisite sunset, after which we wended our way down for *gelato* (ice cream) at the world-famous Vivoli's and experienced overt anxiety over the too-small scoops on the flaky cones and the 425 fruit, nut and chocolate choices that shone brightly just beneath the polished glass. And, of course, on a daily basis, we explored the open-air market of *San Lorenzo*, where Katie picked up 15 lipstick cases, Florentine paper, leather gloves, purses, knapsacks, belts, jackets, suede coats, silk ties, scarves, calendars, t-shirts, gold rings, necklaces, earrings and countless inlaid wooden domes with the urgency of a wife-to-be at the Filene's Basement Bridal Sale. And on each pass by The New Market, a smaller version of *San Lorenzo* and home to the bronzed boar, we would rub the nose of the wild swine to guarantee a return to the city of perfection. Paradise in paradise. Finally, after one more trip into the *Duomo*, one more visit to *David's* Academy, one more glimpse of the Fra Angelico murals, one more picnic on the grounds of the Pitti Palace, cosmopolitan breakfasts on the rooftop terrace of our hotel with the broken elevator, three corns, two blisters and one broken toenail, we decided we'd take a day-trip to Pisa.

We caught an early train and arrived in what, compared to the Germany to Italy marathon, seemed like minutes. Most of the sites of Pisa--the cathedral, the baptistery, The Leaning Tower, can be found in one long stretch in the heart of the town. Their light, spiritual tones demand attention, call the visitors to order--due in large part to the contrasting rich, velvety grass on which they rest.

Despite all the pictures of The Leaning Tower of Pisa and the absolutely clear evidence that it slants to one side, everyone feels compelled to enter into the World Of The Obvious when it is viewed for the first time. "Gee, it really *does* lean." And, gee, it is a tower. And, gee, it is in Pisa. Put them all together and you have an artifact whose name falls all over itself to prevent misconceptions and idiotic observations. If the Washington Monument were renamed The Tall Pointy Obelisk of Washington, I'd like to think that people would avoid similarly obvious decrees as they lounged at the monolith's ankles. All evidence points to the contrary.

The climb to the top of Pisa's gravitational wonder was stranger, still, than the look from the bottom--for although we were going up, the steps were slanted down. We were locked in an M.C. Escher print, leaning in all directions as we either went with the flow or battled the natural forces. We suppressed dizziness and nausea as we pressed onward and sideways and upward to the top, to the rounded, slanted peak and the amazing countryside that unfolded before our eyes.

At the top, The Leaning Tower's lifelong mission seemed reasonable. Toward the earth. Toward the earth. Toward the earth, forever. I, too, wanted to romp in the rich green grasses and smell the smells of the life that was thriving below. Still, we savored the moment on top. Aware of the water to our west, the richness to our east and the confused reality that comes with resting on the peak of one of humanity's most unique, most recognizable spectacles. The Leaning Tower of Pisa. Under our feet. Our slanted feet. With corns, blisters and broken toenail. Surrounded by copper-colored roofs, wedding cake architecture and waves of discovery at every turn.

When we returned to level ground, we surrendered to the temptation. We rolled on the greens outside the cathedral and then steadied ourselves with our backs to the grounds and our eyes toward the incredible sky and the stark white tower that pierces the deepest blues. And my thoughts raced to the genius of Galileo, who once lived and worked and studied in Pisa and shattered all notions of the universe as they were and risked his freedoms to do so, to an awareness of the rare moment within The Leaning Tower's spells, to the cacophony of competing languages that floated by our ears, to the wonders of the Renaissance whose thinkers and doers and movers and shakers, scattered mostly in this country and mostly in this region, changed the course of history, technology, boundaries and our interpretations of no and impossible. Then, in a split-second reversal of mental fitness, my thoughts raced to the different kinds of poses we could assume in front of the tower. Slanting in the same direction.

Pretending to be holding it up. Pretending to be pushing it down. The positions who earned others an *L* for loser when they felt compelled to do the same.

I smirked at the kind of information my brain was willing to hold when it was allowed to breathe. When I was allowed to breathe. From the inspiration of Galileo to the smitten-with-myself sensation I felt when I practiced the alliteration of our lunch order. *"Una fetta di pizza con piselli, per favore."*

It was with her chin resting on her bent arm that The Leaning Tower's gravity moved Katie and then me to a different place. "Do you think Nonno ever visited here, Jo?" "I don't know. I wish we could have asked him." "There's so much we'll never know." "But I have to believe there's so much we can still find out," I whispered. As her eyes fell off to the distance--thinking she was making room for me on his lap. As I made room for her in my dream.

We picked ourselves up off the ground and toured the remaining sights in Pisa, which fall along a short stretch of land leading away from The Leaning Tower and away from The Leaning Tower's lean. Sparing them the fear of a midnight crash. I stepped inside and tried to etch in my mind the features and tones and windows, the crosses and saints and tiles that distinguish that gathering place from the dozens of other Christian strongholds I had visited. It was getting harder and harder as the similar features of the cathedrals across Italy crossed borders in my head and had me place a Venetian neighbor-hood church in Todi and a Perugian house of worship in Orvieto. Without speaking, Katie and I brought matches to the candle's wicks in the darkened space and watched the flame flicker in each other's faces as we prayed for a safe return to The United States in the midst of Khaddaffi's newest anti-American rhetoric.

And then we headed back. At a slant. Laughing and signaling *L*s on our foreheads as we boarded the train.

The need for an emergency pit-stop in the upstairs bathroom of a Florentine *trattoria* confirmed my *L*, for certain. But it was what I overheard Katie saying on the other side of the door that confirmed hers. "Well, I don't know that much about Florence, but when my sister gets out of the bathroom, she can help you with what to see and what to do."

Now, of course she knew a lot about Florence. We had spent the last several days examining every corner of the city and, if nothing else, she could have spoken *ad nauseam* about the wares at the open markets and the jewels on the *Ponte Vecchio*. I didn't want to come out of the bathroom to speak to the man whom I had just toilet-bowled over in the spirit of waste removal. But, I had to. So I emerged, feeling eight pounds thinner, and we did the round of introductions. His name was Steve, and his use of the word "buddy" to describe the friend that was waiting downstairs reeked of shore leave and left my suggestions about Donatello's *David* and the murals of Fra Angelico embarrassed and awkward and probably unheard. I was still battling the demons of assumption.

When I convinced myself that I had been cordial enough, we headed down the steps, out the door and straight back to the *pensione*, leaving the two buddies to their cigarettes and beer. We had barely gotten out onto the street when Katie asked, "That must have been Steve's friend in front of the bar. Did you see his face?" At 5'4", I could've given a blueprint description of the belt he was wearing or how his pants rested on top of his kneecaps or if his socks matched his trousers, but I couldn't have picked him out of a two-person police lineup unless he worked for Frank Baum. When I shrugged a decided "no," Katie looked disappointed in my blindness to his good looks. And in my indifference. And in my height deficiency.

When we got back to the *pensione*, we plopped down on the beds and opted for naps over card-playing. When we awoke three and one-half hours later at 6:00 P.M., sparkling with a post-slumber glow, I wanted to get up, get out and get something to eat--but Katie was not in the mood for any of it. She just wanted to hang out for the night, play some cards, eat a *panino* (sandwich) and drink a couple of Cokes. No alcohol for her tonight, she said. We didn't have to be on the go *all* the time, she said.

So I entered into the begging phase. My youngest-in-the-family status meant that I had it down to an art. And my success rate was indisputable. "Jo, ask Dad if he'll take us out for ice cream after dinner. Ask Mum if we can go play at the Robbins' house. Ask Mum and Dad if we can camp outside in the tree fort tonight. They'll do it if you ask. You're the lovey-dovey one in the family." So, off I'd go for a minute or two while my brothers and sister awaited my return to the paneled den. TV volume lowered, eyes hopeful, faces looking upward from their places on the floor and couch. They were waiting for the sign. And when the moment was right, I would show that sign--a pinky finger thrust into the air with a vigorous twirl signaling that All Systems Were Go, that The Eagle Had Landed and that Houston Did *Not* Have A Problem. The victory always inspired astronaut talk.

It never occurred to us that our parents might have actually wanted an ice cream or wanted us at the Robbins' or wanted us sleeping in the fort. They were in total control and were happy leading us to believe that it was completely in our hands, in my finger, a finger that was merely a pawn in their chess game. Still, Katie thought I was a formidable opponent, so after a few minutes of pursuit, she reluctantly gave in. "OK, I'll go but I don't want to. And I'm *not* changing out of these jeans and red sweatshirt and I am *not* putting on any makeup." Fine. Like I was headed for a ball gown and some eyeliner.

Each cafè we entered that night was teeming with men. Smoking men. Old men. Scruffy men. We'd swing open the door or climb through the woolen strands to a dark gathering and, in an instant, this one would look up from his card game, that one would turn from the bar, that one would push back his chair from the table, this one would scratch the crown of his head and nudge his neighbor and then, inevitably, that one would get up and head toward us at the door. It was at the moment of the advance that we'd do The Tacit Glance Check and casually back up onto the street.

That scene replayed itself 20 times that night. Twenty scratches, 20 nudges, 20 moves toward the woolen strands and the Florentine sidewalks. I was on the verge of suggesting that Katie might have had the right idea to stay home and play cards when we decided we'd go eat at a little place I knew near the *Duomo*. Certainly not off the beaten path. Certainly not a page out of Indiana Jones' Adventure Guide. But we were hungry and thirsty and fed up.

The self-serve cafè with the view of the *Battistero* doors had fluorescent lights, a long buffet, tables for four and poster-size photos of some of the world's greatest landmarks, some of which were well within our reach. We shuffled along the sides of the smorgasbord-under-glass, with not-big-enough plates in hand, and selected at least 10 colorful varieties of delicacies, including roasted vegetables and various versions of squid. I got Katie to change her mind about sampling a little *vino* and moved toward a table carrying two filled plates, two glasses and a bottle of Michelangelo wine. Wine price tag--one dollar.

Within seconds of our first bites and sips, Katie looked up to see the two "buddies" from the *trattoria* slide through the front door of the cafè. She asked if she should invite them over, suddenly stepping up to the microphone to accept the Miss Congeniality Award and putting an insurmountable distance between the broad smile that consumed most of her face right then and her last remarks at the *pensione*. "OK, I'll go but I don't want to." Sure.

Steve and James came right over to the table, asked if they could join us, pulled up two chairs, ordered two mugs of beer and jumped right in on the conversation. Katie met James. James met Katie. A pair whose chemistry was certainly enhanced by but not defined by the three bottles of Michelangelo wine and the countless mugs of Italian beer. We know that because it started well before the potent grapes and hops could have kicked in as they moved up to, through and beyond the opening chatter and superficial exchanges in record-time. The faint remnants of pain after Katie's previous romantic involvement, remnants only I had come to notice in my sister's eyes and lips and bitten fingernails, were blown out into the Italian countryside and then into the Adriatic to rest, forever undisturbed, as all deaths at sea should rest. The tinges of sadness were instantly replaced that night with comfort and conversation and laughter and an unprecedented spectacle of kissing in the middle of the crowded cafè. Before the second bottle of wine was emptied but after their many digressions about family and hopes and traveling in, being in and being alive in Italy, I heard James say that they could tell their children they met in Florence. Across from the *Duomo* and the baptistery, where the bronzed *Gates of Paradise* would forever take on a newer, truer meaning. Before the third bottle of wine was emptied but after more was shared about souls, spirits and Native American beliefs about where both go after life and after death, I wondered about those souls and spirits and journeys. And I wondered where and how and when and why it was that Katie and James had met before, since the cafè rendezvous could not have been their first. Could not have been their beginning--because that night they started in the middle.

Time sped by as a more modest and modern version of the Renaissance, their renaissance, lived on in Florence and as Katie and James made up for a lifetime of missed minutes. We left the restaurant together hours later, completely convinced that love-at-first-sight was alive and that friends and family had just watched friends and family write a page for that book. And we left the restaurant with my sister not even noticing that she was not wearing makeup, not even noticing that her feet were skipping along the stone pavement and not even noticing that the smile on James' face was as sure a sign of complete emotional submission as her skipping feet were.

We wandered through the streets and between the peeling townhouses and wended our way to a wild disco, where we got inside with a free drink coupon and climbed to the upper level. There we separated and continued to dance the night away. When we finally reunited, just before midnight, after Katie's and James' images had been thrust up on an enormous video screen that hovered over the Olympic-size dance floor, I had to grab my sister's hand, tug her from her haven and begin to lead only two of us back to the *pensione* before the door slammed shut for our midnight curfew.

We raced through the sea of bodies, with James and Steve trailing, and remembered to exchange addresses when we got outside. Thank the gods, because early the next morning their Navy ship would sail away from Italy and from my sister. So with the torn sheet of paper bearing her future wedged deeply into her little hand, we headed off into darkness, leaving James still and peering after her.

Just seconds before midnight, we pushed through the large, brown door to our *pensione*, the door that first separated us from my sister's new brand of happiness and an old, more romantic brand of court-ship. Long distance letter-writing. Later that night, she pulled me beside her on the bed. "Jo," she said, with her older, softer, smoother hands covering mine. "He is the one. You have to believe me. He is the one."

One and one-half years later, as I walked down the aisle in front of my sister and father, linked arm-in-arm with *Pachelbel's Canon* in the background, I was glad I did believe her. And I was glad I was the Best Woman--because without me she would have stayed home that night in Florence, Italy, played a few hands of Hearts, eaten a cheese sandwich and called it a day. Instead, she fell in love. With a tall, curly-haired, soft-spoken man. Her David. And, amazingly, that one, too, was touched by the hand of Michelangelo--a Michelangelo who was worth a lot more than his 100-cent price tag.

Chapter Seventeen
Italian Red Tape Versus
The American Middle Finger

Katie talked about James cautiously, wondering to herself if the four-hour whirlwind romance that went on amidst the squid and wine, disco lights and Pointer Sisters, was real or imagined. Fortunately, I was there to refresh her memory and alleviate any fears she had of insanity or hyperbole. Yes, it did happen. Yes, you did fall in love. And, yes, he did pass the initial sister-test. And then I went out and bought a red-hooded *Ooh, Ooh, Ooh, I'm Just A Love Machine* sweatshirt.

The day after, in mid-morning, as James and Steve set sail for destinations unknown to us, we boarded a train for Perugia. The Italian newspaper I bought as we stepped up on the platform had a feature article about a bomb that had gone off in a Berlin disco the night before. It made me recall the headline I had spotted several days earlier, just before we headed into the Doge Palace in Venice, about a bomb that had been placed aboard a TWA plane. Initial speculation was that both acts were linked to Libya. The Pisa prayers that we sent up as we lighted the candles in the back of the cathedral must have leaned in the direction of not being heard.

Our panic escalated rapidly in the compartment of the brain that controls logical thought or in the place that allows for freedom and freedoms. We were hovering at Mach 1,000 when we arrived in Perugia--to placards on the sides of buildings that read "Libya Hates Americans" in Italian. It was the first time I wished I didn't speak the language--since its translation led to paralysis. An inevitable outcome given our possession of the genetic material that insisted upon worrying, that allowed it to be practiced and perfected and raised to an art form and required for existence. We were already picturing fighter pilots encircling Perugia with deadly toxins and gases hooked up to parachutes that were pointed to land on the marble tabletop in my kitchen. To spill out over my *pasta carbonara* and Parmesan cheese. Our thoughts turned to our funerals and feeling sadness for the family and friends we'd leave behind.

When we got back to my apartment, we cranked the *bomba*, a name which came to take on a decidedly different meaning, and planned a dinner menu to take our minds off our panic. We decided on John's and my specialty, *tortellini alla panna con piselli e salsiccia, vino rosso e pane,* and headed out the door to go shopping. Katie fell in love with Perugia as we strolled down *Corso Vannucci* from the end overlooking the city to the end that housed the city's main cathedral--a site whose scaffolding and signs, *in restauro*, in restoration, seemed as much a part of the design as the baroque interior. I took her by the street where the underground water pipe had burst in the fall, a street whose excavation led to the discovery of another Etruscan site just below the more modern cobblestones, which stopped the shovels, pickaxes, drills and 20th century progress. We poked our heads down the city's ancient well and sipped a beer in the underground bar and raced by the front of the *trattoria* where I had wasted my first several thousand *lire* on pate´ and Coke. We sampled *Baci*, the "kisses" candy for which the city is most famous, and had fun translating the Italian wishes and fortunes that were wrapped around the chocolate-nutted heaven. The angst of imminent disaster faded with every fortune, every nut, every dash of milk chocolate on our taste buds.

Katie and I finally turned our attention to dinner-shopping, matching steps on the route that Max and I had walked on dozens of occasions. The bread, *pasta*, meat, cheese, fruit, vegetable and wine shops and the *pasticceria*. I looked for him. Loaded down with brown bags decorated with scores of prices in pencil. Smiling. Scattered in his efforts to hunt down the latest treat, the freshest fruit, the most chocolatey dessert. And more than happy to prepare a spread that would make the three of us so, so happy. But he wasn't there. So the joy came from living through her food-shopping eyes. It helped me bring back into focus that we were still in Italy and should not let fear hold us captive. A mantra I repeated to myself about every six minutes.

Along the way, Katie grew impressed with my popularity. Waves and nods there. Short conversations there. I could've been the Mayor of Perugia, she said. Most of it was from the owners of the various shops. Some of their kindness, at least, stemmed from the fact that Max and I were practically single-handedly responsible, by the *lire* that passed from our hands to theirs, for their being able to purchase that Ferrari, have that surgery, redecorate that storefront, buy that Armani suit. They were grateful for our loyalty. We didn't have to pick *their* particular shops, after all. But we did because they were, according to Max, "the best," as in BMW is "the best," Mercedes is "the best." He'd deliver it with a little smile, finding some humor in his sensitivity toward national pride.

The plastic bags that carried our purchases grew rapidly in quantity and kilos with each stop. The handles drew ruts in our palms as we lumbered over the 2,000,000 Perugian steps and slopes back to my home. When we finally stepped inside, hands numbed by circulation deprivation and cooler temperatures, we cranked the newly christened Betty (a less terroristic name for *la bomba*) higher and set my two-burner hot plate on high to boil the water for the *pasta* and warm the kitchen. As I prepared the fresh sausage for frying, we sipped red wine from chipped glasses and sat around the marble table to reminisce about our time together. Ultimately, it led to one fact.

Next stop Rome. And then home.

I was missing her terribly, even though she was inches from my face, cutting off small pats of butter to add to the white sauce and happily rinsing the peas and warming the bread. I still hadn't mastered the joys of living in the moment, and I knew that after she was gone, I would regret it more than I regretted it right then-- because then I wouldn't have her face to bring me back.

Our only full day in Perugia was spent wandering. Sunning on the steps of the cathedral. Getting haircuts. Last-minute shopping. Dropping off our dirty laundry at a local cleaner. Passing by an open-air market to watch natives select live chickens for the killing. Changing Katie's flight reservations to Swiss Air to try to secure a safer passage home. Just catching my Italian *mamma* as she headed to her real daughter's house for a visit with her grandson. She detoured to kiss my cheeks and say she missed me in her home. Her adopted half-Italian. And then checking my mail at the school post office and finding a letter from Dana and Elsie inviting me to join them in Rome just two days after my sister's flight. And trying to mail a pair of jeans to John who requested the favor via postcard from New Zealand. And not visiting Marco. I was still running. Still avoiding. Still bothered by his invasion of our perfectly good relationship with his perfectly bad jealousy. I turned to John's pants. Thinking that the jeans-request was a reasonable one. It certainly would have been back home. Instead, I swallowed whole one of the most infuriating episodes in the history of Italian-American relations-- partially fueled by the language barrier and partly fueled by arrogance run amok.

The first step was for me to buy a very specific pair of jeans from the Stefanel shop on *Corso Vannucci*. The cost was 55,000 *lire* or about $27.50. Back in New Zealand, the same jeans would have cost 100 American dollars. I brought the jeans to the post office thinking that they might have had a packing envelope, a cushioned one, that would hold and protect the jeans on their long journey. They told me they had no such thing but that the store around the corner, which specialized in packaging for shipment, would be happy to prepare them for mailing. Unfortunately, they were closed until 4:00 P.M. Since it was 3:45 P.M., we decided to wait.

And wait we did--well past 4:00 P.M. and more towards 5:00 P.M. Italy is a country where timetables and rules can mean absolutely nothing until they decide they want them to. And then the opposite extreme is visited. At 4:50 P.M., they opened their doors. No apologies. Just condescension.

They selected a box from their collection that was big enough to hold six pairs of jeans, a down parka, the back quarters of a Morgan horse, a Brittany Spaniel and a small Beagle. They wrapped it with brown paper and sealed it off with some string. Cost--4,000 *lire*. So far, OK. Not perfect, but OK.

We walked back around the corner to the post office and headed for the International Shipment Window. I wrote the address on the outside, placed it on the ledge and told them that I wanted to ship it to New Zealand. They told me that the package wasn't going anywhere. "This, I am afraid, is a packing hazard." Hazard? It was going to bring down the aircraft over the Mediterranean? They told me I had to go back to the store and get it rewrapped. So, I did.

I explained the situation to the employees--that the box was too big for the item inside, causing it to move around like a house in a tornado. They reluctantly undid the string, removed the brown wrapping paper, selected a smaller box, rewrapped the jeans in new brown paper and restrung the box. I asked them if the post office would accept the stringed version and not a taped version. They assured me that they always did.

Back to the post office and the International Shipment Window. After I readdressed the package to New Zealand, they spoke. The string, it turned out, was unacceptable. So in crazed Italian I asked, "Why didn't you tell me that the last time? *Exactly* what does this package need to look like in order to meet your shipping standards?" The pair behind the window smirked as they told me it was just the string. Otherwise, all was well.

I stormed back to the shop around the corner and threw the package on the counter. Slowly, as if they had all the time in the world, which they clearly did, they unstrung the box, took out some packing tape and secured it well enough to survive a nuclear blast.

Back to the post office. Finally, it was packed to their satisfaction. And then they dropped the following. By ship, it would take up to six months to arrive in New Zealand. By air, it would cost well more than the jeans themselves. I grabbed the package from their hands, broke away from the Italian language and spewed forth my best English anger and intolerance, to which they gleefully responded, *"Non parliamo inglese."* At which point I walked to the center of the post office, away from all other human contact, spun around once with my arms out by my side, package in one hand, obscene gestures in the other, and vomited out, at the top of my lungs, an emphatic string of colorful English expletives.

The display was enough to silence and, I might add, even frighten the masses. Except for my sister. Who started to laugh hysterically when I joined her. The hysterical duo. Doubled-over. Skipping down the steps. And happy to be leaving Perugia for Rome the next day.

We went back to the packing store and told them to unwrap the box and return my 4,000 *lire*. Which they did. One-third reluctantly. One-third angrily. One-third repressing hilarity. I was sure they were all sleeping together. International Shipments meets Boxes and String--planning the episode over and over in bed the night before as they unwrapped each other.

My sister ended up taking the jeans home and mailing them from The United States for $10.00. On one side of the scale, I saved 32 dollars. On the other side, I completely alienated myself from the Italian people or, at least, a handful of employees in an Umbrian hilltown. The scary thing is that if I had it to do all over again, I'm afraid I'd do it exactly the same way. Spinning and swearing in the middle of Perugia, as is the occasional right of the baby of the family. Not that they knew about or cared about that status. Or knew about or cared about the power of my pinky. They, instead, were more frighteningly focused on the finger that lived nearby. Two houses down. And on the fact that I, Jo Marshall, was, at that moment, a living, ticking, breathing, unraveling "Packing Hazard." And a first-hand example of our ugliest international reputation.

Houston, We Do Have A Problem. All Systems Are Not Go. And Someone Needs To Shoot That Eagle Before It Does Land.

Chapter Eighteen
Shrinkage--Personal, Clothes, Anxiety And Time

After the initial euphoria that spite and arrogance inspired in the Perugian post office, it didn't take long for me to regroup and reassess. I had lost it and was worried about it. And had come far enough to acknowledge misguided power and my access to it and existence within it. But not far enough to anticipate its flexing or to steer it off at the pass. I was struck by its sense of self-preservation, like trick birthday candles bursting forth again and again. Angering and embarrassing. And making me wish that the candles, the flames, could be extinguished as quickly as possible and once and for all. I wondered if Dana and Elsie could help. Not that they were responsible for my education. For my growing-up. They had enough to do without serving as unpaid teachers to the ignorant masses.

I joined Katie in her packing rituals since I was going to stay in Rome after her flight. Then we strolled the streets of Perugia with the goal of picking up our laundry. I used to watch Mamma do hers in the kitchen at my old apartment. On Wednesday afternoons, like clockwork. When Susanna and Petra would be off in other parts and Mamma and I would chat in the kitchen. About Italy and Italians and how fortunate we felt to have our identities wrapped up in each. About motherhood and cooking and loyalty. "It's the mother that holds the family together, you know. She is at the center of it all. Of the love and the nurturing. God knew what He was doing. Even if He was a male." And then she'd chuckle. As she tried to hide her teeth behind her pinkish lips.

In-between some tender moments, she would set the temperature to the dial that read "Hotter than Hell." Inviting Satan in to stir and heckle. Like most things post-depression--my mother reusing aluminum foil 23 times, my father hammering bent nails back into shape, both my parents being absolutely unwilling to throw away even the tiniest morsel of leftover food, ("Mum, do you want me to wrap up the three peas and four carrot cubes that are left in the serving dish?" "Yes, dear. And use the folded aluminum foil in the top drawer to the left of the sink, please...."), I assumed it had something to do with World War II. I just couldn't figure out the connection between war and water temperature, and it was still too sensitive to ask, even 40 years later. So I never had Mamma do my wash--even though her offers were the clearest sign of her favoritism.

When we arrived at the laundry and caught our first glimpses of the brutalized apparel, I realized I had neglected to specify cooler degrees. It was an error of grotesque proportions. My sister's famous red sweatshirt turned pink and was a suitable over garment for Barbie's best friend, Midge. And my jeans, which already encased my body like kielbasa skin, were thrown out on the way back to my apartment. One advantage of the mass shrinkage was that it opened up room for Katie in her bulging suitcases. Her extra duffels were already jammed with enough Venetian and Florentine paraphernalia to earn her compulsive shopping honors. But, when size 14s became 8s, we found space for that 30th lipstick case and fourth linen tablecloth.

We finished our packing late-morning, called for a taxi and chuckled at our driver's look of utter horror and disbelief when our luggage consumed his car. In the trunk. On the back window near the back seat. On the front seat and front floor. On our laps. It was ridiculous, and it was hysterical, and we realized just how much of each it was when he pulled up in front of three taxi stands on the way to the train station to beep and wave to his pals. It was a Perugian hootenanny. They'd look up, slap their knees, rock their heads and laugh out loud. And then do it again. And again--as they snorted at the man who drove the two Americans whose luggage outweighed the car and passengers combined.

In-between the *Hee Haw* episodes, we saw many more pro-Libyan and anti-American placards and asked the driver if he were afraid of the increasingly threatening situation.

"Not at all. You can't live your life waiting for threats to become real."

"But couldn't it be real one of these times?"

"Yes, it could. But maybe it never will. And if it never is, you'll find that you've wasted your time, wasted your life playing a game of terror. Just don't play the game. If you play, they'll win. So don't play."

The worrying that was a part of our Italian bloodline was not a part of his. I wondered if he were a foreigner as we accepted his soothing refrain. When he dropped us at the train station and lightened his load as much as he had lightened ours, we thanked him by giving him an enormous tip. But not nearly as big, it turned out, as the one he had given us.

After we arrived at Termini via train, we had only the rest of that day and one more full day to spend in Rome before Katie returned to Boston early the next morning. In Perugia, when our Khaddaffi anxiety was running most wild, I had thought about going with her. Seeing if Swiss Air had one more seat to safety for sale. In the end, I decided to stay. There was Marco. A visit from my Mum. And the ultimate dream of going to Sicily still looming in the nearer and nearer distance. But the taxi driver affirmed that my decision to stay was the right one and because of him, we lived out the rest of our Italian adventure, short-term and long-term, with much less fear about the possibilities and a lot more freedom about the future.

The touring in Rome was at world-record pace, and the reactions were in world-record awe. A bombardment of sensations and wonders. Unparalleled statuary and cathedrals and paintings cruising down the candy conveyor belt as Lucy and Ethel tried to do justice to each one. But at some point, no matter how much we struggled to keep up, it overwhelmed. We wished we could have just slowed down the onslaught or taken some sites off of our list or sat and rested a bit. But all of that was hard to do when the clock was ticking off its seconds. And all of that was hard to do when we would have been forced to trade away sites. "OK, we'll see the catacombs the next time." No. Because we didn't know if there would be a next time. So we pressed on and succumbed and realized we did the right thing when we stepped lightly, carefully and with some trepidation below the ground on *Via Appia Antica*, the oldest of Roman roads, and paid respectful tribute to the symmetrically carved-out earthen tombs of thousands. Winding their way in maze-like tracks in the cool environs of the center of our immediate world. Interrupted by tiny chapels or spots where torch lights once hung. Once we saw them, we realized we couldn't have traded them. Everywhere we looked there was something. And that something was something that couldn't have been bartered away. Couldn't have been put on hold to the next time. Because seeing it changed our sense of the past and, therefore, our vision of the future. So, the alternatives were clear. Exhausting. But clear.

We walked more miles in Rome in our last hours than we had in the rest of the trip combined. Knees and ankles were throbbing as were hearts and heads. We'd stop periodically for sustenance. An *espresso*. A *panino*. A Coke. Some stale popcorn and peanuts. They kept us going through every single visit, every single ticket purchase, every single mural, every single candle-lighting ritual, every single dome. The Colosseum, The Roman Forum, Circus Maximus, The Spanish Steps, St. Peter's Cathedral and the Vatican Museums, again. I forgot to bring my ear plugs to The Sistine Chapel, so I was subjected to another brilliant Defender Of The Free World remark when a middle-aged, big eye-glassed woman right near *The Last Judgment* said, "I'd like to read up some more on Mr. Angelo when I get home. I want to find out where he learned to paint so nice."

The greatest site for me was in a leather shop near The Pantheon. When the friendly saleswoman refused to accept the notion that I could be anything other than Italian. *"Ma, tu parli bene l'Italiano e senz'un accento. Tu devi essere Italiano. E tu hai la faccia di un Italiano."* (But you speak Italian well and without an accent. You have to be Italian. And you have the face of an Italian.) "I *am* American. But my grandparents were born in Italy." "I knew it," she said. As she slapped down her hand on the glass counter that protected Italy's famous leather gloves with the lambs' wool lining. "And I know exactly where. Sicily. You have those wonderful, deep Sicilian eyes." I wanted to buy every single glove in the store.

Katie and I treated ourselves to a great last supper on the night before she left. And everything that might have been present at the real Last Supper was there--except for the men and the imminent betrayal. We raised our glasses high and shouted an enthusiastic *cin-cin* (cheen-cheen) as we recalled the last 14 days and nights. The *Hofbräuhaus*, train compartments, card-playing, shopping, *gelati*, Uffizi Gallery, Vatican City, Colosseum, Grand Canal, *Piazza della Signoria* and people we had "met" along the way. David-in-the-flesh

(AKA James), David-in-the-marble, Antonio--the *gondoliere*, Michelangelo--the artist, Michelangelo--the bottle, the post office employees and Khaddaffi, to name a few. It felt as if we had lived a lifetime in those two weeks but, at the same time, I could still see Katie's face radiating through the glass near the Munich luggage carousel as if she had arrived one hour earlier. How is it that time can be accounted for hour-by-hour and then seem as if it has passed in a handful of seconds? The simultaneous experiencing of absolutely opposite sensations. Two things in one tiny space. Crowding each other and battling for control. Each winning out. Each losing.

Except time had passed. And a different Katie sat before me then. When she raised her glass to one more toast and asked me to do the same.

"Let's toast our grandparents. To Antonio and Beatrice. To Nonno and Nonna," she said.

"To Nonno and Nonna. For starting it all. And for ending with us."

And we clinked glasses and I saw the face unfold that proved she was my sister. To anyone who had eyes.

"How can people possibly say we don't look alike, Katie?"

"You think we do?"

"Yes. I was just staring at myself just then."

"So the *gondoliere* was wrong."

"He couldn't have been more wrong." And she smiled. And I smiled. Knowing she had said more than she knew how to say just then. And knowing she knew more of me than she knew before our journey started. It made my difference seem far less lonely. And me feel far less alone.

We barely slept that night. I could tell. Even the sleeping pills that we had purchased in Germany (my sister bought them using body language, first faking sleeping and pretending to snore until the salesclerk walked out from the back with two enormous down pillows) were of no use. We just rolled over and over all night. Neither one willing to say what the cause was. For me, despite the taxi driver's reassuring words, I was having a terrorism relapse. I knew I would be happy when I heard she was back and safe. To Logan Airport and parts of the North End before she was safely ensconced in her own kitchen and living room and on her own down pillow. I was sure Katie was thinking the same thing. But I didn't bring it up. We had an amazing capacity to fuel each other's fires until the entire neighborhood was engulfed. I just let it burn inside of me instead.

I was alone in the hotel room when the phone rang. Lying in my bed. Staring at paint chips on the ceiling and seeing if they formed any interesting shapes. Like clouds in the sky. Instead, I could only picture my sister at Leonardo da Vinci Airport in Rome. Watching her check in. Watching her flash her passport. Watching her walk through security. Watching my security fade away as her tight, pink sweatshirt rounded the corner with one arm raised in a wave and the other raised to her lips. Blowing me kisses good-bye. And then wiping her eyes dry. I had to embrace the reality that the comfort that comes from being with her would have to be replaced, for the time being, with something else. That would fall short. Fall down. Fall apart. I picked up the phone to hear my sister's voice confirm her safe arrival. Before she moved to another matter.

"Jo, ask me the question you asked me when the train first lurched over the Italian border."

"Which question?"

"You know, the one about if I felt a connection to our heritage."

"OK, I'm asking."

"No. Ask. Really."

"OK. Do you feel some kind of a connection to our grandparents now that we're into their homeland?"

And then there was silence. "Katie? Are you there?"

"I just wanted a second chance to answer it right. When you get home, I will answer it right. I love you."

Soon after our connection was canceled, I picked up the phone to let the kitchen know I'd be coming down for an omelet and then smiled when I thought I saw my sister's face in the paint chips above my head. Smiling back at me. And waiting for a bite of my food. At that very moment, a chip released its clutch and fell toward the floor. I moved to save it--with my arm outstretched, hand opened to my sister's smile. And welcomed words.

Chapter Nineteen
Isabella Is A Bella

Despite the fact that I was in Rome, I didn't want to do much for the two days after my sister left and before Dana and Elsie arrived. It should have been hard to justify my whiling away the hours on the rooftop terrace of my *pensione* while the former center of civilization beat right outside my window--just watching a small, black & white TV and memorizing the catchy, Italian jingles for soap detergent, soaking up the rays, writing postcards, updating my journal, reading and being cooked for and waited on by a grandfatherly, 80 year-old man with no hair, no teeth and no cooking know-how outside of the omelet and roasted potatoes realm--but it wasn't hard at all. It was just what I wanted to do. So, I did.

I called Max while whiling and Marco, too. It was great to hear Max's voice. His halting sentences. His emphatic pauses. His high-pitched and rapid-paced speech. He was already well into his internship in the family business and enjoyed his first round with some of the Italian designers. *In Italiano.* Ever hopeful that he had nailed the subtleties of the language and not committed a stylistic faux-pas. Like not saying "I am hot" when he meant to say "It is hot."

Marco was into *his* family business, as well. And, it turned out, so was I. His one and only sister was visiting from Bologna, home to the world's oldest and one of Italy's most prestigious universities. Marco was quick to let people know his sister studied there. He was proud of her and protective of her as were, Marco said, all of his brothers. "It is what we do." Yes. I was aware of that.

When I called, he was just getting ready to ask his sister what she thought of my having gone to Germany with a male friend. I was thrilled to learn he was polling his entire family, if necessary, to make a point about "what it is they do" and "what it is I should do." I certainly did not need the entire island of Sicily buzzing about the

American who shunned one of its natives. All for the sake of some jollies at the *Hofbräuhaus*--a few steins of beer, a biting cigar and a Bavarian jig. My concern was reminiscent of my own mother's regarding our *gondoliere* in Venezia, the one whom she thought would spread the false rumor from Venice, Italy to Boston, Massachusetts that my sister and I were products of different fathers. I had inherited far more than my mother's looks. I was a dead ringer for some of her less tangible inclinations. Like paranoia.

In any event, I was finding that topic of Marco's more and more tedious. He was beginning to brandish a disturbing form of control that I just couldn't deal with. So I found a reason to end the conversation. Nicely. But firmly. That, Marco, is what we do. And then I found a tub. That is also what we do.

Later that night, after a long, hot bath and another omelet with roasted potatoes, I called Dana and Elsie. I knew they'd be back that day but I just didn't know when. Elsie picked up the phone on the first ring. *"Pronto"* with an east coast accent. They had just walked into their apartment after a two-week tour around Naples, but mostly Sicily, and were filled with stories and images and excitement. And were ready to drop their luggage and meet me at the left-most pillar of The Pantheon in five minutes. But we agreed, instead, that it would be better to get together the next day. Outside of Rome. Outside of the hustle and bustle.

We settled on Frascati, home to delicious Frascati wine and to a less cosmopolitan, more homegrown way of being, just 13 miles away from the capital. I'd go by late-morning train, and they'd sleep a bit and come by taxi later on. Dana recommended we meet at two o'clock, at the latest, in the small bar just up the street and off the tiny, steep steps that lead away from the train station. We hung up amidst squeals of anticipation.

The rickety, old coot train to Frascati looked as if it might have been the first train ever off the assembly line. Relegated to a 26-mile round-trip and nothing else. Yet another example of Italy's commitment to the elderly. Like the little old man at the Chianti country winery on Max's and my first road trip. With the thin lips and pencil-thin mustache and tiny scar right under his long, straight, Roman nose. And the eyes that had witnessed a lifetime of hard work and hard play. He could still pour a glass. He could still teach passersby how to swirl, smell and chew his lifetime focus. There was still room for aging well, and Italy was determined to honor that.

I had worked at a few schools back home that were committed to the same. There was the elderly gentleman in New Jersey who could be seen mowing the gravel driveway every morning. Or the one in New York who used to water the ivy on days when it poured or water the windows on days when it didn't. And then there was the sweet, elderly man in Massachusetts who carried in the mail each day and then sat in the lobby chairs, stroking his beard and regaling teachers and students with witty jokes and names like "Sweetie."

As the years have rolled by and my parents have started mowing some driveways and watering rain-soaked ivy, I appreciate even more anyone who gives them a reason to get up. To keep busy. To do their version of the 26-mile round trip.

When we pulled into Frascati, I grabbed my knapsack, which held my journal, a Frascati pamphlet from the *pensione*, that day's newspaper, my Boston Red Sox cap and a camera and headed out the station doors toward the village center. As soon as I stepped out, my peripheral vision picked up two images that stopped me in my tracks. To my right, a ragged, filthy, scrawny, old dog making the moves on a telephone pole. And to my left, his look-alike mounting the side of a bored, unfocused, "OK-But-Just-Pull-My-Nightgown-Down-When-You're-Done" female. It reminded me of a ritual I observed on a rooftop terrace of a Florence hotel. Two pigeons. The larger one chasing the smaller one. The smaller one flittering away, flapping her wings, hiding under a fallen napkin or a tablecloth, beating him off with her beak. It went on throughout my first hard roll, my second hard roll and the four crackers that were wrapped in cellophane. It went on throughout my fresh orange juice, my *latte* and an enormous glass of water. And as I rambled off the terrace, with a folded newspaper under my arm, a wrapped croissant in my hand and visions of touring on my brain, it still went on and made me wonder about mating ritual nuances. Was it a mutually understood game of flirtation? Was she playing hard to get? Or was she truly trying to get away? Trying to jam his pigeon toes under his pigeon door and go back to her pigeon home to be under someone else's pigeon wing?

Do even boy pigeons think that "no means yes?" A wing-snap and a beak-jab are misread as foreplay?

Pigeons. Dogs. Women. Men. Telephone poles. And Marco. Why was touching a body more important than touching a soul? Where were his rules before? Why then? Why ever? Why didn't I have wings, too?

I just shook my head and walked along. Smirking somewhat. Wondering if there were some kind of global genetic mutation hidden in the x-y chromosomal connection but absent in the x-x bond. I was grateful for consonants that could never be used as vowels.

When I glanced back one more time, the male dogs were wrestling each other and pausing only to sniff or lick. The female had moved up next to me. Headed up the steps. Looking back and forth. Moseying. I knew she had some things to say. And it seemed that each of us needed someone to listen.

It was uncharacteristically hot for April. I was dressed in crushed gray, cotton pants that I had bought the one time I had ventured out of the *pensione* over the last day-and-a-half. They had a drawstring waist and little cuffs that gently gripped my ankles. And I was wearing a black, short-sleeved t-shirt which started with the sleeves hanging just above my elbows but were then rolled up over my shoulders. Like James Dean without the cigarette pack.

It was one of those days that I showered, exited the tub completely refreshed and then instantly found myself dripping, dripping, dripping tiny droplets of clean water invaded by 10,000 salty beads. It was attractive. I wanted to coat my entire self in Unscented Secret Deodorant to form a perspiration quarantine. Instead, I was a walking sweatbox.

An umbrella in an outdoor cafè just beyond the bar where I'd meet Dana and Elsie beckoned me to its shade. I ordered a liter of cold *acqua naturale* and a *pesto* pizza (a choice that reflected the marriage of two of my favorite foods), and I emptied the first bottle of water while I read back through my journal. Reliving parts of the trip to Italy.

Journal rereading is a very embarrassing exercise--pages riddled with what seemed (at the time) to be provocative, earth-shattering observations but weeks later were shallow, overt signs of an immense immaturity. And dinkdom. And that was only weeks later. What would I think when I read it years later? When I was well into my forties and fifties? *"Within days, thank-yous quickly turned to grazies."* Or, *"I ran into two Americans from California and spent the afternoon with them. They were nice but both a little weird. She struck me as a typical like-wicked-into-nature-granola-munching-west-coaster."* Lord.

It made me want to secure my journal with a password or an explosive device that could be ignited only by someone else's fingerprints. Would Category Four (thinks cool, not cool) be stamped on my forehead if others' eyes were privy to my writings? Perhaps I should just direct them to the following, "If read against my will or without my knowledge, shoot me, cremate me and scatter me with the singed, humiliating pages of my journal-life. Many thanks."

I ordered another bottle of water while I waited for my pizza and moved my seat to a different corner of the outdoor terrace. A man at the table next door had been sucking on his teeth to beat the band, and his cohort felt the need to follow suit. They were out of sight. But still not out of ear. I was afraid they had already ruined my lunch.

I returned to my journal but focused, instead, on the entry about Dana, Elsie and John and the weekend we had spent together in Rome. Those entries still rang true. I thought they'd probably stand the test of time. Wouldn't get singed in the cremation.

Just then, a little red-haired girl with blue eyes and a vaguely freckled nose brought the *pesto* pizza to my table. She was dwarfed by the white apron whose darts rested on her waist and whose hem screeched to a halt just shy of the ground. Her arms were so skinny I feared they'd snap with the weight of the large pizza and the thick green sauce that was calling my name. Her name was Isabella, she said. "My *padre* made the pizza," she insisted, with her chicken arms folded over her flat chest, "but my *mamma* owns the shop."

The pizza had been cooked over a raging, open fire in the back of the restaurant. On most days, that would have seemed so romantic, so enticing, but on the sweltering, muggy, too-soon-for-summer-weather day, it made me feel bad for her dad. But not for me. I used a fork and sharp knife to cut through the thin, perfectly browned crust and bring a triangular slice of *pesto* and melted cheese ecstasy through my lips. Resting the tiny taste on my tongue and letting it melt there. And it did. Right through my tongue, my mouth and the inside of my cheeks. Right into my soul.

Soul food.

I grabbed Isabella's hand and squeezed her fingers from side-to-side. "This," I said, "is the most delicious pizza I have ever had in my life." With that, Isabella slid her hand out from under mine and drew her pointer finger into the mode that earned it its name, landing it just two inches from my face. "OK," she said, smacking her lips loudly, "my *padre* made the pizza, but my *mamma* made the sauce." Isabella--my first Italian feminist.

The little girl hovered over my table as I cut triangle after triangle, as I continued to savor every morsel of what was one of the most delicious combinations of textures and spices and aromas that had ever been assembled for my perusal. I broke away only to listen to Isabella's summary of her life. She was 10. She liked school. Her favorite subject was math. She had one younger brother. He was five. His name was Stefano. Her grandfather also worked in the restaurant, and she had no interest in learning English or in going to The United States. "No," she said emphatically, "I prefer French and France." She was talking 10 kilometers a minute.

At the moment when there was more pizza in my stomach than there was on my plate, I put my fork down, devoted all of my attention to her and stalled for time, delaying the inevitable look of emptiness on my flour-dusted ceramic plate. "And," she said, "I also like to dance. Do you want to see?" she asked with a tilted head. And, without waiting for a response, she took to the street with a performance in mind.

"This is a little dance we do outside my house. We don't do it exactly right, but, you put your hands on your waist like this, and everyone gets in a circle and sings,

"Tacco, punto, tacco, punto, uno, due, tre, tre, tre.

"Tacco, punto, tacco, punto, uno, due, tre, tre, tre.

"Each time you say *tacco*, you kick your foot out to its heel. Each time you say *punto*, you bend your leg onto the toe. Each time you say *uno, due, tre, tre, tre,* you slide to the sides, and slap your hands on your knees like this. And then you sing *la, la, la.* Like this. See? Like this."

It was a moment to behold. The free-spiritedness of a human being without a care in the world. Without one molecule of inhibition or self-consciousness. Without any sense that the eyes of her tiny life were turning to rest on her boundless energy and spinning arms and legs.

She wasn't long into her routine of kicking and pointing and sliding before her mother was on the street, yanking on her arm and apologizing to me for the disturbance--so profoundly embarrassed by what she perceived to be her daughter's intrusive behavior. Just as she leaned forward to pull her off the street and back into the restaurant, I convinced her that it was in no way intrusive by jumping up and taking Isabella's hands in mine, to create a *Tacco-Punto* of our own that crossed age and partisan and dexterity lines.

So there we were, an American klutz, half-loaded up with *pesto* pizza and a liter and a half of water, and an Italian prancer, fully-loaded up with a zest for life and a liter and a half of feistiness, *taccoing* and *puntoing* our way around the streets of Frascati. Bouncing. *La-la-la-ing* Knee-slapping. And not thinking about anything at all. Just throwing our heads back in quarter-howls, quarter-laughs, half-humiliating thrusts. Holding hands and pointing and heeling around in circles. And circles. And circles.

Such a great feeling.

Such a profound return to the wonder of youth.

Such an unabashed spectacle of human idiocy.

Such a delightful exhibition of utter happiness.

Utter, utter happiness.

Under the arm of the Italian skies and the Italian people. Big and small. Old and young. Laughing. And laughing. And dancing through life.

When the last crumb had been expunged from my *pesto* pizza plate and Isabella made her appearance with the check, I paid up and thanked Isabella, her mum *and* her dad (even though he didn't make the sauce and didn't own the pizzeria) for a lunch to remember. Isabella whispered something to her mother and when she nodded, Isabella stepped forward with her head bent down a bit to let play out something they must have planned just moments earlier. I bent at the knees so that my eyes would meet hers on the same level when she finally looked up.

"I have something for you. Do you want it?" she said.

"Of course I want it. If it's from you."

"It's just a picture of me. My school picture. I wrote my address on the back. Do you still want it?"

"More than ever now that I know what it is. And I have something for you, too. Do you want it?"

"Yes, please."

With that, I reached into my knapsack and pulled out the only thing I had tucked inside that was of any personal value at all. My Red Sox baseball cap. Mine for 15 years. I had bought it on the day of my first-ever professional baseball game when I sat along the third base side with my best friend, the one with the not-so-hairy arms, and just missed catching a Carl Yastrzemski foul ball that grazed the fingers of my right hand. If I had taken off the cap and tried to catch the ball with that instead, I'd have a great souvenir in my wooden footlocker back home. Now, I just have the memory of the thrill of almost.

"I'd like you to have this, Isabella. I got this when I was about your age. I hope you change your mind and study English one day--because if you do, then maybe you can come see me in The United States, in Boston, and go to a game with me."

I don't think she knew what Boston was or what game I was talking about or if she ever had any intention of coming to The United States or even could--but it didn't seem to matter. She gracefully took the hat from my hand, placed it on her head and stepped forward to wrap both her skinny little arms around my neck. As she squeezed and squeezed and squeezed, I wrapped both my arms around her body. A body that was so tiny I could touch the fingers of both hands to the elbows of my opposite arms as she rested inside with room to spare. We rocked back and forth and back and forth until we started to pull away. And then, out-of-the-blue, she planted the sweetest little kiss on my right cheek and then on my left cheek and then on my right cheek and turned, before we could look at each other again, before I had a chance to kiss her back, and skipped away. With one hand out to the side and the other holding the too-big hat on top of her head with the plastic adjustable strap flapping from side-to-side.

When I stood up, tears were streaming down my face. And I didn't have any idea why. Maybe it had something to do with wishing I were 10 years-old again.

And free.

To dance. To swing. To twirl about without a care in the world.

To fly away.

La-la-la-la-la-la-la-la.

Chapter Twenty
Truth, Dare, Consequences
Promises But No Repeats

Dana and Elsie were waiting for me with big hugs, some modified dancing and some louder-than-average hoots. They looked great. Not the least bit destylized by the clothes-plastering humidity that was hovering outside. And settling in for a few days. Renting some space. Maybe they were wearing a Secret Deodorant shield. Or maybe they were just cool.

The bar was relatively small and was littered with wobbly, wooden tables for four, a well-stocked assortment of alcohol, a great-looking, spankingly clean *cappuccino-espresso* machine and dozens of hanging plants. It was also decorated with Italians. Only Italians. I didn't expect to hear any *Volare* or see any sequin-cummerbunded accordionists with bad hair and saccharin smiles either. I actually hadn't heard one word of English since I had boarded the train in Rome. It was wonderful. As if it didn't exist. Until the three of us opened our mouths and invaded the purity of the scene.

We ordered drinks and grabbed a table in the front room, in the corner, where we were wedged between two walls that were covered with the names and sketches of those who had stopped by before we did. We boxed off one small area, and the three of us wrote our names in crayon. *Dana, Elsie e Jo--Frascati, Italia.* I resisted any temptation to sketch a memory. The adult education fiasco still loomed largely in my head.

Some chitchat followed that spanned the spectra of insanity and sarcasm--from Elsie mistakenly buying birth control pills in Sicily for the treatment of her headache to Dana's shot at the Italian highways to my relationship with Marco. We got caught on that for awhile as Elsie and I worked on trying to understand men while Dana worked on trying to defend them.

"It started off great," I said. "Nice. Patient. Thoughtful. Different. But, he got angry when I went off to Germany with a friend."

"Was it a guy friend?" Dana asked.

So I did my best to explain the platonic nature of Max's and my relationship. About the newness of Marco's and my relationship. And my concerns about his lack of trust and his desire to control.

"I'm not sure that he didn't trust you," Dana said. "He didn't trust Max."

"You know guys don't feel anything until they have sex," Elsie said. "And women don't want to have sex until they feel something."

"Pigeons," I said. "And telephone poles. And dogs."

The confusion on Dana's face was profound. But Elsie was bobbing her head and was off and running. Talking about a TV show about the mating rituals of koalas. A male approach met by a squealing, spitting, scratching female. So the male tries again and mounts one who doesn't run away. And calls it a day 10 seconds later after being hissed by the female who has already had enough. Then she mentioned the dogs down by the telephone pole. Having sex with a hole in some wood.

"I seriously think more men would step to the altar if that were waiting for them at the end in a nice, white dress." Elsie's and my explosive laughter interrupted the otherwise docile scene, and if Dana hadn't stepped in to squelch the direction, we could have upped the ante until the sarcasm was beyond stupid, until we had become the exact people that I can't stand in restaurants. Those who think the entire world is enjoying their experience. Cool when *you're* doing it. Not the least bit cool when *others* are.

It's the same force that drives couples to kiss each other in public while the uncoupled friend, trapped across the table, only inches from the exchange of hormones, doesn't know where to rest her or his eyes--inspecting pleats, reading signs, visiting the bathroom, moving food around the plate, folding napkins--even after they, said couple, have themselves suffered as pleat-inspecting, sign-reading, head-scratching, food-moving, napkin-folding specimens. It should have been Commandment 11. There Shalt Be No Public Displays Of Affection--Particularly, But Not Exclusively, When There Is An Odd Number Of People Assembled. Amen.

In any event, we knew it was fair to redirect the conversation given the 2 to 1 odds. So we did.

"OK, tell me all about Sicily," I begged while a round of drinks made it to our table.

"Great," said Elsie. "Absolutely great. Your mother and you are going to have an incredible time. The people are friendly. You won't hear a word of English. It's easy to get around the island. And the countryside is beautiful. Especially the interior."

And so they started--touring me around the island from city to city, from village to village, from temple to temple. I was like an excited little kid in bed, all tucked in with fresh sheets, tightly wrapped over my body, holding me safe as the story unfolded. I learned about Geraci Siculo, the tiny town in Sicily's interior that sported one *trattoria* in the front room of someone's house. There they got an *antipasto*, bread, a main meal, dessert, wine and an after-dinner drink for the cost of three subway tickets back home and then retired to the main *piazza* for mingling near the fountain, spontaneous after-dinner music and seasonal fruits that were sold along the side streets. I heard about Sperlinga, the town where some citizens still adhere to the centuries-old custom of living in caves. Carved right into the natural stone and separated from the more modern conveniences by antiquated wooden doors and hanging woolen strands. And there was Agrigento, with its Valley of The Temples, a long, long stretch of some of the most remarkably preserved Greek sites in the world. Temples whose other-worldliness was reinforced by the hot African winds that danced inside the sacred places. And Noto, the baroque city near the water that screamed of a more opulent time, where fashion outdid practicality and humans breathed in the shadows of its splendor. And Erice, the town that rested precariously on top of the world, smiling down on earth from the distant skies. Replete with sloping cobblestoned streets, a cathedral that held heavenly court on the city's edge and a people that bore the kind of confidence and contentment that only those who exist that way from day-to-day could possibly exude.

I listened without interruption as they told their tale--a tale I had been waiting to hear for as long as I could remember. I didn't want it to end. And, of course, it wouldn't have to. Since I'd be there soon enough. With my mother. To meet our relatives. My mother's and my cousins. And an aunt. The wife of my grandfather's brother.

So then they settled in, under the sheets, to listen to the story I loved to tell. From start to finish. About my grandfather--all of the familiar ones and others I had yet to tell. Including his refusal to master the nuances of the English language or to speak it without sticking a thick Italian accent on top. Pronouncing every syllable of English the way he pronounced every syllable of Italian. People was pee-aw-pa-lee. Right was ree-ga-ta. And the abbreviated French-fried potatoes was fr-fr-pots. He was strict about the men my mother could date and would sit up in the front room until she got home. Inventing adorable ways of learning the details of the evening--despite the unwavering consistency of my mother's response. "If you think I was doing what I think you think I was doing, I wasn't."

He bought his son a fancy convertible when he got his advanced degree. And sent his daughters to college during a time when most were passed by. And loved to rock his grandchildren. And loved to hold their hands. He was affectionate. And smart. And courageous. And his heart gave out too early. And he died too young. Under an oxygen tent. With his family unwilling to let go of the man whose heart would beat forever.

Dana and Elsie handled the story as I knew they would. As Max did. And as Katie did--once she learned I had a story to tell. I knew they had their nevers. And I had mine. So we mourned the presence of those nevers and respected the silence that followed.

In time, we ordered another round of drinks, and the conversation took an interesting shift away from never and toward sometimes or always. The differences between males and females, the idea of what our society values, control and power and a little bit, at my initiation, about the connection between all of that and race. And then we'd circle back. To power again. And gender. And first impressions. And first assumptions.

We were fed by our sharing of personal experiences--such as the time I was only one woman with four men in a room going over the credentials of a "questionable" female teaching candidate who spent half of her interview touching the arms of the male interviewers and not making eye contact with the females. When I told them she was flirting her way into a job and suggested that they might even be somewhat blinded by the advances, they said I was "overacting" or being "too sensitive" or possibly even "threatened." They were completely oblivious to the power they held in the imbalance. Numbers, alone. Never mind anything else.

Dana and Elsie, with caution, also shared some stories. Some of which were old to me, some of which were new to me. I didn't know which won the battle. My sadness over my ignorance or my happiness that at least a tiny fraction of a line was being moved. Or faded. I wanted to live up to the moment. I wanted to prove to them *and* to myself that I had learned something. That the kick from Italy's boot had not been in vain.

During one rare lull in the conversation, we glanced at our watches and only then realized that hours had slipped by. Our words had moved in and out and in and out. Like tracing the fingers of the right hand with the left. Out to the extremities. In toward safety. As my eyes scanned the walls of the bar, I stepped out toward one last precipice as I thought about my own first impressions and assumptions. Dana. Elsie. Max. James. And I watched the last drips of red wine form sugary legs on the inside of my glass and wondered if my face were the same color as the wine that lingered within.

When we left the restaurant, one-half day after we had first entered it and changed by the words that had passed over our tongues and into our ears, I boarded the train with my eyes wide open. And I watched. I watched the watchers. I watched the watchers watch us. From our view. Our side. First impressions and assumptions.

In the 13 miles of silence back to Rome, I turned to the land and watched Italy pass outside of me. And inside of me--as I saw a picture of myself. A picture I recognized in the window's reflection. *To define myself. To know my important pieces. And to know the ones that overlapped with others and the ones that were completely different. And to notice the differences. And wonder--about other people's personal journeys and personal attacks. And the spectra of respect and assumption. Of love and abuse.* And then I focused on a distant cypress tree. While the Italian language sang all around me. And the wine's flavors still visited my mouth and nose. As my feet vibrated against the floor of the rickety train. And all five senses ran full throttle. Alive. Awake. Finally, I thought, the words and the music were starting to come together. To form a song. A song that maybe I could dance to one day. Maybe.

And Italy passed outside of me. And inside of me. As the train that had lived a full life carried us forward. But with the gentleness that comes with age. And experience. And wisdom. And respect.

Chapter Twenty-One
You Can Run But You Cannot Hide

I stayed in Rome with Dana and Elsie for about a week. More lingering conversations into uncharted territory, strolls through the Roman streets, picnics along Tevere, water splashes from the fountains in *Piazza Navona* and forced-intimacy on crowded bus rides brought us closer and closer, making it very hard to say good-bye when I finally convinced myself that I had to get back to Perugia, to stop running away from what I had to face. It helped to know that I'd see them in Boston. In the North End. On Columbus Weekend. At a restaurant on Causeway Street that has the best *focaccia* around. We exchanged our real home phone numbers, and I was off to Perugia to spend some heartbeats around town before my mother would arrive in a few weeks for our lifetime adventure.

The train ride to Perugia gave me a chance to plan a strategy for returning to a city and to people that were shifting in front of my eyes. The innocent parts of the earliest Perugian days were changing. Mastery of possessive pronouns had turned to worries about relationships. The past, present and future tenses took a back seat to life decisions about friendships and to going home. Home home. Not Perugia home.

I decided that I'd start with John and then work up to Marco, so I was relieved when he answered the door to his apartment the day after I returned. He invited me in for tea and talked about the great time he had had in New Zealand. People had commented on his mahogany-handled umbrella and his unnecessary weight loss, unaware that the former was partially responsible for the latter. But I was also peeved when he answered the door to his apartment the day after I returned. If I had known how soon he was going to be back, I would have had him buy his own damn jeans, particularly when he shrugged off the post office debacle, giving it minimal attention, and particularly when I figured out that he and his jeans crossed each other in international air space. "It was worth it," he said. "But, John, I spewed massive obscenities in the middle of a crowded government building." "But imagine how good I will look wearing them." His sartorial splendor for my international incident. His selfishness for everything else.

At times I wondered why I even bothered to hold on. Maybe it was for moments that we had when we traveled, such as the summit hike in Todi, the fishing expedition near Lake Trasimeno and the Etruscan burial sites in Orvieto. Or maybe it was for our teas. Or *tortellini*. Or wine. But the good was always invaded by the difficult and the insensitive. It was relentless and, at times, misguided. And it was implemented with great regularity. I don't know why it remained so unexpected when it was so common.

"How can you expect me to respect your culture, Jo, when you issue economic sanctions against my home country for our stance on nuclear power? Cutting off our bloodline because of an ideological difference." "And so you want us completely out of your country's business?" "Yes." "Completely out." "Yes." "And what would you expect us to do if your borders came under siege?" And without hesitation. "Well, of course, I'd expect America to defend us." "And you don't see the hypocrisy there? You ask me how I can expect you to respect my culture? How can you expect me to respect you?"

When we were together in bed that famous weekend in Rome and found each other staring at each other, glazed and exhausted and hurt, we hugged, and I cried, and I thought we'd talk later. But we never did. And we never would. And we wouldn't speak again once we left Perugia. I had run out of energy just when I realized that his energy would forever be higher than mine.

So I turned to Marco when I realized that the anticipated pain of that conversation was, at least, more palatable than the pain of my conversations with John. At least I was sure that relationship was based on some degree of genuine affection, whereas John's and my relationship was built on some degree of something else. There was a coolness to Marco's tone when he picked up the phone. But he couldn't completely disguise his excitement. Nor could I disguise mine. It left me confused about my original intention--to call it off-- since I was, at that moment, able to picture the face that went along with the voice.

We decided to meet at the underground bar in the center of Perugia. I didn't want to see him at his apartment, for a lot of reasons, and thought that the bar might give me an advantage. Since Max and I had been there about 20 times, it was practically a second home to me. Not as neutral a place as Marco might have hoped for-- if he had any clue at all.

I got there first and always enjoyed the steady descent to the main seating area. Narrow and uneven brick steps with brick walls on either side. Very dark, alluring lighting. Not the least bit scary. Just calming. At the bottom, there was a turn to the right and magic. Wonderful brick and tiled floors, long, wooden tables and benches that forced strangers to sit next to each other, that instigated the crossing of boundaries, painting a leisurely United Nations, absent Kruschev and the pounding shoe. There were also a long, richly dark, wooden bar with brass-polished beer taps, stainless steel-polished coffee-makers and silver necklaces on the hard liquor bottles that spelled their names. The best of all, though, for me, were the brick arches that spanned from side-to-side, up and over and down and up again, in intricate patterns of curves and perfectly placed blocks. The Etruscans invented the arch, and they would be proud to see how Perugia, a former Etruscan stronghold, perfected it in that bar.

Primo, the bartender, waved as I rounded the corner and finally brought my eyes down from the ceiling to the bar. His genuine, friendly, lively way was enough to make people fall in love with him on the first meeting. I always felt that he and his name were a dead match. He was the king of Category One. Primo. He was cool and ever-so-coolly knew it.

I sat at one of the stools and ordered a glass of white wine, the same as the first drink I had ever ordered there, the night I had come with eight Germans and one Greek and was driven to insanity within minutes by jerking English and inane Italian. So, I thought I'd order it again. Come full circle, given the increasingly nagging suspicion that that would be my last visit and that I was slowly but surely saying good-bye to my home away from home.

With one sip left in the first glass of wine, Marco surprised me by coming up from behind and touching his right hand to my right arm and his lips to my left cheek. Primo immediately turned his attention to someone else as shivers ran from the top of my head down my spine to my knees. He knew it would not be a particularly light and easy conversation--even if the initial greeting was all of that.

I stood and turned to him for a soulful, longer hug and with our bodies pressed firmly up against each other, I could count and feel each of the days we had been apart. It had been well over a month, he whispered, as we moved away from the bar to one of the two tables that was nestled right into the wall. As statues are often nestled. The space was so small that our knees rested up against each other under the table, as did our feet and hands.

Marco was so smooth. And so handsome. And he had eyes that were so dark and so bottomless that they immediately rendered worthless any advantage I thought I had by choosing that familiar bar. His eyes. His lips. His cheeks where a faint beard shone through. His eyebrows that moved to their own beat when he spoke. Sometimes coming together to form an upside-down V. Sometimes working independently to form letters with more curves. They were all weapons. I wasn't armed enough.

The first part of the conversation was safe. Stilted. Almost formal. I talked about Germany (but not Max), travels with my sister, her having met James and his situation in the Navy. And then I talked about Dana and Elsie and their trip to Sicily. And I talked about my mother's and my trip there, only three weeks away. He talked about school and exams and his visit with his sister. He was brief. He had spent a quieter month than I had. Again, it was always easier to leave than to be left, which was made clear when two minutes into his summary he asked about us. It started way too quickly.

"So, what's going on? Have you changed your mind about me? I thought that something was happening with us. Was I wrong?"

"No. You weren't wrong."

"The farmhouse. Dinners at my apartment. Walks. Talks. Dreams about Sicily. Did I do something wrong?"

There was a sad and frantic look on his face that made me want to lie. To fix everything. No, you didn't start to push. No, you didn't start to possess. No, you didn't brandish a version of control that was reminiscent of Abdul's.

"At first, no."

"So, what? Was it Germany? And my reaction to that guy?"

"Max. Yes. That was partly it."

"Well can we talk about it? Will you talk about it?"

"I just wanted to travel with him. He's a good friend."

"It just doesn't look good. To me, my friends, my family." And then he looked straight into my eyes and reached under the table to place his hand on my hand, as my half-bitten fingernails tried to dig a trench in my kneecaps. And he looked away. And shook his head from side-to-side as he spoke quietly and massaged the tension out of my fingers.

And then let go.

"You don't have any idea how much you mean to me," he said. With his face resting in both of his hands and the heels of his palms wedged into the hollows of those eyes, he talked about love. And in love. And about never having felt that way before. About my smile. And how we talk. And laugh. And how my small hands fit so perfectly into his. About Sicily. And about wanting to be with me.

And then, as emotionally and passionately and abruptly as he had just tossed his life onto the table, he stood up. And waited for me to respond. And I couldn't. I stared up at him as his eyes welled up. And mine welled up. So he had to turn, slowly, and step out of the space that was ideal for statues. Statues of my variety. And then he turned back and leaned down and brought his warm, smooth lips onto my own. And kissed me with a kind of soul and passion and warmth that was new. And deep. And different.

And then he left. Wiping his face with my favorite flannel shirt. Disappearing into the stairwell that, just minutes before, had seemed so safe and calming, despite the imperfections in the brick, but then seemed so dark and scary. And cold.

I sat at the table for two more hours. Wishing I had longer fingernails to carve grooves in the wood. Wishing I hadn't already emptied a whole bottle of wine. Wishing I could understand what had just happened. Wishing I always felt what Marco felt and not just sometimes felt what Marco felt.

I had lived most of my adult life thinking I would give anything to hear those words. To have someone hold me up as the object of that kind of unconditional love. But when it happened, so honestly, so openly, so unabashedly, in that romantic bar in that romantic city in that romantic country with those romantic eyes, it scared me. A lot. I was worried that I wasn't worth it. And that he would find that out. And that it would kill him. And me.

I waited at home for a few days. Watching April turn into May. And then I went to his house. When I got there and stepped inside the apartment foyer, his landlady emerged from her door and offered the following. Abruptly. And coolly.

"È in Sicilia, per una settimana." (He's in Sicily, for a week.)

Albert Einstein once said at the time of his proposal of the Theory of Relativity in 1929, "If my Theory of Relativity is proven correct, Germany will claim me as a German and France will declare that I am a citizen of the world. Should my theory prove untrue, France will say that I am a German and Germany will declare that I am a Jew."[1]

In her eyes, I had gone, in an instant, from *una paesana*, the affable, lovable, transplanted Italian, to one big, mean, ignorant, unappreciative Yankee. I told her I'd be back. And I smiled.

She did not.

So I waited. Some auditing of the upper level Italian courses. A phone call to Max. Letter-writing. Journal-writing. Some packing. Some loneliness. Marco was at his kitchen table studying when I walked in seven days later. When he saw who it was, he shot up from his chair, pushing it back against the kitchen cabinets, and brought one tiny fingertip to my face and then two fingers and then one hand.

"Well?" he said, as we rocked back and forth in each other's arms, as he wiped the salty tears off of my cheeks. I didn't know. I didn't know why I couldn't throw myself at him so fully. So I asked if we could just stay like that for awhile. Which we did. For several days.

Until it was my turn to go to Sicily.

1 (Sorbonne, Early December, 1929. New York Times, February 16, 1930.)

Chapter Twenty-Two
Crusty Gusts And Lusty Busts

I was greatly relieved to be moving away from something. Relieved to be moving toward something. Relieved that Alitalia Airlines had brought my mother to me safely. We had thought about canceling her trip due to lingering warnings to Americans traveling abroad. Threats still coming at us in our foreign travels. We tossed the dice and opted for broadening our boundaries instead of narrowing them. And hoped that the dice weren't loaded.

She rounded the corner at Leonardo da Vinci Airport in Rome with her luggage in her hand and as big a smile as I ever remember. She was dressed adorably. Worn jeans. Black Umbro sneakers with white socks. And a cotton shirt which would hang on most people just down below the waist but hung on my increasingly shrinking mother just down below her down below, as she called it. Her hair had been smooshed from the long flight, a flight which was, inevitably, replete with tiny seats, recycled air, anywhere from two to five squirming, sniffling infants, a bulbous-nosed man who was drinking too much, a movie she couldn't see because of the bouffant in front of her, and a next-door neighbor whose elbow found its way into the middle of her ribcage, way over his armrest, way over his well-defined boundary-marker. So, the smooshed hair was understandable. And, in her case, endearing.

I ran to her and was already crying. I hadn't seen her since January. Four months and a lifetime. But then, my mother, my Italian-rooted mother, had her feet planted in Rome, Italy, and was separated from me by only meters instead of oceans, and then millimeters, as I wrapped my arms around her little body and felt her incredibly soft cheeks up against my own. We could feel each other shaking inside the embrace. When we pulled away, I placed my hands on the sides of her face. And held the precious package as delicately as I could. As always, I saw my face in her face. Hers was just a little more wrinkled, a little more "broken," as my nephew once said. A little more worn from her extra hours of living. *"Ti voglio bene, mamma."* (I love you, Mum.) *"Ti voglio bene, Gio."* (I love you, Jo.) "Thank you so much for coming." "Thank me? Thank you." I picked up her little suitcase and picked up her little hand and we started to walk away. And to walk toward. For here was the start of my dream. But we weren't close to sleeping.

My mother and I spent five weeks together in Italy as the boot readied itself for the June onslaught of summer and summer guests. We toured the country, from top to bottom, as if we were two recent high school graduates who were taking a year-off before heading to college--except that we steered clear of the hostels, took regular showers and did not carry one-third of our worldly possessions on our backs. We were a great traveling team that mastered the minutiae of the game. The packing and carrying of the luggage were borderline scientific. We developed a system for expenses that eliminated tit-for-tat economics. We set a daily schedule for sightseeing which was leisurely and enlightening and included at least one wonderful meal and a little glass (or two) of the local libations. And we set aside time for postcards and phone calls to let our family know the whereabouts of the nomadic mother and child.

We romped from Venezia to Verona to Bologna to Firenze to Roma, again, and to Napoli before we headed to Sicilia. We spent hours and hours together--walking, sleeping, eating, laughing, reading and talking--about life, love, how my parents met, what we were like as children, why she cut short her education, what she would do with her life if she had it to do over again. ("I'd do it exactly the same way. Otherwise I wouldn't have the four of you.") As a result, I had an intense and unique insight into my mother that no one else had. And, as a result, the genetic and behavioral origins of some of my idiosyncratic tendencies, my endearing idiosyncratic tendencies, came to light.

Like in Rome, when she slid underneath the metro turnstile because we didn't have exact change for the subway. There she was. Ass up. *Espresso*-to-go in her hand. Moving like a cat. Or when she was determined, at 68 years-old, to climb to the top of St. Peter's without use of an elevator. And did so with great ease, blowing by teenagers who were one-quarter of her age. Or when she wore her clothes into the shower in Florence so that she could wash them *and* herself at the same time. When she emerged, she looked as if she had just survived her own version of the Iron Woman Triathlon--biking, running and swimming simultaneously in the interest of speed. Or when the gates to The Baths of Caracalla flung open for admission to the live, open-air performance of *Aida*. It was a first come-first served event. The Italian version of The Running of the Bulls. My mother led the pack by swinging her purse like a weapon, slaying countless beasts along the way, and leading us to the best of the cheapest seats in the house.

And then there was Verona and the *calzone* cafè.

The morning there was glorious. The sky was bright blue with puffy, puffy clouds looming in the distance. We took advantage of the idyllic setting as the town took advantage of us--suckering us in to the Romeo and Juliet scam by paying money to visit the real life, fictitious balcony and the burial plots of the imagined. In time, we returned to the main *piazza* where we seated ourselves at an outdoor cafè to enjoy a *calzone* that we had spied on our way through the town square.

The cafè was very crowded, and we were lucky to have found a table at all. But we did. A table-for-two with a linen cloth and big white, ceramic dishes that could barely contain the specialty luncheons. My mother's *calzone* was the kitchen-sink deal. Everything that could possibly be squeezed inside the moon-shaped dough including Genoa *salame*, *prosciutto*, roasted peppers, *mortadella*, sauteed onions and a sea of cholesterol. Mine was the four cheeses, a meal that armed my digestive system for an attack of the pellets. We also ordered a bottle of water.

By the time our food arrived, the weather was starting to change. The sky was darkening, it was growing cooler, and we had to hold onto our napkins to prevent them from blowing off our laps. There was a lively "oooh" from the Italian patrons. The sound that is heard after the first minor swoop on a roller coaster.

Three bites later, the situation was growing a little more serious. It started to drizzle, the tablecloths were blowing up over the sides of the table and onto the food, and more than one customer decided to take lunch inside. The roller coaster "ooohs" were replaced with agitated sneers and worried looks. My mother and I remained. Methodically cutting our *calzone*. Methodically chewing each bite.

Two swallows later, the door to hell cracked open. It started to pour, and the wind was beginning to blow with more gusto. Our *calzone* were getting rained on as were the sides of our legs. My water glass was tossed on its side, the top and side flaps of the tent were swinging wildly, and most of the clientele abandoned their food and possessions and ran for cover. At that point I asked my mother, "Should we go inside?" "No, dear, we're OK."

I looked around to find an abandoned ship. Only the captain, the maitre d', was still in sight. Staring at the two of us as we gingerly cut our pockets of cholesterol. One swallow later, the tent succumbed to a major thrust of wind and toppled partially, but not completely, onto its side. The plates, glasses, paper products and food from the other tables were thrown in our direction, forcing us into an impromptu, projectile-dodging routine. The rain was torrential. I couldn't even see the enormous, ancient arena that, I assumed, continued to rest only a few meters from our table. My mother's head was completely soaked. My t-shirt looked frighteningly like *papier-mâché*. I yelled to her, frantically. "Mum, come on! We have to go inside!" She looked through her steamed-up glasses, stood, reluctantly, and started to move in the right direction. But, in an instant, she stopped dead in her tracks. Turned. And reached back for the fraction of the *calzone* that remained on her plate. To escort her life-blood to safety.

So, on one Italian afternoon, in the shadows of the open-air theater, under the angry European skies, and beneath the kind of protection that only a canvas barricade can offer, I discovered *exactly* whence my deep, intense, systemic obsession with food had come. My mother. In the wondrous town of Verona, where Juliet uttered in angst and in hope, "Romeo, Romeo, wherefore art thou, Romeo?", a woman's daughter would never be hard pressed to answer that question if ever rephrased for her liking. "Mamma, mamma, wherefore art thou, mamma?" Under the tent. Eating lunch. Romancing some bread and cheese and risking life for the taking.

My mother and I wended our way from north to south--soaking in the wonders of Italy with every stop. In Venezia, we found our *gondoliere*, Antonio, so that my mother could testify to the fact that Katie and I did, unequivocally, have the same mother, same father. In Bologna, we marveled at the inlaid wooden art collection in the city's cathedral, touched the walls of the world's oldest university and had a Big Brother moment when I turned on CNN to find my former Headmaster pontificating about the need for parents to put money away for higher education. In Firenze, we revisited what had become familiar sites, stopped in a pharmacy after my mother's upper arm was bitten by a horse in *Piazza della Signoria* and returned to *Latini* for some *pasta e fagioli*. In Roma, we mourned the relegation of *La Pietà* to a screened-off corner after a crazed tourist had sought to destroy it, strolled through Circus Maximus and took a day-trip to Tivoli Gardens and Hadrian's Villa to catch a glimpse of the very high life. And in Napoli, we spent a couple of days touring the waterfront, visiting friends and sightseeing in Pompei before we boarded a ship for Palermo, Sicilia.

We couldn't believe it was almost within reach. That the September dream had turned into a June reality and we were actually on our way. Excitement, nervousness, fear, and oddly enough, sadness overcame us. The mixture of feelings you get when you know you're about to do something you've wanted to do your whole life. And you're afraid it can't live up. Or you're afraid it will live up. Either way, its happening was imminent, and then it would be over. Perhaps the wanting had become more important than the getting. Perhaps it had taken on insurmountable proportions that could not possibly meet the test.

The ship to Palermo did its job--despite the putrid orange and blue interior. We booked too late to get the most comfortable lodging for the half-day sail, but we did manage to grab two cushioned seats near a large window. The view helped to entertain us during the daylight hours when we had run out of games and discussions to bide our time. That didn't happen too often since my mother and I could make a game out of anything. The Alphabet Game. The Famous Person Game. The Singing Game. The Guess That Occupation Game. No matter how many times we played, we'd laugh ourselves silly by naming completely illogical careers for completely illogical people. The grandmother weight-lifter. The bleached-blonde nun. It didn't take much.

My mum's favorite games had to do with words. My dad's favorite games had to do with numbers. When I was little and I'd ask to be excused from the table to get some milk, he'd request (with a smile) that I recite the 12s tables up to 240 in 10 seconds or fewer. Or he'd show me the tricks for multiples of nine or teach me about prime numbers. Or he'd drill me with split-second, rapid-fire basic skills. "Take the number three, add two, double that, double that, square that, cut it in half, cut it in half again and take the square root." Between the two of them, I was well-armed for the SAT and for entertaining myself when I drove across The United States from Michigan to Maine without company and without a radio.

The most popular game on the Naples to Palermo ship was a variation of Jumbles. We'd state a real word and see if the other person could unscramble it to spell another real word. "Opted," for example, could be rearranged to spell "depot." When I played that game with my mother, I was careful about my word selection. Sure, "pines" could be rearranged to spell "spine," but it didn't take long for a more graphic member of the sexual apparatus family to emerge. It was a word of that family of words, in fact, when I was seven years-old, that led to an unexplained Jumbles hiatus.

It was the summer of 1966. I was doing the newspaper Jumbles in the den while my mother was preparing a roast pork dinner. My hesitation on one particular combination forced me to yell to her through the walls. "Mum, is there any such word as sperm?" Her potato-parer fell into the sink with an assertive thrust, and she marched right into the den, apron askew, hair slightly mussed and with vegetable skins clinging to her wrist. "You listen to me, young lady. I want you to stop hanging around with that Karen Amherst! Do you hear me?" A confusing response for a seven year-old, but not for my psychic mother--who had anticipated Karen's sleazy career well before it came to fruition--as she shucked some corn on a summer night.

After disembarking and hailing a taxi from the dock, we headed east along the water toward the lodging we had selected from my trusted guidebook. Ten minutes later, after numerous rights and lefts but mostly rights, we ended up infinitesimally close to where we had started--at a hotel from whose windows we could have spat on the ship we had just gotten off. Taxi bill--thousands of *lire.* Taxi distance--40 meters.

The small hotel lobby was typical except that we were stared at relentlessly as we approached the sign-in desk. Not only by the unshaven, hairy-armed, hairy-backed, sleeveless t-shirted man who worked behind the desk, but also by the three relatively unattractive, middle-aged women who were posing on the Victorian couch off to the side. Who looked at us and then to each other and then whispered as we started to check-in. Not in a gossiping way. But in a confused way. Almost concerned. It felt weird. It was weird.

We got warnings from the man behind the desk about guarding our possessions in Palermo. Watch your jewelry. Don't carry your purses outside. Don't go out at night. Although they were intended to help, they ended up nearly paralyzing us. I had to talk myself back to calm by comparing those warnings to the ones I always get when I visit New York. A city where I am always on-guard but which, by and large, has proved very safe and very pleasant. I figured it would be the same.

I was more concerned, frankly, about the people *in* the hotel. Did the three women work there? Did they clean the rooms and make the beds? Between the mini-skirts, fishnet stockings, pumps and heavy-blue eye shadow, they weren't offering that they dust, vacuum and fluff pillows for a living.

So I told my mother to wait in the room and that I would be right back. Two of the remaining three women plus the desk clerk hairball watched me as I ran down the steps to the street on my way to a four-star establishment that loomed a block and a half away. I knew it would fly way outside our budget. But I didn't care. I wanted security. I wanted air-conditioning. And I wanted our first experience in Nonno's birthplace to be laced with class and dignity. So I booked us a suite and ran back to get my mother.

I found her sitting on the bed. Next to her closed suitcase. Legs together. Hands resting on her knees. Looking up at the door as I entered. "Mum, let's get out of here. This place gives me the creeps. I just booked us a room in a hotel that's five minutes from here."

"OK, dear. I wasn't liking this place too much myself."

When the door to our new air-conditioned suite flung open to greet us from our places on the designer carpet in the designer hallway, the relief was palpable. Enormous beds. Shower stalls as large as our last *pensione*. And a window view of Palermo's diverse architectural offerings--the combination of which reflected Sicily's history of outside domination, an island steppingstone on the way to bigger and better battles.

It wasn't until we felt presentable, not long after hot showers, fresh clothes and a cup of tea with croissants and fresh whipped butter, that we decided to call our cousin, Angelo, the son of my grandfather's brother. A brother, Giuseppe, who was born in Italy (along with another sister, Giuseppina) after my grandfather had come to The United States to begin a new, more hopeful life. They never met--Nonno, Giuseppe, Giuseppina--even though the blood of the same parents coursed through their bodies. The moment had finally arrived, and within seconds I would be speaking with one of my mother's first cousins, cousins separated by an enormous expanse of ocean and an enormous expanse of cultural differences. But also cousins who were connected by blood, by family, by loyalty.

I dialed nervously, listening impatiently to the distinctly Italian ring until a man picked up the phone on the third beat and uttered a greeting in his native tongue. Different from my native tongue. My cousin. Angelo. After a lifetime of preparation. On the other end of an increasingly shrinking cord. New family but old family. Family that spends life nestled between the beautiful mountains and breath-taking coasts of Sicily. The decibel levels in our exchanges once I told him who I was spoke volumes of our excitement, of our understanding of the moment, practically rendering the phone lines unnecessary. My mother sat beside me on my bed, shaking her head from side-to-side, forehead resting in her palms. Offering her own contribution to the unique energy in our tiny space.

Angelo arranged to pick us up early in the morning at our hotel, a choice he greatly favored over our previous option. He spoke of taking us to the family's summer home on the northern coast where the rest of the relatives would be gathered. They were anxiously awaiting our phone call. On the way, we'd pass Tusa--my grand-father's birthplace. We clarified plans again and then hung up. To find a woman, a daughter, a mother, who was beside herself with anticipation, not only about meeting Angelo, but also about catching her first glimpse of Tusa. Her father's home until he left for Ellis

Island. She was still reveling in the reality of tomorrow when I invaded her thoughts and caught her way off-guard.

"Mum, let's play one more round of Jumbles."

"Now?"

"Yuh, listen. Angelo shed some light on the goings-on at the last hotel. Here's a hint. Unscramble the letters in the word 'shower' to spell another word."

"Shower?"

"Yes."

Her brow furrowed as I watched her rehearse different combinations. Tilting her head to one side and then the other as if the reorientation would unscramble the letters. I could tell she was on the verge of giving up when she jumped up from the bed, slapped her hands to her thighs and then clapped her fingers together five times before she knocked back her head and wailed.

"Oh, my God! Oh, my God!!! WHORES! WHORES! They were whores?"

God, she was good at that game. Jumbles, that is.

Our first hotel was a whore house. A brothel. The t-shirted hairball was a pimp, and the three women on the red velour couch were genuine Sicilian harlots. The unrealized image of our cousin, Angelo, whirling around the corner early the next day to find his elderly first-cousin and his younger first-cousin-once-removed waving fond good-byes to the hirsute Palermo Pimp from the street, gave us a good laugh and flew in the face of the exact ring of class and dignity I had been seeking.

When we turned off the light that night, with the brothel-recommending guidebook consuming most of the trash can, we decided, given the events of the day, to invent a subcategory of our favorite game. Jumbles with a trampish twist. Vixen Mixin'. We went back and forth for a few minutes. Entertaining ourselves. Trying to stump each other. But it was my Catholic, church-going, God-fearing, 68 year-old, *calzone*-worshiping mother who offered up the award-winner.

"Honey, did you know that Tulsa spelled backwards is 'A Slut?'"

And with that, we erupted again. Writhing under the sheets. Wiping tears from our eyes with the silky pillow cases. And scrambling ourselves to sleep.

Chapter Twenty-Three
There's No Place Like Home

Right on schedule, our cousin pulled up in front of the hotel at 7:00 A.M. Not that we wouldn't have been ready if he had come early. My mother's and my eyes met at 4:15 A.M. when I squinted at the clock for the tenth time to see how much longer we had to wait to get going. We decided we'd rather wait showered than wait sleepy. So we dressed and seated ourselves on the edges of our beds with time to spare. And bided our time by finding dozens of people who shared my mother's maiden name in the phone book. Her name was as common there as my father's name was common in The United States. It was a visual for their connections. A visual for their identities.

Angelo said we would recognize him by his American jeans, his blue, cotton, short-sleeved shirt and his Fiat. When he stepped out of the car, my mother and I moved toward him. Hesitantly. He didn't look the way I had expected, and we wanted to be sure that the man we threw our arms around was *our* family member with the American jeans, short-sleeved shirt and the Fiat and not someone else's. When we stepped slowly off the curb, he nodded his head, and my mother reached up to put her arms around his neck. *"Mamma, questo è tuo cugino, Angelo,"* I mustered with quivering voice as my stomach moved its way up to rest next to my tonsils. Their hug was fiercely intense. Fiercely connected. And it lingered. Slow-motion.

When they finally released each other, after swaying and crying, saying things that neither one understood and holding each other's cheeks between their shaking fingers, I stepped forward for my hug-- a hug which already carried love and comfort and history. Family.

Angelo was small, by American standards, but, my mother said, she could tell by the reach of her grasp that he was the same height as my grandfather. With similar brown, waning hair and rounded eyeglasses. With a similar contour to his face made more perfect by an olive complexion. We climbed into his car and headed out of

Palermo where, on the outskirts, we stopped for an *espresso* and a pastry. Angelo's treat. Everything tasted better than usual.

As we drove along the northern coast of Sicily, I struggled to communicate with Angelo. I wanted to impress him but had a lot of trouble separating the real Italian from the dialect which occasionally forced its way into his conversation. When I reluctantly admitted that I didn't understand a phrase or two, he would say it again, sometimes the exact same way, until I finally pretended I understood it all or until I finally did understand it all. My mother was in the back seat and was of little to no help, largely due to her infatuation with the extraordinary Sicilian landscape and her fluency in dialectical profanity.

The road along the coast was sandwiched in-between the best of what the earth has to offer. To the north, ragged coastlines, jetties, sandy beaches and rich, aqua-blue water and to the south, a mountainous, craggy and vast interior with vineyards and wineries off in the distance. Along the way, we sorted out the family tree and learned some things we had never known. That one of my grandfather's brothers had been the vice-mayor of the family's hilltop town. That we had other cousins who lived in Messina, children of my grandfather's sister, Giuseppina. That my grandfather had been well-known in the region for his intelligence--which proved to be a burden to the younger siblings who followed him in school who, according to them, paled by comparison. That my great-grandfather was a very successful ice cream salesman, which may explain the outright obsession both my mother and I have with any flavor on a cone. Especially in Italy.

And then, suddenly, Angelo pointed to a tiny village at the top of a hill. That, he said, is the town where my mother's father, my *nonno*, his uncle, was born. We stared out the windows. Trying to take it all in--not knowing if we would ever have the chance to go to the summit. My mother's hand slid around the side of the front seat of the car and grazed my face. Gently. And she whispered. "Thank you." I could tell she was crying. And with that, Angelo put on his right blinker and began the ascent. He was taking us to the top. The very top.

We climbed up and up and up at crazed Italian driving speeds and wound our way through the steep and curved streets of Tusa to the oldest part of town. Angelo parked the car and walked us to an archaic home in the midst of an ancient block. The tan exterior was crumbling. Continuing to acquiesce to the ravages of time. The hundreds of years of its history.

Angelo pointed up. That, he directed to my mother, is the balcony to your father's room. And that is the *piazza* where he played ball with his younger siblings and friends. And that is where the family used to go to church every Sunday. And that woman in the store across the way remembers playing with your father's youngest sister. And that is where your father's parents will rest forever.

Thousands of miles from home, barely a stone's throw from the island's watery borders. At the home that had held my grandfather securely and had nurtured him throughout his first 14 years of life. That fed him delicious dinners and taught him about the importance of family. And of love. And of humor. That sent him off to school each day. And that, eventually, nudged him out the door to America where, his parents were convinced, he would find a better life. A better chance at success. And where he would ultimately continue the line that led to my mother. That led to me. A moment that was never to be understood by those who hadn't made this same trek themselves. Never.

My mother started to weep openly and, in shocking spontaneity, she dropped to her knees, with her head in her hands, and sobbed. Her body moved to the beat of her pain and her happiness. Which was transferred to me--when I walked up behind her and placed my hands on her two shoulders. And bent my head down on top of hers. And wept along with her. As Angelo waited off in the distance. Patient. And understanding.

In time, we stood again, and my mother searched for some words between her tears. What finally came out was heart-breaking and joyous. "He feels so near to me right now. As if he has just died. The pain is raw. So fresh. I can feel him. See him. Hear his voice."

He had held my brothers. He had held my sister just days before he died. His flesh had touched their very own. Had held their tiny bodies. But never me. Never rested his eyes on my hair, my nose, my little fingernails and knees. Until there in his hilltown of Tusa, at the summit of the summit, when I felt him, too. Holding me, too. Finally. Finally. After all those years. He was alive again.

After dozens of pictures and an *espresso* near my grandfather's play area, we got into the car and twisted our bodies around to peer out the back window, straining to get one more look at still another place we can call home. And then we continued to head east, in silence, to the relatives who waited. Trying to make sense of what had just happened. And then trying to make sure Angelo knew how much it meant to us to have stopped. He knew. We knew he knew.

Within an hour, we arrived at the summer home of Angelo's only sister, Maria, another of my mother's first cousins. In a blink, Maria shattered the American stereotype of Italians and, most particularly, Sicilians. She had light-colored skin, cheeky cheeks of satin, blonde hair, a brightly colored, flowing dress and, we soon found out, one of the most distinctive kisses known to mankind. She grabbed my mother's face in-between her two hands and kissed, no, smooched, no, sucked, her right cheek and then her left cheek and then her right cheek and then her left cheek. Again and again. Nearly drawing my mother's skin into her mouth. Before she began the chant that she repeated all day long. *"Lo stesso sangue! Lo stesso sangue!"* (The same blood! The same blood!) Her greeting had as much energy as Angelo's had restraint. Brother and sister. Night and day. Except for *lo stesso sangue.* That meant everything to both. And had always meant everything to us. Nonno. Nonna. My mother and father. My brother and brother and sister. And too many aunts and uncles and cousins to name. And new cousins. Whose old blood was familiar.

Maria then walked my mother to her mother. Arm-in-arm. To the wife of my *nonno's* brother. The only surviving member of that generation. Zia Rosina. Whose greeting was more delicate. More controlled. Out of respect for the more elderly and frail woman who sat before us in her sleeveless, black dress and her flat, leather sandals. She was the picture of class in her perfect hair, her dainty gold necklace and her simple, gold wedding ring that was swimming on her skinny, aged fingers. It was delicate, controlled, but not one bit less emotional. Immeasurable moments.

And then to Maria's husband and their son. Nine years-old with pale, white skin and thick, straight, blonde hair. Who carried the same name and the same eyes as my grandfather. My grandfather. It was hard for us to breathe.

Soft sofas held our bodies as we talked. And just looked at one another. Trying to find some familiar characteristics. More signs of the blood that binds us. Maria found it in my mother's and her hairlines and foreheads. And in the tiny varicose veins they had on the exact same place on the outer part of their left thighs. With those discoveries there was more smooching, more hugging, more proof of what races within us all.

In time, we moved into the dining room for dinner. A small, cozy space with drawn curtains. To shut out the relentless sunshine of the northern coast. A mahogany table was protected by a silk cloth, daintily decorated with hand-stitched flowers on skinny vines with light colors of pink and yellow and pale green. Handmade, ceramic dishes from a nearby village marked our places as did heavy sterling silver. Two forks. Two knives. Two spoons. And candlesticks holding candle flames that stood still in the thick Sicilian air. Cotton napkins were tented on our plates.

Maria orchestrated where we'd sit. With Zia and my mother in the seats of honor. Unaware of the temporary but willing dethroning of Maria's husband from his normal spot. Our chairs were stately. Tall backs with sculpted feet. And just the perfect height for a group that hovered closer to smaller than taller. They held us well as Maria nourished us. For the first time.

For hours we received her love. As we were treated to another Italian feast--augmented by a Sicilian flair. And a Sicilian family. The food a little more spicy. The bread a little more tasty. The wine a little more potent. The dessert a little more rich. I served as the translator throughout the spread. Head bobbing back and forth. Both parties, the English-speakers and the Italian-speakers, were requesting the same things of me. "Gio, tell this, tell that, tell this." Or "Gio, what'd they say, he say, she say?" We were thrilled to learn the details of the lives that had, to that point, been hidden by the miles and the language. And we were sad to learn of the fairly recent deaths of close relatives--including my grandfather's brother. Zio. Relatives who could have helped us fill in the gaps, bridge the cultures, complete the family tree, find more varicose veins and special hairlines. Relatives who could have smooched just as loudly, hugged just as intensely, held us just as gently. I was exhausted as the meal began to end. And I was filled. In every way.

When the last bite of sugary dessert was washed with the remnants of the wine, there was one last gesture. While we were all together. The new family. The old family. Who would be assembled with only those very people at that very time. One last tribute that transcended translation. That transcended the barriers.

Maria rose slowly at her end of the table with a glass of red wine in her hand. She got our attention when her voice fell to a whisper. And she said, in the most beautiful Italian I had ever heard...

"L'unico desiderio di mio padre è stato quello di vedere un figlio di suo fratello prima di morire. Benvenuto, figlia di suo fratello. È figlia della figlia. Papà, spero che tu ci stai guardando. Alla famiglia. Sempre alla famiglia."

My mother waited with anticipation throughout Maria's toast. Her fingers wrapped in mine under the table. When it was time, I brought her hand to both of mine and faced her. And shared the message. As each word changed the look on her face ever so slightly. And as each word came through with the translation of her dreams.

My father's one wish in life was to see a child of his brother before he died. Welcome, child of his brother. And child of a child. Papa, I hope you're watching. To family. Always to family.

With that, each one of us stood. To join Maria. One by one. Around the table. First Zia. And then my mother. And then I. And then Angelo. And then Antonio and his dad, Mauro. One by one. Until all seven of us were standing. With our glasses raised high. First barely speaking. And then watching it grow to song.

"Alla famiglia. Sempre alla famiglia."

My throat was killing me from holding back the tears.

Earlier in the day, Maria had spoken of another American cousin, another Angelo, who had come to visit them in Sicily. Their tie was through Angelo's mother and their father. My mother's connection was through her father and their father--where the blood is stronger, they believe. And so it made our visit different to them.

Maria told us that when Angelo left Sicily to return to America, he was overwrought with sadness. "We were all *so* sad that day," Maria said. "We cried for hours after he left." Despite her warning, I was completely unprepared for the moment of departure. The moment when Angelo said, "OK, we need to be getting back to

Palermo now." My mother and I moved from person to person. Touching. Hugging. Kissing. Crying. Repeating expressions of love and reminders of the blood connection. More crying. And more hugging. Holding Zia Rosina's hand. And promising to return.

We climbed into his car with far more reluctance than we had expected. Toes dragging on the Sicilian earth. Lips quivering with the frenzy of devastation. And turned back for one more glimpse, one more kiss, one more wave. Dancing at the extremes of emotion. Sadness to ecstasy to sadness, again. Finally, we were out of sight of Zia, whom we would never see again, and whose generation we would never see again, and Maria and her husband and child. We barely spoke on the drive back. And broke the silence only with the sounds that tears can make.

We looked, again, to the beautiful Sicilian countryside to comfort us. And it did. Especially when we waved good-bye to Tusa, resting proud and regal at the top of an elegant hill. And we waved, but not good-bye, to Nonno's spirit, also resting proud and regal at the top. The very top. We looked for and found comfort in the birthplace of a lineage, our lineage, that was decorated with the greens and purples and blacks and browns and blues of the nearby vineyards and trees and water. And we kept driving.

When we said good-bye to our cousin in the hotel lobby, my mother and I continued to dance at the emotional extremes, and Angelo led with the masculine version of the steps. As we watched him get into his Fiat to drive away, his car's derogatory acronym (Fix It Again Tony) took on a whole different meaning. We knew he had fixed it, my grandfather, Antonio, as utter emotional exhaustion slowed our steps back to our suite.

We got ready for bed without speaking and climbed in after turning off the light. No Jumbles tonight. No Occupation Game. No singing. Only seconds later I felt something come to rest near my feet. My mother. In her little flowered nightgown. With her hands on her knees and her head bent down on her chest. And clutching an envelope in her left hand. A mother's hand. With its peculiar veins and wrinkles and little birthmark that we fiddled with when we sat next to her in church or when she read *Home For A Bunny* or when we begged her to sing *Ole Mamie Riley* and bounce us in our beds one more time, just one more time, before the lights went out and we said good-bye to her comfort for a nighttime. That hand was clutching the envelope. The handwritten envelope.

A' I Figli Del Mio Caro Fratello
(To The Children Of My Dear Brother)

My mother said that Maria had slid it into my mother's pocket before we drove away. A precious, precious treasure. She held out her arm and asked me to open up the envelope to find the note inside. Fragile. Yellow. And to read it to her. So I did. But only after I brought the paper to my face, my nose, my cheek. Only after I steadied myself and readied myself for a trip I'd never taken and with a person I'd never met. Only after I squeezed next to my mother on the bed so that I could take her along.

Alla Mia Cara Famiglia-

Sono molto dispiacente che ho lasciato questa terra prima della vostra venuta. Mi avrebbe fatto molto felice di aver potuto abbracciarvi e poter vedere nei vostri visi la faccia di mio fratello che non ho mai conosciuto. Ma voi siete qui adesso. Tutti insieme. Ed io sono sicuro che voi farete un brindisi insieme alla famiglia. Sempre alla famiglia.
   Vi voglio bene.
   Zio

To My Dear Family-

I regret that I left this earth before you came. I would have loved to hold you in my hands and to see in your faces the face of my brother I never knew. But you are here now. All together. And I am sure that you will make a toast to family. Always to family.
   I love you.
   Zio

When we turned off the light again to try and sleep, I thought back to my fears about a dream-fulfilled. But when my eyes adjusted to the light, and I saw the silhouette of my mother curled up in her bed, with her head literally resting on her uncle's words, I realized I should have known better.

To family.

Always to family.

Goodnight, Mum.

Goodnight.

Chapter Twenty-Four
Good-cries, Good-sighs, Good-ties, Good-byes

Our Sicilian adventure. We talked about it and cried about it and wrote about it as we rode the ship back to Napoli and rode the train back to Roma and rode the taxi to our hotel near the train station. We knew we had lived through something, together, that no one could understand. And knew we had just carved a memory that changed us and united us in a way family and friends would never identify or feel. That felt special. And lonely. And frustrating.

We wished we had planned more than a day-long visit with the cousins. We hadn't come close to predicting the emotional impact of meeting them. So the few days that remained of our travels felt different. Our breakneck touring pace lacked the thrill of before. An air-conditioned bus tour of the Seven Hills of Rome, a mapped exploration of the Roman Forum, a deciphering of the Arch of Titus and an iced *cappuccino* near the more decorated Spanish Steps paled and failed in their attempts to match our other journey. It was only the side-trip to Abruzzi and Campo di Giove, the birthplace of my *nonna*, that gave us back some energy.

We left a 91-degree Rome that day in sleeveless t-shirts and skirts and arrived in the mountainous eastern region after several different train rides featuring vehicles of old to very old to should-be-retired to should-be-dead. Fifty-degree temperatures greeted us as did people in flannel shirts and woolen pants. Two new sweatshirts assuaged the frigidity and allowed us to meander through the stone streets of my grandmother's hometown to take in the perfectly stacked fireplace and wood stove logs and the flowers that grow only along mountain-sides. And to take in whatever information we could about my grandmother's maiden name, which was no longer current in the village of 900, and my great grandmother's maiden name, which seemed familiar to the ticket collector at the train station. "I know everyone, and that name is still around."

That night back in Rome, my mother took a red, felt-tip pen from my knapsack to write one simple question in my journal. It stuck out amidst the black ink from Nonno's fountain pen that normally records my memories. "Did I walk on the streets that my dear mother did when she was a girl?" Did her footsteps match her mother's nearly 100 years later? Did we sit in the same pew in the same church that her family paraded into when she was small? Did we rest on the same benches my grandmother rested upon as we gazed over the valleys of Abruzzi and swallowed the rich diversity and splendor of the land? Questions that could be answered in Sicily by those who knew the truth. Questions that tugged at me and beckoned me to answer. My attention could turn to them now.

Before we knew it, my mother was packing to leave. I watched her the night she reluctantly tossed her little luggage onto the bed and started to fold her clothes in limp patterns, flat and disheveled. It was so unlike her--so famous in our small circle for her scientific folding techniques. With the exception of the blue and white silk skirt, the Campo di Giove sweatshirt and the enormous multicolored scarf she bought in the *San Lorenzo* Market in Florence, the only other new item she'd carry onboard was a Christmas ornament from her cousin, Angelo. An ornament he left for her at the front desk of our Palermo hotel. It carried the face of the patron saint of Palermo. Santa Rosalia. The saint of miracles.

The next day I took my mother to the airport and walked her as far as I could before they forced us to separate. She was wearing the same outfit she had worn when she touched down in Rome. Jeans, sneakers, white socks and that cotton shirt that then hung even farther down below her down below. It was her traveling outfit, she said. Augmented only by the Santa Rosalia ornament that was in her side pocket.

We hugged good-bye and, as always, I was surprised that my head rested on top of her head, her hair just under my chin, instead of the other way around. I wondered if there were a part of me that would never stop seeing my parents the way I saw them when I was five or 12 or 17. Or when I was just shorter than they were.

When we pulled away from the hug, tears spilled down our cheeks, giving me reason to pause and think about how much is packed in one salty droplet. Gratitude. Missing. Worry. Love. Pride.

If her parents hadn't left Italy, the very country on which our very feet were not-so-firmly planted at that very moment, she would not have been there. So I would not have been there. And none of this would have happened.

Life is so random.

My mother was practically back home in The United States before I was back home in Perugia. I had a long time to think after I left her-- as I returned to the hotel to gather my things, as I waited for the train to leave Termini, as I rested my head against the window and watched Italy pass.

On a visit Max had made back to Perugia once, long after it had begun to empty itself of the people we had met there, the transient people, the people in our classes, the people in the discos, the people in the bars, the people in our favorite outdoor cafè, he said that the city had changed. "It was a body without a soul," he said.

And it was a body whose soul had thrived during a cycle that was comfortable. A cycle of September to June. Novice to expert. Open-to-newness to ready-to-leave. Primed for promotion after passing life's tests. So as I made my way back to that increasingly hollow body, most of my thoughts were consumed by the notion of going home. I was missing my family, my friends and the peace of things familiar. I had done what I had come to do and much more than I had expected. It was time. Time for a new dream. Time for a new direction. Long before the train slowed into the Perugian train station, I had decided to leave and was determined to make that a reality as fast as I could. Any insecurity about being impulsive was steam-rolled by the energy of my relief.

I spent the next few days putting things in order. Resurrecting the kind of unparalleled energy and organizational skills and single-minded focusing that had made college and teaching easier each year. There were logistical things and personal things. Make a plane reservation. Return Betty (the heater) to the store. Pay my last month's rent and clean the apartment. Close my bank account. Get the mail that had collected in my school mailbox. And, most important, reconnect, possibly one last time, with people in Perugia whom I cared about. Except for Max. Who had already left. Whose body was in Germany but whose soul was there with me. And reconnect in a way that was unique and true to us. To our history. To our time together. I started with Mamma--since it had started with Mamma. With her hot and cold water, clean kitchen floors, boiling sauces, clear rules, sparkling bidets, protective arms, Wednesday afternoon laundry conversations and unequivocal pride in all things Italian. Including me.

She was happy when she got my phone call. I hadn't seen her in awhile, and she was wondering if I had already left Perugia. We set a date for dinner, and I told her that I would bring the ingredients. A little basil, a little Parmesan, a little parsley, olive oil, garlic, *pignoli* and butter, a little bread, a little red wine. I also bought two gifts--a new bath mat to match the bathroom tiles and a new shower curtain, thicker than Saran Wrap and reinforced around the hooks.

When I got there she wasn't wearing her green muu-muu. She had on a blue and white checkered muu-muu with blue flats. Her hair was done, and she was wearing a gold necklace and bracelet. All dressed up and looking absolutely adorable. We took to the kitchen after two or three sips of the wine I had brought and began preparing dinner from inspiration alone--since the *Making Pesto With Feeling (And A Little Wine) Recipe Card* remained tucked into the front pocket of my peach-colored Benetton vest where I could see it but not read it. With confidence I cut off the brown parts of the basil leaves. Casually I threw in the Parmesan and melted the butter. And in the end, cockily I flipped the Cuisinart switch and watched it give birth to *pesto*.

While I was cutting and tossing and flipping in the kitchen, Mamma was moving between the activity there and setting the table in her corner of the house. Nice china. Linen tablecloth and napkins. Polished silver. Crystal water and wine glasses. We carried the food inside, sat down and took each other's hands as she said grace in Italian. Then she moved toward the TV, turned it on, and we started to watch as the title to a Katharine Hepburn movie rolled up the screen. We spoke only during the commercials, and I had a chance to tell her I had met Katharine Hepburn in college when she had come to receive the highest award that the college offers. That I had escorted her across campus to the reception area, arm-in-arm. She had a chance to tell me she had finally booted Susanna out of the house. The last straw was when Susanna told Mamma she talked too loudly in the afternoon. That she needed to tone it down a bit while she studied. Mamma responded with a bite. "Why don't you pack your things and go? Then you won't ever have to hear my voice again." She left the next day. Tone that.

When dinner and the movie were over, I reached under my chair and pulled out the gifts I had covered in Florentine wrapping paper. Mamma took the presents from my hands, without any evidence of modesty or shyness, and tore them open. She threw back her head and laughed out loud and then got up from her chair and smooched my cheeks just as cousin Maria had done in Sicily. I finally told her she had surprised me the day I had obliterated Bathroom Rule Number One. The day she jiggled past me merely to wash the bath mat and replace the shower curtain. *"Perchè,"* she said. *"Tu sei Italiana."* (Why? You're Italian.)

When I left her that night, after cleaning up the dishes and freezing the leftover *pesto*, which I labeled with love, I stopped just outside her door and turned around.

"Sei stata come una mamma." (You were like a mother.)

"Sei stata come una figlia." (You were like a daughter.)

"Ritornerò presto." (I will come back soon.)

"Spero di si." (I hope so.)

"Arrivederci." (I'll see you later.)

"Va, cara, con un sacco di baci." (Go, dear, with a sack of kisses.)

I walked the 117 stairs to the bottom, to the dark lobby, illuminated only by the tiny bulb on the light switch, enclosed by the large brown door that led to the street. When I got outside, I knew that in my last moments inside that foyer, just outside the confines of Mamma's big, flapping arm, her hot water, her new closets and warm kitchen, it was the first time in a long time that Abdul hadn't been there with me. Haunting me. Waiting for me. Calling my name. Instead, I heard only Mamma and some of her last words.

"Tu sei Italiana."

Yes, Mamma. I am.

John was next. It was hard to think up something that would be unique to us. Something that would reflect the turbulent nature of our existence. Maybe we could hold hands and then slap each other and then hold hands again and slap each other again. Or maybe we could sip some nice, hot, soothing tea and then spit it into each other's face. Or maybe we could just stand inches from each other's lips and watch as first kisses were freed and then scathing words. The insanity of our relationship. The verbal sado-masochism.

When I went over to John's house the day after dinner with Mamma, he was sitting on his unmade bed in his boxer shorts and a t-shirt. Smoking a cigarette and scratching his head. And although an Italian grammar book was opened on his makeshift desk, he was studying, instead, both a Beethoven concerto and a dull-looking pamphlet on the student rates for motor-scooter rentals.

The next day we found ourselves on the back of one of those scooters with a courier bag over my shoulder, some bottled water, a camera, a map of Assisi and a whistled version of some of Beethoven's best. The trip through Assisi was a gas--made that way by the .0008 horsepower engine on the motorbike and the fact that its hill-climbing machismo was pathetic at best. We laughed ourselves to hysteria, doubled-over in convulsions, as old men on bikes, kids on foot and women loaded down with plastic shopping bags kept pace with us as we tried to climb up to the city center built along the slopes of Mount Subasio. Our less-than-impressive mode of transportation bonded us in some way to St. Francis himself, the son of a merchant who shunned wealth and embraced, instead, a life of minimalism and poverty. As Mercedes Benz automobiles, tourist buses and more fancy motorcycles than ours nearly edged us outside the confines of the city's *Rocca* (fortress), we thought we could feel St. Francis smiling down on us and approving of our more modest choice for movement.

The long, slow climb to our destination gave us plenty of time to enjoy what sprawled around us. The valley's home to olive groves and vineyards and tobacco fields and grains. The faintly tinted stone homes and the smattering of ancient churches that dot the skyline. And, most stunning of all, by its sheer size, the protective wall that surrounds the city and still serves to ward off and control the onslaught of 20th century tourists--invaders whose goals are the same as the enemies of old. Sample the town's riches and leave in a hurry.

John and I climbed off of our scooter long enough to pay tribute to St. Clare, the less well-known founder of the Franciscan order of

Friars and nuns, whose remains lay visible for all to see in the *Basilica di Santa Chiara*. And then we passed through the tall entrance to the *Basilica di San Francesco*--decorated with the revolutionary paintings of Giotto, whose drive toward humanity as subject and away from religious icons as subject helped shift the future of creativity. St. Francis' pleas for simplicity were lost in the echoes of the enormous basilica--whose frescoes and colors and dignity mellowed our moods. Holy, ancient, charitable, inspirational. Goodness couldn't help but enter our skin and our veins as St. Francis and St. Clare visited us as we visited them. It made me wonder how John and I might have been different if we had seen Assisi on our first day together instead of on our last. Maybe the city, the aura and the pervasive elements of tenderness and sacrifice could have steered us to a different course.

We eventually climbed up out of the center of Assisi to a delightful, outdoor, open-grill restaurant off the beaten path. We hiked up a small hill to a table for two on a terrace that was protected from the hot sun by ivy-covered trellises and ordered our favorite meal. Watching as someone else prepared our *tortellini* with sausage and peas at the open fire-pit that extended the entire width of the terrace. We spoke very little as we waited. So I focused on the tiny roses and ivy that flapped gently in the breeze. And I focused on the fact that sooner, rather than later, I would be saying good-bye to settings such as that one and would be exchanging them for a pace of life that was much more frenetic and much less in-the-moment.

The food arrived and our forks broke the silence. After a first taste and a moment or two to assess the quality of the preparation, we concluded that although it was good, it simply was not as good as ours--a victory that somehow validated our friendship, gave us a reason to have coexisted. With each bite, we shared another memory of our time together. Our first tea. Our first trip. Our first Dutch drag. As the last bits of cheese-filled *tortellini* with a sliver of sausage, one pea and white sauce made their way to my stomach, I finally understood what there was between us. As a couple of friends, we never, ever mastered the beauty of the consistency of kindness. Of sensitivity. Of understanding. But we did give birth to several great kids--among them *pasta*, tea, trains and cheap wine--kids who were the only real glue, the only real stability, the only real light in our otherwise volatile relationship.

So, when we finally said good-bye, in the waning moments of our time together, I thought of it more as an amicable divorce. An awareness that while we'd always have the memories of our children, we'd never have a future all our own. And so we parted--with joint custody.

The only other person to see just before I closed my last piece of luggage, just before I boarded the train to Rome, just before I stepped on the plane that would take me home to Boston, was Marco. He was happy to get my call. He wanted to hear all about Sicily. All about my visit with the relatives and my reaction to his land, his *paesani*, his air and water and mountains. His excitement and interest were reminiscent of what we had before jealousy arrived. Before his focus on Max grew bigger than his focus on me.

We planned to meet each other that night on the steps of the main cathedral at the end of *Corso Vannucci*. On the very step where we had first laid eyes on each other. Where he had beamed a smile of relief that I was happy to meet a Sicilian. I told him I would bring a blanket, a bottle of wine, two glasses and some news that might be difficult for both of us. He placed down the receiver so gently that I wasn't sure he had hung up. Until I heard the long, flat dial tone that paralleled our emotions at the time.

The rest of the day I played out our visit as I packed and cleaned and paid overdue bills. I forced myself to imagine the exact scene and the perfect time to tell him I'd be gone from Perugia within a few hours. That I'd soon be far away from the streets and the people and the conversations and the *espressi* that had changed my life or tried to change my life. I couldn't get it to play out clearly in my head. It had to do with my inability to predict my reaction to being with him or my inability to predict his reaction to being with me. Forces that never evolved in predictable ways and always destroyed my best-laid plans.

I got to the cathedral first that evening and sat wrapped in a striped, wool blanket with frayed silk edging. A wine bottle was in-between my feet and two wine glasses rested against my back. It was a beautiful night--a little brisk, but the June sky could not have been clearer. Loaded with stars. So close. And sparkling.

I dropped my head down from the sky just in time to see Marco as he glided along *Corso Vannucci*. As he strolled the long, broad passageway to the end. With a hand in his pocket and a bag strapped over his shoulder. Unable to resist the temptation to window-shop along the way. It was a national pastime. A national law.

When he got closer to the cathedral, he moved away from the stores and into the center of the path and looked up. Tipping his head to the side and smiling a different smile. I couldn't tell if it were about embarrassment or sadness or knowing more than I knew he knew. Or all of that. My smile was a sign that I had forgotten how handsome he was. Is. And that I had forgotten how much he had gotten to me.

We hugged on the steps, and I asked him in Italian if he happened to know the translation of Land Rover. He laughed and said he had used that line about five times that day, but I was the only one who didn't shrink back when he mentioned he was Sicilian. Their loss, I thought.

We followed the familiar routes that brought us to familiar places. The more than 100 tiny steps that led to the Italian university. The elevated walkway that overlooked the city. The ancient Etruscan arch. My old apartment. The homemade *pasta* shop. The wall that enclosed Perugia. Most of the time we were silent. Most of the time we walked hand-in-hand. And occasionally, one of us would stop and point out a certain star in the sky--a sky and a star that were pressing down on us from above.

We walked to a part of the wall we could climb over onto the sloping hillsides of the Umbrian village. And we did. And opened the blanket and the wine and laid on our backs--just sipping our drinks and staring at the stars. Stars that were so busy, so clear, so bustling that they brightened the ground. And lit up our faces.

As the minutes and then hours slipped by, we shifted our positions. From backs to sides to spoons. And then to backs again. Right before the first time I shivered, he reached into his bag and pulled out two flannel shirts that carried his powder. His soap. We put them on, and I left mine on almost constantly until I touched down in Boston. It was our first visit together to the place I call home.

We made shapes out of the stars that night. Arrows. Spaghetti strands. Faces. And one cluster that looked a little like Sicily, we thought. And so we went there. It was our first visit together to the place he calls home.

Just before the darkness fell away and the morning sun started to invade our staring, silent, clear moments, Marco decided to find one star in the sky that would be ours. That we could point to at night, from Sicily and from New England, and feel each other. On that blanket. Outside that wall. In Perugia.

"Right there," he said. "The last star of what you called the Big Dipper. The one at the end of the handle. That is where our hands should rest," he said. "Would rest," he said. "Together at the end."

He knew I was leaving.

And I hadn't said a word.

We stretched our hands toward that star at the end of that handle. My hand covered by his. Gently. Completely. And as our hands fell slowly to the earth, I had to try to remember why it hadn't worked out. Why I had been looking for a reason, any reason, to escape. To fly away. To exercise my pigeon wings.

After a few minutes of wondering about the irretrievable minutes that had ticked by in my life, I looked back up at our star at the end of the handle and then back at Marco at the edge of the blanket. Sleeping behind me. I wedged my hand inside of his and told him, from my heart, just a hair away from those closed and bottomless eyes, the things he deserved to hear as he lay sleeping, dreaming, smiling. Fingers wrapped around my own.

And the stars lit up his face and spilled light upon my soul.

As I struggled to let go. As I struggled for an explanation.

Chapter Twenty-Five
What's It All About, Nonno?

When I let my head fall onto the pillow the night before I left for home, I tried to recall the person who first arrived in Italy--the person who had surrounded herself with several pieces of baggage that were intended to bring peace and familiarity thousands of miles away from regular routines and unthinking rituals. But she was gone. No specific number of cotton balls or worn t-shirts, no Top Ten music, telephone Calling Cards and old journal entries had done what she unknowingly had intended them to do. To protect her from the unfamiliar. To protect her from difference. The possessions she had stowed in the overhead luggage compartment were symptomatic of her discomfort with discomfort. And the airport carousel episode was Italy's first message that things had to change, in a big way, whether she could handle them or not.

My mind, that night in Perugia, then turned to images of the last several months of my life, the last several months of me. It was filled with the sounds and smells and tastes and feels of all the people who had walked me down those Italian roads or run me off of them or pointed me toward different roads altogether. And it was filled with the sounds and smells and tastes and feels of an Italy that romped way inside and outside the romantic stereotypes of the land and the guidebook descriptions of a people, a history, a spirit, a way of living.

The images were crossing and confused. And improbable. My Italian *mamma* making *pesto* with my real *mamma*. John sipping tea with Max. Antonio, the *gondoliere*, slamming Abdul on the side of his head with his oar. Katie christening the U.S.S. America with a bottle of Michelangelo wine. Dana and Elsie dining with the statue of David. Marco with me, on a blanket, in flannel shirts, under the autumn trees of New England. My grandfather, holding in his hands the cheeks of a brother he never knew.

They were in motion. Each with a direction. A calm direction. Gliding, effortlessly, toward a time that seemed endless and a space that seemed weightless. And leading it were the people I already knew or had come to know, already loved or had come to love. Nonno. And Nonna. And Max and Mamma, Petra, John, Signora Gala, Marco, my sister, my mother, *mia zia e mio zio e i nostri cugini*, Dana, Elsie and the gods. And in the background, others turned the other way.

I listened in on the soft conversation of those I loved. They were offering glimpses. Fragments. Pieces of a puzzle, a puzzle of me, that was different for everyone there. For some, our journey was about language and culture, food and wine, friendship and falling in love. For others it was about patriotism and its risks, privileges and opportunities and those denied. And silence. For still others, it was about fear and failure, the death of naivete´. Or a vision, a shared vision and different visions. It was about eyesight and avoiding self-deception. For others, it was about family.

They were committed to convincing each other--to extracting the perfect description of what it all had meant to me and had been for me. And how it had changed me. My puzzle. My life. My path. My me.

When the last syllable of the last word was spoken, I stepped up beside my *nonno*, placed my hand in his and tugged on it. Gently. And he looked down, through his round glasses and his brown eyes, and smiled. And I spoke to him. One more time. In Italian. *Lines, Nonno. Lines. We need to walk them, skip them, run them, paint them. Erase them and meld them. Connect them and dance them. Up. Down. On. Off. Above. Below. And across. Even when we're alone. Even when we're alone.* And then I paused, a long pause, and looked up, into his Sicilian eyes, our Sicilian eyes.

And he took both my hands in his and in one sure voice, with a heavenly Italian accent, he whispered. Simple. Proud. *Mia nipote. La mia più giovane nipote. Mia Gio.* (My granddaughter. My youngest granddaughter. My Jo.) And then our hands separated gracefully. The tips of my fingers passing over the smoothness of his palm. And I found myself alone. And complete. And very wide awake.

Just before I finally drifted off to sleep that last night, I glanced over at the one item I had yet to pack--an item that was partially illuminated by the stars and the moon. The photo. The photo of my grandfather, Nonno, and his five grandchildren. All on or around his giant lap. Surrounding him with love. I reached for it and saw something for the first time in the background. My *nonna*. Standing watch over the gentle scene as she rested her back against the door jamb to her kitchen. Her strong arm stretched out and her hand reaching for something that was hidden behind the dining room wall. And then I noticed a tiny space. Right in the middle of Nonno's lap. Right between my sister, Katie, and my cousin, Laura. And then I noticed that nearly everyone's eyes were focused on a different site. A different spot. Off in the distance or off to the side. Looking.

As I leaned the photo back up against my green duffel and let my lids fall closed over the eyes that had watched my world unfold and grow, I felt my head slink back against the pillow and let the mattress accept my body as it smoothed itself out along the ridges.

He died before I was born.

But he lived because I was born.

It is a fact that makes me unique in my family. Different.

And now I know why it mattered so much.

Adesso, lo so.

- FINE -
(End)

ACKNOWLEDGMENTS

With love and special thanks, for giving me my Italian roots, to *mio nonno*, my grandfather, Antonio Ragonese, and *mia nonna*, my grandmother, Beatrice Rubeo Ragonese.

Thanks also to Stephan Mientus--for your spirit, your soul and your friendship in the year that changed our lives. To Louise (*Mamma*) and Romolo (*Papà*) Venditti and family--for bringing Italy to life for me back home and for feeding me in incomparable ways when my home was just above you. To Sally and Tod Wellman--for allowing me the coastal setting of a lifetime to write this book. To Justin Ferrelli--for your research and Cajun openness. To Lucille Ragonese and Bastian Duehmert--for your help with tricky spellings. To Fernanda Conley--for perfecting my use of the most beautiful language in the world. To Bernadette Bourque--for a spin through your journal's memories. To David Saul--for being willing to put your broad photographic skills to play on three difficult subjects. To Tom Wiseley--for your patience with my Macintosh-biased and IBM-illiterate questions. To Aunt Lu, Joseph Cummings, III, Anthony Cummings, Cindy Cummings Neprash, Marcia Falzone and Laura Ragonese--for allowing me to use the photo that inspired this work. To Lisa Jo Ahearn and Nora Dale Hoffmann--for acquiescing to my excerpt-listening sessions. To Mary Ward Burns--for your laughter when laughter was intended. To Denise Childress--for your valuable opinions and proofreading talents in the final hour. To Martha Hirschman--for helping me see the need to bring the images to life. To Gail Starkey--for your graphic design talents on the covers and your patience with my numerous requests. To Wendy Wilderotter--for your opinions surrounding some of the most challenging parts. To Jodi Reamer--for offering the kind of comprehensive and intelligent feedback that helped change the quality of my efforts. To Louise Cohen--for your inspiration. And to Editor, Adolfo Caso--for your direction, for believing and for giving me a chance.

Finally, to Cindy Cummings Neprash--for your constant support and for being the only sister I would choose again and again. And to the rest of my family--my mother, Antoinette Ragonese Cummings, my father, Joseph Cummings, Jr., my brothers and all aunts, uncles and cousins Ragonese--thank you for giving this near youngest a chance to watch the best. *Alla famiglia. Sempre alla famiglia...*